D1367125

Severe Learning Disability and Psychological Handicap

John Clements
Institute of Psychiatry,
London

JOHN WILEY & SONS
Chichester · New York · Brisbane · Toronto · Singapore

Copyright © 1987 by John Wiley & Sons Ltd.

All rights reserved.

No part of this book may be reproduced by any means,
or transmitted, or translated into a machine
language without the written permission of the publisher.

Library of Congress Cataloging-in-Publication Data:

Clements, John.
 Severe learning disability and psychological handicap.

 (Wiley series in clinical psychology)
 Includes index.
 1. Learning disabilities.   I. Title.
II. Series.   [DNLM: 1. Learning Disorders — psychology. WS 110 C626s]
RJ506.L4C58   1987   616.85'89   87-8330

 ISBN 0 471 91354 5

British Library Cataloguing in Publication Data:

Clements, John
 Severe learning disability and psychological handicap
 — (Wiley series in clinical psychology).
 1. Learning disabilities   2. Clinical
 psychology
 I. Title
 371.9   LC4815

ISBN 0 471 91354 5

Typeset by Witwell Ltd., Liverpool.

Printed in Great Britain by St Edmundsbury Press,
Bury St Edmunds, Suffolk.

Contents

Series Preface vii
Preface ix
1 Introduction 1
2 Facts and Values 8

PART ONE: THE NATURE OF IMPAIRMENT 15
3 General Cognitive Functioning 19
4 Social Cognition 43
5 Biological Aspects of Severe Learning Disabilities 60

PART TWO: REMEDIATING SEVERE LEARNING AND 79
    BEHAVIOURAL DISABILITIES: GENERAL OVERVIEW
6 Developing New Skills 85
7 Managing Problem Behaviours 97
8 Implementing and Generalizing Programmes of Behaviour 116
  Change

PART THREE: REMEDIATING SEVERE LEARNING AND 129
     BEHAVIOURAL DISABILITIES: A REVIEW OF TWO
     SPECIFIC AREAS
9 Language and Communication 133
10 Self-Control 155

11 Conclusions 174

Index 178

Series Preface

This is the first of a new series of texts in clinical psychology. Some, such as this one by John Clements, will present an authoritative, up-to-date introduction to one of the core fields of clinical psychology. Others will present distillations of work on more specialist areas where exciting advances are currently being made. Where possible, the books will be written by a single author or by a small group of authors working as a team, and will therefore have the coherence which is often lacking in edited books. However, there will be others that require a range of expertise and points of view that can only be achieved with an edited book.

Clinical psychology is a field with permeable frontiers. It has close links with many other professions and scientific disciplines. We hope, therefore, that the series will have a broad appeal to all those who are concerned with the application of psychological knowledge to clinical problems.

People with severe learning disabilities have proved difficult to identify in clear and effective terminology. In the past, they might have been called the 'subnormal' or the 'severely retarded'. Such terms are objectionable on the grounds of being too pejorative and stigmatizing. They do not sufficiently recognize that people with severe learning disabilities are, above all, *people*. However, prejudiced attitudes are not changed simply by changing terminology. If attitudes remain unreformed, new terminology will become as prejudiced as the old and will need to be discarded in turn. 'Severe learning disabilities' is still a relatively virginal concept that has not yet been soiled by prejudicial attitudes, but it may not remain so for long.

It might perhaps also be criticized for emphasizing quasi-educational difficulties to the exclusion of other facets, such as the broad range of behavioural problems often found in conjunction with severe learning disabilities. The contents of this book do not reflect any such limited psychological focus. The phrase 'psychological handicap' has been used in the title to try to capture the broader range of psychological and behavioural problems with which severe learning disabilities are often associated.

There has been a tendency in work with severe learning disabilities for professionals to pursue one particular approach to the exclusion of others. Some have focused exclusively on the rights of people with severe learning disabilities to a normal life in the community. Others have used the technology of behaviour modification to the exclusion of all other approaches. There is a danger when one approach is pursued single-mindedly that the broad basis of relevant psychological knowledge will be ignored. This has happened to a disturbing extent with severe learning disabilities.

The problem has been compounded by a severe shortage of books that present, in an accessible form, basic psychological knowledge about severe learning disabilities and the broad range of relevant professional psychological work that can be undertaken. In particular, trainee professionals entering the field require a clear presentation of the general scientific background for their professional work.

John Clements has succeeded admirably in meeting this need, and has provided the field with a text which is (a) broad based and eschews blinkered commitments, (b) scholarly, providing a judicious appraisal and summary of a large body of scientific literature, and (c) clear and readable. I predict that such a book, like corn in Egypt, will be eagerly devoured.

Fraser Watts

Series Editor

Preface

This book is concerned with psychological research relevant to the functioning of people with severe learning disabilities. The knowledge base is small, but this book is written in the belief that it is expanding in exciting ways. Many creative innovations in practice are possible if a dialogue is maintained between experimental and applied endeavours. This book tries to promote such a dialogue.

It is not intended to be comprehensive in its coverage of learning disability. Without denying the importance of other perspectives, this book is purely about psychology. Even in terms of psychology, it reflects the author's own limited knowledge and interests. However, it does try to bring together information which is scattered across many sources, and often difficult to access for the practitioner.

The book is targeted upon those for whom psychology is an integral part of everyday working practice. This includes professional psychologists, teachers, speech therapists, occupational therapists and psychiatrists. It is hoped it might be of interest to those in training and those already qualified.

Many people contributed to the outcome you are now reading. The Hilda Lewis House team, colleagues in Southwark, and clinical psychology students at the Institute of Psychiatry, all provided important 'setting conditions'. There are several very specific contributions. Fraser Watts somehow persuaded me to write the book in the first place, and has provided help and encouragement throughout. Jean Foley helped with typing some of the early drafts of the manuscript. There are then three very special credits. T.C. provided the home support team without which no intervention can be maintained. Jean Morgan wrestled tirelessly with indecipherable manuscripts and audio tapes, with much good humour and sound advice. She provided most of the earlier drafts and the complete final manuscript. Ewa Zarkowska read the first draft of every chapter, commented constructively and provided much general encouragement and support. To all these people I offer my sincerest thanks for turning a mid-life crisis to productive use!

Chapter 1

Introduction

The people with whom this book concerns itself are easily recognized in any society. For administrative and research purposes they are often held to constitute a 'population'. Defining such a 'population' proves much more difficult than recognizing the people themselves. They are people who progress very slowly—they take longer to learn skills and pass through the stages of human development. Their difficulties are evident from early in life and their levels of attainment are well below those of their peers at nearly all ages. They will score very low on standardized tests of intelligence, usually below IQ 55. Most will have some evidence of biological factors which influence the functioning of their central nervous system. This may involve gross damage to the system or a variety of structural and functional anomalies. All will require a great deal more help, support and supervision than others of their age; and few will attain full independence even in adult life. Many will have additional physical, sensory, medical or psychological problems; and in this sense they are people vulnerable to a wide range of difficulties.

These people attract a range of labels. These include 'severely mentally handicapped', 'moderately, severely or profoundly retarded' and 'severely learning disabled'. For the purposes of this book use will be made of the World Health Organization guidelines on terminology (WHO, 1980). The nature of the difficulty affecting these people is seen as one of severe intellectual impairment where impairment is taken to mean 'any loss or abnormality of psychological, physiological or anatomical structure or function'. Given this impairment people experience severe difficulties in learning, i.e. they have severe learning disabilities, where the term disability refers to 'any restriction or lack (resulting from an impairment) of ability to perform an activity in the manner or within the range considered normal for a human being'. Those affected by such disabilities are likely to be handicapped, where handicap means 'a disadvantage for an individual resulting from an impairment or disability, that limits or prevents fulfilment of a role that is normal (depending on age, sex and social and cultural factors) for that individual'. It can be seen from this that the degree of handicap will be as much determined by the help and opportunities offered to those affected as it will be by the actual disability itself.

This interaction between a disability and society's response to that disability does much to determine what constitutes the psychology of severe intellectual impairment. The most common response of a society is to regard people who have such impairments and disabilities as members of a single population. This is based upon the many needs that such people have in common. They need a great deal of support, and there is a low probability that they will become fully independent members of society. Such needs will require from a society a planned response and in any humane setting this will mean a social policy and allocation of resources. It is easier to develop such a policy and allocate resources if the people affected can be considered a group. In this sense it is administratively convenient to aggregate such people together on the basis of the extent of their needs, irrespective of the factors underlying these needs. The psychological ramifications of such a view are seen in the focus of interest upon one of the psychological features that these people have in common—their low scores on tests of general intellectual functioning. Such tests have been used as a major means of defining membership of the population and much psychological work has gone into understanding the processes which might underlie performance on such IQ tests.

Aggregating people into such administrative groups both reflects and encourages the forming of general social models which will mediate the interpretation of the presenting phenomena and provide some kind of philosophical framework to guide and rationalize society's response. Such models may also serve a deeper symbolic function for a society, particularly where it enables a society to find a scapegoat during times of general social crisis. Thus people with a severe intellectual impairment always have tended to be regarded as a population but there have been a number of models used for socially interpreting the nature of the problem faced by this population (Wolfensberger, 1975). Such social models have exerted a powerful influence upon how people so affected have led their lives. At various times and in various societies a single predominant model may be detected; or a range of models may be seen in operation. There are religious, medical, sociological, zoological and educational models. Religious models have offered a range of interpretations for the phenomena of intellectual impairment. People affected have been seen as agents of the devil or, alternatively, as having a special relationship with God. This has led to their being driven from society or offered a special and protected place within a society. Services based upon charity (sometimes 'cold' charity), derive from the notion that caring for the disabled constitutes 'good work' and thus endows the carer with grace for the after-life. More zoological approaches have looked at those with severe learning disabilities from a species point of view. This has suggested that such people are not fully human. This can be seen in the ready equation of sub-normal with sub-human and can also be seen in current ethical debates about what constitutes a human life—the struggle for a definition that will determine whether or not interventions will take place to conserve an individual's life. Such zoological thinking has encouraged segregation and the provision of the sorts of environments provided for animals in captivity.

There are a number of sociological models of which one has regarded those with intellectual impairment as a socially deviant group. Work on genetics in the late nineteenth and early twentieth centuries drew a link between intellectual impairment and crime and saw those that were impaired as a threat to society. Viewed in this light, practices such as enforced segregation and sterilization were encouraged. An alternative formulation, growing up particularly in the 1960s, drew attention to those with intellectual impairment as a deprived minority group and emphasized the human rights element as a key determinant of service provision and resource allocation. Such a view stresses the humanity of those affected and their right to a place in society and a fair share of resources, using a logic very similar to that used to argue against racial and sexual prejudice. Medical models have indicated that the phenomena of severe intellectual impairment should be interpreted in the same way as other illnesses. Such a view emphasizes the need for specialized professional treatment operating primarily within a health context. On the other hand, educational models view intellectual impairment from the point of view of the major disability that follows—that of learning. It suggests the need for 'education' not 'treatment' and stresses the need for services to be provided within an educational rather than a health context.

At the present time many Western industrial capitalist societies are in the midst of a major shift in social models. The medical model is giving way to an educational model linked to a human rights sociological approach. The outcome of this shift can be seen in the sometimes rapid move towards increased community care and integration; and the increased control of services by education and social welfare agencies as opposed to health agencies. Although this represents the dominant trend, many other models can be seen in operation at more local or individual levels as in the operation of specific religious-based communities for people with severe learning disabilities.

The psychology of intellectual impairment is bound to be influenced by the predominant social model. The questions studied, the theories proposed will be determined to some extent by this broad social interpretative framework. In response to the administrative aggregation of affected people psychological theories have tended to be rather unidimensional and suggest that there is *a* theory of severe intellectual impairment. As already mentioned, low IQ has been taken as the defining feature and psychology has sought to explain factors that underlie low measured intelligence with the implicit belief that a single explanation may suffice, irrespective of the origin and exact nature of the intellectual impairment. When such a view is linked to a belief in the relatively unchangeable nature of IQ then such a psychology can be seen as primarily descriptive rather than oriented towards remediation and change.

Two major psychological theories have been proposed to explain severe intellectual impairment. The deviancy theory suggests that those with such problems have one or more deviant mental processes which underlie the low IQ. Such a theory suggests that the processes are different from those in the normal population and research has been directed to pinpointing such deviant processes and endeavouring to quantify the nature of this deviance. The method of study has been to use control group research designs, comparing a group of people with impairments to other non-impaired people matched for age or level of mental development. Such a theory is consistent with the emphasis of the medical model or the sociological-deviancy model. It serves to emphasize the differences rather than the commonalities between those who are affected and other members of society.

The major alternative to deviancy theory is the developmental delay theory which proposes that people with severe intellectual impairment have the same mental processes as other people and go through the same stages of development as others but at a rather slower rate. Methods of study similar to those above are used but the emphasis is upon the commonalities with, rather than the differences from, the general population. Such a model coheres with a sociological human rights model and, to some extent, educational models in so far as knowledge of developmental processes is regarded as relevant to education.

The main problem is not whether such theories are true or correct. Both may be drawing attention to important phenomena. The difficulty lies in the idea that severe intellectual impairment can be understood in terms of a unidimensional model applicable to all those affected. One aspect of the current shift in social models and social policies is the emphasis placed upon individual needs, the recognition that the administratively labelled population represent in fact a very varied group. While recognizing the basic common human needs, emphasis is placed upon the unique needs of each individual, some of which may be completely unique, some of which may have much in common with those in the so-called normal population, some of which may relate to needs present in other defined groups. Many dimensions of such variation are suggested—the overall degree of impairment, the pattern or profile of learning difficulties, the additional physical, sensory, medical or psychological problems to which people with a severe intellectual impairment can be vulnerable. Such an emphasis has not only drawn attention to the variation which may be inherent within the individual but has also drawn attention to the fact that, as for normal people, the functioning of the individual is very much determined by environmental circumstances. These may include quality of relationships, level and type of stimulation and the sort of remedial help offered.

Thus the need arises for a psychological framework which will adequately represent such individual variation. No simple undimensional theory or model will suffice. The key psychological questions are not now focused upon how to explain low IQ. Rather, they are concerned with how to understand the functioning of a particular individual in a particular situation. The increasing recognition of the dynamic nature of human behaviour, its relative changeability and instability, makes such a psychology more change oriented and concerned with applied rather than purely experimental issues. Where such a psychology becomes allied to a human rights approach to social policy then it becomes a key means of developing the detailed strategies and techniques that will make a reality of that social policy. What is needed, therefore, is some kind of multidimensional framework which will facilitate the study of individual differences and the analysis of individual needs. The focus has shifted to the individual, with any groupings determined on an empirical, as opposed to an administrative, basis. There may well be groups of people who have a number of individual needs in common and for whom group membership might constitute an advantage. Such groupings would be flexible, would not constitute the whole basis of an individual's existence and would be based upon comprehensive individual analysis rather than being determined a priori on the basis of one single characteristic such as level of dependency or IQ score.

It is one of the aims of this book to try and specify some of the dimensions which may be relevant to a psychological approach useful for people with a severe degree of intellectual impairment. There is no pretence to a comprehensive analysis. It is more an attempt to explore the implications of such a conceptualization but from a limited and personal perspective. Much that emerges may well appear trite. Thus it will be suggested that any approach to understanding the individual will require analysis of a range of personal and environmental characteristics. The individual's presentation at any one point in time will be seen as the product of an interaction between the individual and the environment. This is hardly novel, and such interaction is commonplace in 'normal' psychology. In the study of intellectual impairment, however, it represents an attempt to overcome the influence of simpler social models upon psychological conceptualizations.

The powerful administrative labels applied to people affected by severe learning disabilities have done much to overshadow their psychology and render difficult the study of the uniqueness of each individual.

Such an interactionist position may be obvious at a general level, yet its more detailed application to severe intellectual impairment has so far been very limited. There is a large amount of scattered information but little in the way of a coherent framework to permit the integration of knowledge so far obtained. A relevant psychology will be called upon to assess the many facets of individual and environmental functioning. It will also be called upon to develop strategies for change based upon this analysis. It will need to know the relevant dimensions of individuals and environments which require assessment; it will need methods which adequately reflect and reliably represent such dimensions; it will need validated strategies for effecting change. Some of this information is already available but much has yet to be discovered. This book will endeavour to describe some of the areas of knowledge that may be relevant for such a psychology. There is no pretence to completeness or even correctness—that is, some of the areas suggested as promising in this book may yet prove to be blind alleys. Nevertheless it is written in the firm conviction that such a psychology is possible and that it will require the integration of knowledge from many domains. Ecological psychology, neuropsychology, cognitive, social and developmental psychology all have a contribution to make. It is unfortunate that integration of knowledge from these areas is hampered by the relative isolation of those who work in these various branches of psychology. There is some indication that artificial academic barriers are breaking down but much more progress will be needed in that direction if the potential of psychology in relation to severe intellectual impairment is to be developed.

Although many different branches of psychology are necessary if an understanding of the phenomena of severe intellectual impairment is to be advanced, the methods by which such advances will be secured must also be considered. This book is written from the perspective of psychology as a science. It is implicit in what is said that advances in understanding will take place through the application of scientific methods to the questions raised. Such methods may range from careful naturalistic observations to controlled group or individual experimentation. The methods vary but all are based upon the underlying concept of objective measurement. Attaining objectivity is a difficult struggle in any area of science but none more so than in the field of psychology where so many phenomena (for example thoughts, feelings, attitudes, expectations) would seem accessible only through subjective experience. Despite the difficulties of the scientific approach it is the firm belief of the author that this is the road to advancement of knowledge, and thus the content of this book is concerned very much with available scientific research and the inferences that this permits.

However, there is no pretence that objectivity can ever be complete or that science is value-free. The scientific method is seen as a means of effecting significant advances in our understanding but there is no implication that such endeavours exist in isolation from the world of values. It has already been indicated that the questions asked by a scientific psychology are deeply influenced by the prevailing social and cultural context—in particular the predominant social model of intellectual impairment. It has also been indicated that some social models (and thus some psychological studies) can be gravely detrimental to what is now conceived of as the interests of people with such impairments. Science cannot escape questions of value and it therefore seems important in a text which is based upon scientific studies and advocates scientific methods that some consideration should be given to the value perspective from which the book is written. At the very least this may help the reader to recognize the author's prejudices; and may assist in the delicate process of disentangling statements which reflect current scientific understanding from those which more truly represent personal preferences and values.

REFERENCES

WHO (1980) *International Classification of Impairments, Disabilities and Handicaps.* Geneva: World Health Organization.
Wolfensberger, W. (1975) *The Origin and Nature of our Institutional Models.* Syracuse, NY: Human Policy Press.

Chapter 2

Facts and Values

Severe intellectual impairment raises many ethical issues for individuals and for society in general. Some of these issues are specific to this particular kind of personal difficulty. Other issues are more general, concerned with the nature of being and of society. The last 30 years have seen a growing awareness of such ethical issues and to some extent this growth can be analysed chronologically.

The first concerns arose out of the living conditions that were being imposed by many societies upon people with severe intellectual impairment. Such concerns were highlighted by scientific studies demonstrating the damaging effects of large-scale institutions upon the personal development of those with severe learning disabilities. They were highlighted by the public scandals over living conditions in many of these institutions. Such revelations elicited feelings of compassion and motivated a more humanitarian approach. The first reaction, particularly in the late 1960s and early 1970s, was to review social policy and immediately to allocate more resources to improving the services already available. However, through the 1970s a more pro-active response grew out of the development of a human rights approach to these issues. Thus institutional forms of living became not just inadequate but in violation of the fundamental rights of people affected by severe learning disabilities. Many such rights have been articulated—for example the right to care in, and by, the community, the right to an 'ordinary' life, the right to integration, the right to work, the right to an individual programme plan. Such an approach was given coherence through the philosophy of normalization and the insights it provided into the social devaluation and role expectations of people with learning disabilities (Nirje, 1969; Wolfensberger, 1972). This produced both empirical guidelines as to what should be done to enhance the competence and image of those with disabilities (Wolfensberger, 1983), and a strong moral force for change.

At the same time that the inadequacies of general living conditions were being highlighted so too was knowledge being accumulated that, rather than being ineducable or untreatable, people with severe learning disabilities could learn new skills and overcome behavioural difficulties. Behavioural research was demonstrating quite clearly that there were specific techniques which could dramatically affect personal development. Such knowledge indicated that maximizing development was not just a question of improving general living conditions but also of applying specific and detailed intervention technologies. In articulating such technologies many ethical issues arose out of both the goals and methods to be used for behaviour change. An early concern arose out of the use of punishment techniques, in particular the use of physically painful stimuli, to suppress problem behaviours such as self-injury. Another early concern was the goals towards which programmes of behaviour change might be directed, and in particular a fear that such programmes were used to reinforce institutional goals such as passivity which might be at variance with the true interests of the individual. Such concern with the ethics of intervention, particularly behavioural interventions, provided an important theme through to the late 1970s. It stimulated the development of a range of ethical control procedures such as ethical committees, codes of practice and systems of inspection. As well as focusing attention upon issues about the goals and methods of behaviour change, it also illustrated the difficulty over what might constitute permission for people with inherently limited abilities to speak for themselves.

The late 1970s and 1980s have been marked by growing awareness of the ethical issues that arise with recent advances in biomedical technologies. The development of antenatal screening techniques such as amniocentesis has made a reality of preventing some kinds of impairment through abortion. There is of course the general issue over the ethics of abortion. However, even if abortion in general is accepted within a society there is still the issue of what constitutes grounds for an abortion. This in turn raises consideration of what constitutes quality of life for both the parents and the child. Does the possession of an extra chromosome and the likelihood of a moderate to severe degree of intellectual impairment mean such a poor quality of life for the child and family that such a life should not be allowed to develop? Such issues are also raised by major advances in life-preserving techniques. Progress in this area has been continuous but it is only the more recent advances in high technology medicine which have attracted considerable attention. Thus the advent of antibiotics radically altered the life expectancy of many people with severe intellectual impairment, in particular those with Down's syndrome. Similar effects followed from advances in heart surgery. Improvements in the ability to care for low birth weight babies have saved many normal children but have also kept alive already impaired infants who would otherwise have died. New life support systems have aided the survival of many normal infants stricken with devastating infections and subsequent brain damage who also would have otherwise died. In the face of these advances many questions have been raised about what should constitute adequate grounds for initiating or sustaining heroic interventions which will keep alive those who are clearly impaired. Such dilemmas become particularly acute in times of limited economic resources and have forced the issue of quality of life and what constitutes a human life on to the open agenda of social policy (Laura and Ashman, 1985).

Thus ethical issues pervade many areas of work with people affected by severe learning disabilities. For a scientific psychology in this field some of these are particuarly relevant. Concern about the goals and methods of psychological interventions has already been mentioned. Thus interventions which inflict pain or which increase passivity, have come to be viewed with increasing distaste. There are perhaps more fundamental issues which are not so frequently discussed. The difficult issue of permission arises in both applied and research settings. It is alarming to note the very large literature, much of it concerned with institutionalized populations, which makes no mention of how permission was obtained for the involvement of people with severe learning disabilities. It is also alarming to note the many studies which would appear to be of marginal practical utility to those involved where no mention was made of any recompense to the subjects for their involvement. In working with a disadvantaged population, which is essentially what people with severe learning disabilities often are, psychology like any other science must be aware of the danger of exploitation which is inherent in being disadvantaged. Much greater care is needed to protect the rights of those to be involved and to ensure that people with learning disabilities who participate in clinical or experimental studies are entitled to the same consideration as everyone else.

The issue of consent is a particular focus for concern and there needs to be a much greater awareness of the potential negative side-effects of any psychological study or intervention. Such side effects may be directly upon the individual involved. Thus administration of a drug or the inflicting of pain may not only influence particular behaviours targeted for change but also create a number of other disturbances within the individual which are, in general, detrimental to his or her functioning. These situations are relatively clear-cut. However, there are other considerations which are relevant. In Chapter 1 there was some discussion about the social models which have influenced attitudes towards, and provision for, people with severe intellectual impairment. Some of these models, and the prevailing stereotypes through which they are expressed, would appear actively detrimental to the well-being of people with severe learning disabilities. An important ethical issue arises as to whether particular applied and research questions or methods of work contribute to an unhelpful image of people with severe learning disabilities (see Wolfensberger, 1983). Some of the most significant objections to the use of pain-shock have nothing to do with the infliction of pain. In using such a universally feared stimulus, further stigmatization of those involved is a likely outcome. In applying such a stimulus through a vehicle such as a cattle prod, it is virtually guaranteed and can only suggest a sub-human stereotype for the person whose behaviour is being changed in this way. Such a stereotype has guided some of the worst provision for people with severe learning disabilities. In a similar vein some of the strongest objections to the use of food reinforcement in treatment programmes are not dental but the powerful image of animal training so suggested. Excessive use of social attention with adults who have severe learning disabilities fosters the notion of them as perpetual children. Irrespective of whether a particular technique works, or a particular study produces a significant result, it is always important to consider whether the methods used foster the right self and social image of people with severe learning disabilities. In the questions it asks and the methods it uses a psychology of severe intellectual impairment must not contribute to a negative image of those affected.

The issues so far raised reflect ethical concerns at a very general level. However, values are also highly personal and those held by an individual will not necessarily coincide with more general values which are expressed through social attitudes and social policies. Individual values will affect the questions that an individual asks and the way that facts are interpreted. As this is a book written by an individual, it seems important that there be some articulation of the author's own values in this area. This will help, perhaps, to clarify the general approach adopted in the book and the selection of information presented. This in its turn will hopefully enable the reader to go some way to separating fact from opinion and make it easier to reject opinion without necessarily rejecting the facts themselves. For example, one may dispute whether a particular study of memory functioning supports the idea of deviant mental processes in people with severe learning disabilities. One may contest whether one should be attempting to establish such deviancy anyway. However, this should not stop one from recognizing that some people with severe learning disabilities may well have the memory problems which are illustrated in the particular study. What follows, therefore, is an attempt to articulate some of the values and attitudes which underlie this book. There is no implication that these are right nor is there any pretence to a coherent philosophy of general interest. Although understandably the product of many influences it is essentially a personal statement made in an attempt to help the reader overcome the author's prejudices.

A central theme is that people with severe learning disabilities are first and foremost human beings with at least the same needs and rights as other members of society. They are entitled to lead as ordinary a life as possible within the main stream of society. Indeed it will only be possible to understand the full nature of severe learning disabilities when those affected are exposed to normal living conditions. Only in this situation can one avoid confounding problems of learning disability with secondary handicaps which might derive from living in disadvantaged circumstances. Having a right to a place in society does not require that it be taken up in any rigid or stereotyped fashion. Thus it is a strong belief of the author that different living arrangements will suit different people, and that there should be respect for such individual differences. It is seen as the job of a relevant psychology to explore which aspects of living environments produce which sorts of outcomes for those living in them, outcomes in terms of personal development, personal satisfaction or social standing (dependent variables which are not always highly correlated). Individual freedom of choice is a recurring theme. Thus any narrow interpretation of community care as requiring people to live individually or in very small groups in the places where they were born is rejected. There is no particular commitment in this text to individual or small-group living in urban housing. If some people benefit from and prefer to live out of town, and/or in larger group settings, then that is a legitimate outcome of study and research. If some people benefit from and prefer living in settings with relationships other than those based upon a conception of the nuclear family, then this too is a legitimate and possible outcome.

Indeed, it is belief in the importance of the individual which pervades many areas of this book. This means that the interests of people with severe intellectual impairment are most likely to be served if they themselves are able to exert counter-control over those who live, work and plan with them. This is true whether these others are family members, professional staff or politicians and social planners. Exerting such counter-control is extremely difficult for people with these kinds of disabilities. It may well require special advocacy arrangements. Nevertheless, much can be done to assist individuals to do this for themselves. It is no accident that in the part looking at the interface between severe intellectual impairment and educational technologies (Part 3) the examples chosen are communication and self-management skills.

In recognizing the worth of the individual, however, there is no simple equation of worth with attainment. The rate at which a person progresses, the degree of independence achieved, is not seen as critical to that person's value as an individual. This is a very difficult dilemma, particularly in an advanced capitalist culture which lays so much stress upon individual attainment and very closely equates personal value with personal progress. This dilemma made writing the chapter on intervention technologies particularly difficult. It is very tempting to exaggerate claims for efficacy and to gloss over limitations when attempting to achieve a more satisfactory place for a disadvantaged group in society. Perhaps, indeed, this is justifiable sometimes and positive discrimination may well be an important way forward for some groups. However, it has to be accepted that severe intellectual impairment cannot, as yet, be cured. Many affected people can make more progress than they have in the past and can attain a far higher degree of independence. Many, however, will not attain full independence and some will make extremely slow progress and remain heavily dependent throughout their lives. Those who remain so dependent are no less valuable as people. Acknowledging limitations is a spur to innovation, not an admission of defeat. It is a challenge for any society to find a place in it for those who are heavily dependent. This challenge cannot be avoided by pretending that dependency can be eliminated. It is in this spirit that the appraisal of intervention technologies is a critical one. It would perhaps have been better also had more of the book been devoted to relevant aspects of psychological functioning other than attainment. The fact that the study of attainment still predominates so much in this text perhaps reflects the author's dilemmas in this area.

If any term characterizes this attitude to the individual it is the term 'respect'. For the author, attaining respect for the individual is an ongoing struggle rather than an already achieved state. At the personal level it involves acknowledging the basic humanity and societal rights of those affected by severe learning disabilities. It involves recognizing the individuality of the people affected in the midst of very obvious and often multiple disabilities. It means trying to find ways of satisfactorily relating to people whose attainments will always be limited. At a more professional level it requires full recognition of the complexity of the phenomena with which one is faced. Respect often becomes awe in the face of trying to interpret the many and complex factors which go towards determining individual behaviour in real-world settings. It is clear that there will be no easy answers and professional respect dictates that the approaches developed give adequate recognition to the complexity of the phenomena. People with intellectual impairments have sometimes been labelled as 'simple'. Likewise, the psychology proposed for people so affected has often been 'simple'. It is hoped that this text, and many others like it, go some way towards illustrating the irony of such a description. If that engenders certain feelings of professional bewilderment and inadequacy, then that more truly reflects the state of the art in the psychology of severe intellectual impairment than any more comforting notions based upon an assured knowledge base.

The foregoing represents some of the value themes of which the author is consciously aware as exerting influence in the production of this book.

There may well be others in operation. It is hoped that by describing such values two effects will have been achieved. One is to reinforce the general need for continuing dialogue between scientific enterprises and moral debate, to keep science in a value-laden context. The second is to elucidate some of the author's personal prejudices in order to help the reader discount these and reach a personal appraisal of the facts presented. With this in mind, the three parts of the book go on to look at some of the relevant areas of psychological knowledge in relation to severe intellectual impairment.

REFERENCES

Laura, R.S., and Ashman, A.F. (eds) (1985) *Moral Issues in Mental Retardation*. London: Croom Helm.

Nirje, B. (1969) The normalization principle and its human service implications. In R. Kugel and W. Wolfensberger (eds.) *Changing Patterns in Residential Services for the Mentally Retarded*. Washington, DC: Government Printing Office.

Wolfensberger, W. (1972) *The Principle of Normalization in Human Services*. Toronto: National Institute on Mental Retardation.

Wolfensberger, W. (1983) Social role valorization: a proposed new term for the principle of normalization. *Mental Retardation*, 21, 234–239.

Part One

The Nature of Impairment

INTRODUCTION TO PART 1

This part tries to examine some of the factors which may be related to difficulty with learning and behaving adaptively. It is often speculative, drawing upon different areas of research to provide a framework for analysing these factors. It is always arbitrary to make a sharp distinction between what may be part of a basic impairment and what is the result of experience. The features described in this section are not necessarily uninfluenced or uninfluenceable by experience. Indeed, most of the factors selected for review are those which offer significant possibilities for change as this is a major theme of the present book. Nevertheless, it is felt that these are factors closer to the nature of a basic underlying impairment; and that they are factors which may be related to many areas of difficulty in everyday functioning. However, it is felt that understanding them will significantly improve the ability to understand individual differences and to direct help in a more rational and individualized way.

Chapter 3

General Cognitive Functioning

The area of work to be discussed in this chapter deals with the mental activities involved in selecting, analysing and interpreting information and planning responses appropriate to presented situations. Cognitive functioning includes, among other things, attending to and discriminating between objects and events, solving problems, learning and remembering. It thus encompasses what are often thought of as 'rational' activities. This is obviously relevant to understanding the difficulties experienced by people with intellectual impairment and learning disabilities. Standard definitions of mental handicap and mental retardation always incorporate the fact that the people concerned have general difficulty in learning and in acting in a socially competent manner. Popular conceptions about people with these disabilities often refer to their problems in attending, understanding and remembering. If learning disabilities are to be better understood, it would seem essential to define more clearly the nature of cognitive functioning, to find means of assessing it and to use this as a guide for modifying it.

DEFINING COGNITIVE FUNCTIONING

Figure 1 presents a schematic model of the cognitive system. It incorporates three distinct elements:
1. *Structures* These are analogous to the hardware aspects of the computer system or the physical components of bureaucracy (such as filing cabinets and employees). They are physical elements which have a limited capacity (Broadbent, 1958). They include sensory receptors, the channels along which information travels and the various memory stores in which information is held.
2. *Processes* These are analogous to some of the software elements in a computer system or the operating procedures in a bureaucracy (such as memos, job descriptions, operational procedures). They represent the

rules by which the system operates. Because capacities are limited attention is selective so that some information is received and passed on for processing while other information is blocked out. Such selection is an active process. Remembering material may require active rehearsal — this is therefore a process for getting information into temporary or permanent storage. Solving problems will require reference to earlier experience — retrieval is the process by which information is brought from storage to aid in decision making.

3. *Higher order strategies* These are analogous to control systems or the management element in a bureaucracy (general plans). They refer to the overall control of the cognitive system. Such strategies provide 'instructions' which determine which processes operate in which order. They monitor the general functioning of the system and adjust it according to the results being achieved.

The whole system can be seen to operate in a series of stages. Two examples may help to make this clearer. The first deals with a standard

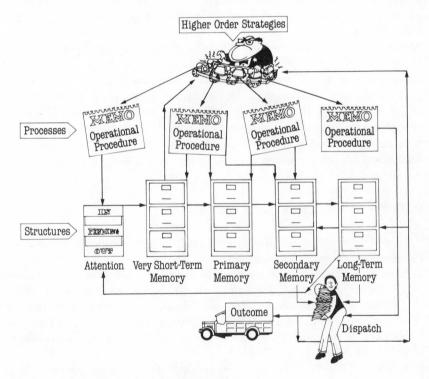

Figure 1   Schematic model of human cognitive system.

laboratory situation where a person has to remember a list of pictures presented one after the other. The first stage is to define the general requirements of the situation, i.e. this is a picture task which means looking closely at what the researcher presents and trying to get the greatest number of successful responses possible. Such an analysis orients the cognitive system towards a particular range of information, sets the broad limits within which information will be selected and sets the standards for evaluating response efficacy. As the pictures come up on the screen, attention is focused on to them and other information (such as traffic noise) is blocked out. The information selected is then processed in a series of stages. It is first held in a sensory register from which information decays very rapidly. It passes from there to a short-term, rehearsal buffer memory where it is organized and analysed before proceeding, if necessary, to a longer term store. Thus as the pictures flash up on the screen in rapid succession they will be processed in a number of ways. Note may be taken of the name of the picture (e.g. cat), its conceptual category (animal), its position on the screen (top-right), its position in the sequence (third) — all these and many other features may be noted and stored. As the task is one of memorizing, the items may need to be rehearsed and repeated in order to consolidate them and it may be a better strategy to chunk them, for example into blocks of three, for such rehearsal. Thus a range of processes can be called upon to effect memory, and the higher order strategy will determine exactly which processes are used. At the end of the picture sequence when the subject has to repeat the picture list, the retrieval process begins. Again, this may be carried out in a number of ways as determined by the higher order strategy. For example, the subject might recall the list in order of presentation or recall it by conceptual category (all the animals first, then all the plants). At the end of recall the subject will evaluate the performance and such an evaluation will feed back to influence the ways in which the system operates on the next run through the list. For example, if five out of eight were right but the middle three were forgotten then the system might be oriented to devote more time to rehearsing the middle three of the list next time around. This illustrates some of the complexities of organization and the interplay between structures, processes and higher order strategies.

A more mundane example can be given in terms of shopping in a supermarket. The person must first define the situation, in this example as a large crowded shop where a list of items is to be purchased as quickly and cheaply as possible. Attention is then focussed on to the list of items for purchase and information on other aspects of the environment, such as other goods available, may be blocked out (depending upon the strong will of the shopper and the sophistication of the marketing tactics!). A decision will need to be made as to whether to purchase items in the order they are presented on the shopping list or whether some other order, for example type of food or physical layout of the supermarket, should determine how the task is to be tackled. Once it has been decided how to tackle the order of shopping, then the first item is selected for purchase and information will have to be retrieved on its likely location (for example, last time the cheese was at the top of the third aisle counting from the right). Having found the cheese, then information on type, weight and price will need to be analysed to compare with the shopping requirement and other factors retrieved from memory (for example prices elsewhere). Following from this, the item will be selected for purchase. As items continue to be purchased a running check will need to be maintained of items already purchased so that it is clear when the shopping is complete. Once through the checkout a general evaluation of the expedition can be taken in terms of the number of list items obtained, the time taken and the money spent. Such information may be used to adjust the way subsequent expeditions are undertaken.

These two examples provide some indication of the working of the cognitive system. A comprehensive model has yet to be developed but at least some of the elements are beginning to be understood. It is clear that the system can malfunction in a number of ways. A situation may be incorrectly defined, the wrong information may be selected, the system may not be big enough to handle all the information necessary, information may be organized and processed inappropriately so that it fails to get into memory or information may not be successfully retrieved from memory. There may be an inaccurate evaluation of the outcome of actions. This is a reminder that there can be many cognitive factors underlying a performance difficulty and that learning can break down in a number of ways.

This model of cognitive functioning can be applied to a wide range of problem-solving situations. For present purposes, a distinction will be made between physical and social cognition. Physical cognition is the ability to understand and to act upon the world of objects, to understand things inanimate and mechanical. Social cognition is the ability to understand and relate to people, to solve problems that arise in a social context. Clearly there is overlap between these two areas. Many problems have both social and physcial dimensions and there may be many common structures and processes involved in both domains. Even remembering a list of words presented by an experimenter is not just a mechanical task and incorporates knowledge of social rules to do with cooperating and being well regarded. It does appear, however, that during child development physical and social cognition can be seen as separable domains (Dunst, 1984). More particularly, amongst people with severe learning disabilities there are a significant number with specific additional problems in understanding and relating to people. For these, and other reasons, a separate chapter is devoted to social cognition and the present chapter will be primarily concerned with physical cognition.

A further important point concerns the role of motivation. Task performance is not purely determined by cognitive factors. Motivation determines whether the cognitive system works to optimum capacity. A technically sophisticated management system achieves little unless those operating it are committed and ambitious. Task performance may rise or fall according to whether the person is interested in the task, wants to do well, is indifferent or overanxious. Understanding performance difficulties must therefore try to integrate both cognitive and motivational factors. In any particular situation it is very difficult to separate these two methodologically and the bulk of research has concerned itself with cognitive aspects and interpreted its findings in purely cognitive terms. There has been a relative neglect of motivational factors and the interplay between cognition and motivation. Thus most of this chapter will discuss the types of cognitive difficulty thought to be involved in severe intellectual impairment and learning disabilities. There will be a shorter section on the motivational factors relevant to understanding these types of problems which more reflects lack of attention to this area rather than lack of importance.

However, before any relevant research findings can be discussed it is necessary to comment upon how the cognitive system has been studied.

THE STUDY OF COGNITIVE FUNCTIONING

Much of the literature reviewed in this chapter is based upon the study of cognitive functioning in laboratory settings. This literature has a number of general limitations for the present purpose, which is to look for ways of understanding and remediating the difficulties of the individual learner affected by severe intellectual impairment. This purpose is not one that underlies many experimental studies. Most cognitive research is designed to test out predictions from general theories of cognitive and intellectual functioning. In this tradition, score on IQ tests is the performance to be explained. Other areas of functioning are not considered nor do such theories have any significant remedial implications. In the opening chapter the need for a more comprehensive psychological view of severe learning disabilities was stressed. The large individual differences between people with these problems was emphasized. The target for present explanations is the difference between people, not the factor that they have in common (that is, low IQ). This difference in purpose clearly limits the likely utility of findings from general experimental research.

A second set of problems concerns the subjects that have been involved in experimental research. Such research often takes place in laboratory settings where subjects work individually with minimal assistance and distraction. They are often given limited instructions about what is expected in order not to bias their responding. On the other hand, the subjects are undoubtedly expected to understand that the task is important and that they should do their best. These general demand characteristics of laboratory settings may be very difficult for people with severe learning disabilities to manage. Much of the research, therefore, has involved people with milder degrees of disability and deliberately excluded those whose difficulties are considered severe. Thus caution is needed in extrapolating from findings on one client group to a quite different population.

The third important limiting characteristic has been the tasks traditionally used in laboratory research. The emphasis of researchers has been upon tasks which tap one particular cognitive function, which can be presented in a very controlled way and which minimize the effects of earlier learning and experience. The tasks used include reacting to lights, judging lines for similarity in length, memorizing word, picture or number lists. Such tasks and their method of presentation are far removed from human problem solving in real-world situations and there is almost an inverse relationship between degree of experimental control and likely relevance. This, again, urges caution when interpreting laboratory findings and seeking to apply them in real-world situations.

These, and a number of other concerns about experimental cognitive research, have been much discussed in recent years (see Brooks and Baumeister, 1977; House, 1977; Baumeister, 1984; McMillan and Meyers, 1984; Dunst, 1984). Although caution is clearly necessary when generalizing findings it would be foolish to reject as altogether irrelevant the information accumulated in this literature. This work has helped to develop understanding of the many varied processes involved in human problem-solving activities. It has begun to develop a conceptual framework within which such differences can be understood. It provides a range of insights and ideas into the factors which might underlie the performance problems of some pople with intellectual impairment. Most recently it has begun to explore ways of remediating some of the cognitive difficulties that have been suggested (Brooks and McCauley, 1984). It may be that much more could be achieved if those working in applied settings could take up the concepts developed in the experimental literature and seek to apply them to real-world situations. Undoubtedly these concepts would be 'stretched' and modified in the process. However, this is exactly the way in which applied behavioural work grew out of experimental laboratory-based behavioural work and such a movement has proved much to the advantage of people with severe learning disabilities (see Chapters 6, 7 and 8; see also

McMillan and Meyers, 1984). It is in this spirit that the subsequent sections of this chapter and the chapter on social cognition are presented.

EXPERIMENTAL STUDIES OF COGNITIVE FUNCTIONING

Dealing with Incoming Information

A number of structural and process difficulties have been suggested in this area. People with learning disabilities may have greater difficulty in holding and analysing information at the very earliest level of the brief sensory register (See Figure 1). In a situation where two lines are briefly flashed on a screen and a judgement has to be made as to whether their length is equal, people with learning disabilities require a longer exposure time before their judgements are accurate (Lally and Nettlebeck, 1977; Nettlebeck and Lally, 1979). Experiments where subjects must judge whether an item shown is a member of a group previously viewed have found that those with learning disabilities are more adversely affected by any impairment in the quality of the presented item. They are also more affected by increases in the number of items in the original group (see Maisto and Baumeister, 1984, for a review of these findings). These problems are not explained by the subjects' level of development but rather relate to the severity of their disability compared to their peers, i.e. they are related to IQ not mental age. It is suggested from these tasks that people with learning disabilities are slow to encode information and to scan through information held in the first store. Whether this represents a structural capacity problem or poor ways of processing information is not clear. As yet, no remedial implications have been articulated, but one could envisage these in terms of the speed and clarity with which information is presented.

A more central difficulty with attentional processes is put forward by Zeaman and his colleagues (see Zeaman and House, 1963; Fisher and Zeaman, 1973; Zeaman and House, 1979). Attention in these terms refers not just to the sensory impact of the stimuli but to the analysis of these incoming stimuli. This analysis involves two steps. First, the stimulus is analysed in terms of general dimensions (colour, form, position, etc.). Secondly, the different aspects of a stimulus within a given dimension are analysed (e.g. red versus blue, round versus square, left versus right). In solving a discrimination problem a subject must attend to the relevant dimension and then select the correct cue along that dimension. Much of the work of Zeaman and colleagues uses tasks where the subject is presented visually with items and must choose the correct one — the problem lies in finding out which one the experimenter has designated as correct (it may, for example, be a particular colour, shape or pattern). A key finding from their early researches is illustrated in Figures 2 and 3. Figure 2 shows the picture obtained from a group of subjects with data summarized across the group. A smooth curve is produced suggesting that success steadily increases over the number of trials presented. If, however, the learning curves for individual subjects are examined a quite different picture emerges (see Figure 3). Subjects appear to spend a period of time responding at chance level and then rapidly improve to criterion. The important early finding was that the difference between subjects with and without learning disabilities lay not in the rate at which improvement occurs once it beings. It lay in a longer initial period of chance level responding for those at lower developmental levels. This finding was interpreted by the authors as implicating attentional processes. It is with the selection of the right dimension that difficulties are suggested at lower developmental levels, not the actual rate of learning which cue is the right one. Again, it is not certain whether this reflects structural or process difficulties. Zeaman and colleagues have some evidence that those with

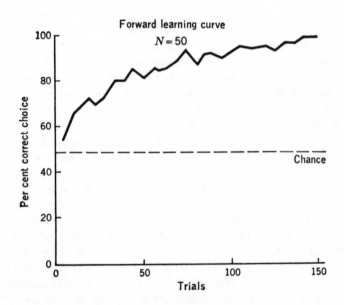

Figure 2   Discrimination learning curve obtained by averaging performance across a group of subjects. (From Zeaman and House, 1963. Reproduced by permission of McGraw-Hill).

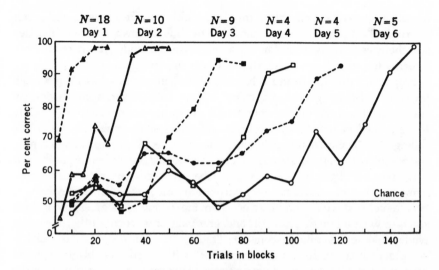

Figure 3   Discrimination learning curves obtained by sub-groups requiring various numbers of training days and trials to reach criterion. (From Zeaman and House, 1963. Reproduced by permission of McGraw-Hill).

learning difficulties may process a more limited range of cues at any one time. Alternatively, it may be that they can process to the same degree but do not deploy their capacities in a systematic problem-oriented fashion.

This body of research has produced a number of other interesting findings. Among those of potential applied relevance are studies which show the very strong attraction of certain aspects of the stimulus. For example, a novel stimulus is very likely to catch the attention of a subject and be responded to. Likewise, subjects often select items according to position rather than any other characteristic such as shape, size or colour. There appears also to be some developmental ordering to discriminations. Form discriminations appear earlier in the course of development than colour discriminations; and three-dimensional are easier than two-dimensional representations. Prolonged failure on a problem has been found to be followed by a failure on problems which have previously been solved by subjects. Although only one aspect of a stimulus may be relevant in solving a problem it has been found that subjects, particularly as one advances developmentally, also learn about other aspects of the stimulus, i.e. they may be able to process a larger amount of information about a variety of aspects of a stimulus. For example, on a colour discrimination they may also learn about the shape and position differences between stimuli. It has been shown that one can speed acquisition of a discrimination by offering extra help built into the stimulus. Teaching a red/green discrimination proceeds more quickly if the reds are always shown as circles and the greens as squares. There are many ways of adding such 'redundant' information which may speed up the learning process.

Improving the speed and reliability of discriminations has been a main focus of laboratory research based on an entirely different theoretical tradition. This is the field of operant discrimination training and particularly those areas labelled stimulus control and errorless training (Terrace, 1966; Rilling, 1977). Given the difficulties faced by people with severe learning disabilities and their failure to learn by traditional trial-and-error methods it was natural that interest should be aroused in procedures that demonstrated successful mastery without errors. A range of strategies have been developed which minimize errors made during training. These include starting with a simple situation and gradually introducing other elements while holding responding constant ('fading in'). For example, to teach a red/green discrimination one might start with a red and blank card and then gradually introduce colour on to the blank card while ensuring that the learner continues to select the red card. An alternative approach is to start with a discrimination which the student can already make and link this to the target discrimination so that the student is faced with complex stimuli full of redundant information which is progressively 'faded out'. Thus one approach to teaching reading is to pair pictures with words and gradually fade out the pictures. 'Stimulus shaping' refers to the procedure whereby the physical aspects of the stimulus are gradually altered over learning trials while the nature of the discrimination remains the same. For example, to teach someone to discriminate between a circle and an ellipse one might start with a simpler discrimination (for example, circle and square) and gradually alter the properties of one or both stimuli towards the final discrimination (for example, remove the edges and gradually curve the sides of the square). Finally, the strategy of physical prompting and fading relies on physically guiding or constraining students so that a correct response always occurs and then systematically reducing the level of guidance over time (this may just be a special example of redundancy fading procedures). For example, a student may have his hand guided to pick up the correct object out of two choices and then have the amount of help gradually reduced over trials while ensuring that he or she continues to select the correct object. Figure 4 illustrates some of these different strategies in relation to a word discrimination study with autistic children by Rincover (1978).

All these strategies may serve to minimize errors. It certainly appears that such errorless training may teach discriminations which are not acquired through trial-and-error learning or are acquired much more slowly (e.g. Schilmoeller et al., 1979; Zawlocki and Walls, 1983). However, a

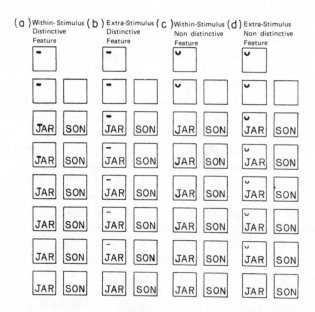

Figure 4   Illustrations of four fading procedures:

(a) **Within-stimulus distinctive feature**   *An intrinsic part of the final discrimination which differentiates the two elements is introduced at the outset, other features are added, and the distinctive feature itself is reduced to be fully integrated into the stimulus.*

(b) **Extra-stimulus distinctive feature** *An initial discrimination is established with a feature, the target discrimination is then introduced coupled to the feature which is then progressively reduced, while kept physically separated from the target stimuli.*

(c) **Within-stimulus non-distinctive feature**   *An intrinsic part of the final discrimination but one which is common to both elements is introduced first. Procedure is then as for (a).*

(d) **Extra-stimulus non-distinctive feature**   *The initial discrimination is established with a feature which is common to both elements in the final discrimination. Procedure is then as for (b). (From A. Rincover (1978) Variables affecting stimulus fading and discriminative responding in psychotic children.* **Journal of Abnormal Psychology,** *87, 541–553. Copyright (1978) by the American Psychological Association. Reprinted by permission of the author).*

number of difficulties have emerged with some of these procedures. In particular it has been found that on occasions learning will proceed with minimal errors up to the point of the final discrimination, when students revert to chance level (see Etzel and Leblanc, 1979, for a useful review of issues involved in such discrimination learning). This problem is much more likely to occur where errors were minimized by using redundant information that was not relevant to the fnal discrimination. Thus in Rincover's (1978) study this problem occurred in the condition where an extra-simulus feature (a mark in the corner of the card) was provided and gradually faded in intensity (Figure 4 (b) and (d)). As soon as it disappeared the discrimination broke down. Successful training of target discriminations is much more likely where criterion-relevant redundant cues are used (Figure 4 (a) and (c)) and stimulus shaping appears to be a particularly effective way of doing this (see Schilmoeller and Etzel, 1977; Schilmoeller *et al.*, 1979; Doran and Holland, 1979; Mosk and Bucher, 1984). These findings suggest that some learners, particularly those at low developmental levels, may only process very limited aspects of the stimuli available to them. This relates closely to Zeaman's finding of the difficulty experienced by disabled learners in selecting the most relevant stimulus for processing. What is perhaps most interesting is that such a phenomenon can be observed in real-world situations when teaching people with severe learning disabilities. Examples from personal experience include the difficulty that sometimes arises in eliminating physical or other kinds of prompts during the teaching of self-help or play skills. The ability of a student to follow instructions can also be dramatically different according to whether the instruction is given from in front or behind, the difference lying in the availability of non-verbal signals.

Such 'over-selectivity' has been regarded as a particular difficulty for those who are labelled autistic. Indeed it has been posited as an explanation for many of the problems presented by such people (see Lovaas, Koegel and Schreibman, 1979). However, it is certainly not a problem found only in this population. It is found in young normal children and people with intellectual impairments varying widely in age, level and type of disability (Meisel, 1981; Bailey, 1981; Gersten, 1983). Nor is it necessarily a stable feature of the individual student's learning: some show over-selectivity on one task but not necessarily on another (Anderson and Rincover, 1982). Multiple factors may determine the breadth of attention and exactly how much information a student extracts from a given situation. These include general level of development (narrower attention at lower development levels), type of task, previous learning history and motivational factors such as degree of arousal (narrower attention at higher levels — see, for example, Easterbrook, 1959; Venables, 1967).

The discussion on over-selectivity brings into focus the issues arising from the study of cognitive processes at the level of incoming information. The research described illustrates a number of possible areas of difficulty for the learner — speed of processing, rate of scanning, breadth of attention, priority in processing. Many of these problems are shown in highly individualized situations and there is no indication as to whether such problems generalize across tasks. Likewise, the explanation of these phenomena might be offered at a number of levels. One might suggest that they illustrate underlying structural limitations in the learner. Alternatively, one might suggest that they reflect strategy problems. For example, Borkowski, Peck and Damberg (1983) point out that subjects with learning disabilities show much more off-task glancing on a range of reaction time and discrimination tasks (i.e. in a test situation they may not orient themselves appropriately or scan arrays in a systematic fashion). Attention performance may also be affected by type of task, by learning conditions (e.g. type of incentive) and by more social factors such as familiarity with the testing situation and the experimenter and understanding the 'rules of the game'. State factors such as degree of arousal may also play a part. Thus no simple explanation can be offered as regards the phenomena reported. Nevertheless a number of useful ways of conceptualizing the difficulties that an individual student might face have emerged. There are also indications of possible strategies for overcoming these difficulties. At present, these are informed guesswork as there is little experimental evidence on attempts to influence attentional performance. However, it may be worth speculating in order to generate the kind of 'bridging' thinking alluded to earlier in the chapter.

Prolonged failure is clearly detrimental and avoidable. Care as to how information is presented provides one set of strategies for teacher and student. Information should be presented so that the important aspects of the situation are clear, the student's attention should be actively drawn to the relevant aspects of the situation, and while extra help and redundant information may be useful they should be provided in a way that does not confuse the learner as to the true nature of the task. Information needs to be presented slowly and in a context which does not induce high levels of arousal in the learner. These may seem fairly gross and obvious statements. However, many of the teaching tactics adopted with handicapped learners do not recognize the attentional difficulties that the student may face. For example, a common way of teaching early reading skills is to pair pictures with words. For some learners this may positively inhibit attention to word shapes. Teaching road crossing may begin with teaching students to use controlled crossings and respond to the light and auditory cues present at these crossings. For some students this may positively distract from the relevant aspects of the situation which are the speed and distance of approaching traffic. Teaching an industrial assembly task using a lot of verbal instructions may draw attention away from key features of the components such as size, shape, colour or sequence position. An interesting example of an approach which incorporates knowledge from the attentional literature is the look and say reading scheme proposed by Jeffree and Skeffington (1980); see Figure 5. This initially presents words with alterations and additions made in such a way that the word resembles the object itself. The additional 'redundant' features can be gradually withdrawn while holding the student's attention on the word shape. This shows how in an imaginative fashion the attention of the student is drawn to the relevant aspects of the situation in a way that minimizes errors. An alternative approach would be to train students to process a wider range of stimuli. Some success with this has been achieved in studies with autistic children using over-training (Schover and Newsom, 1976); or by directly teaching discriminations where multiple cues must be processed as, for example, in conditional discriminations (Koegel and Schreibman, 1977).

These suggestions are not put forward as general rules about the performance of people with learning disabilities. Many such people will learn in exactly the same way as others, from a range of instructional strategies. However, where an individual's learning breaks down then one area to analyse is that of how incoming information is presented and how the student deals with such information. The tools of analysis may be crude

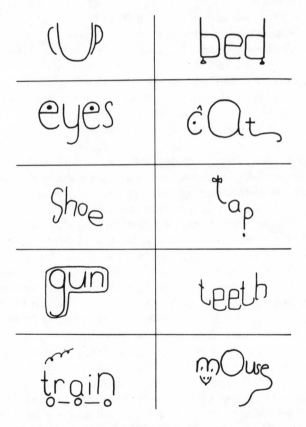

Figure 5 Using within-stimulus redundant features to aid word reading. (From Jeffree and Skeffington, 1980, Let Me Read). Reproduced by permission of Souvenir Press Ltd.

but at least a start can be made and some ideas of where to look have been suggested.

The response to incoming information is, of course, only one stage of cognitive processing. The storage of new information and retrieval of old information is essential to any problem-solving exercise and this area is reviewed in the next section.

Storage and Retrieval of Information

It is a common stereotype of people with severe learning disabilities that they do not remember things very well. This has been attributed to limited storage capacity (a structural deficit). One of the earliest experimental theories about the cognitive problems underlying learning difficulties suggested that a major problem lay in short-term memory because of rapid fading of the stimulus trace (Ellis, 1963). Since that time, theoretical models of memory have developed to the point where it is thought that there are at least four memory stores (see Figure 1 and Ellis, 1970). The literature is both large and confusing with evidence for and against deficits in every kind of store (see Detterman, 1979; Borkowski et al., 1983). It is a major problem to find tasks which are valid and reliable measures of each kind of memory store; and, as yet, no attention has been given to ways of remedying hypothesized storage limitations. Nevertheless, such limitations in particular areas of memory must be recognized as a potential factor underlying performance difficulties. Further development of assessment and remedial strategies would certainly be of interest.

Knowledge of greater applied potential has emerged from the much more robust finding that, apart from any limitations in capacity, people with severe learning disabilities do tend to show much less evidence of using helpful strategies in processing information which has to be remembered. On many kinds of list-learning tasks it has been found that while those with learning disabilities may do as well as others at remembering the last few items, they are almost always worse at recalling items from the beginning of the list (Ellis, 1970). It is thought that remembering such items requires the learner to organize them into groups and actively rehearse them in some way. If the rate at which a list is presented is slowed down (thus giving more opportunity for rehearsal), subjects with learning disabilities are less likely than others of similar developmental level to improve their performance (Detterman, 1979; Borkowski et al., 1983). On tasks where remembering might be aided by organizing items into related groups (e.g. animals, flowers) it has been found that those with severe learning disabilities may show less evidence of spontaneous use of such clustering strategies (e.g. Herriott, Green and McConkey, 1973).

Thus the focus in much experimental work has shifted from the study of structural capacity to the study of the processes used to handle information. As these processes seem potentially more open to remediation this is, therefore, an area of considerable applied interest.

The difficulty for people with learning disabilities that seems to emerge from a range of studies is not so much to do with whether certain processing strategies are present but rather whether the person knows when it is appropriate to use them. Hermelin and O'Connor (1975) found that on a task to remember numbers presented visually, people with severe learning disabilities tended not to encode the numbers in verbal form even though they had the verbal skills to do so. Herriot *et al.* (1973) found when testing their adult subjects with vocabulary skills between the five- and eight-year level that subjects at the lower level tended to show less spontaneous evidence of clustering related items together. However, when reminded to cluster items, either at the time when information was being presented or just before recall testing, subjects appeared perfectly able to carry out such clustering and for the more able subjects this did help the amount they remembered. Even a general instruction that it was possible to categorize the material was sufficient to improve both clustering and recall.

Studies have begun to look at the effects of training people with learning disabilities on processing strategies thought relevant to remembering. Glidden (1979) identifies six such strategies which have been taught:

1. actively labelling and repeating presented items;
2. grouping items at presentation;
3. using category cues at the time of recall;
4. repeating items presented earlier in the task (cumulative rehearsal);
5. developing distinctive visual images to accompany presented items;
6. developing verbal links between items.

People with mild degrees of intellectual impairment have been shown to be perfectly capable of acquiring such strategies with very limited training input. Training does seem to improve performance on the training tasks themselves. However, the evidence that use of such strategies is retained over time or that the strategies are applied to different tasks is much more variable. Such generalization seems more likely for those who are more developmentally advanced (e.g. around the eight- to nine-year level — Brown, Campione and Barclay, 1979; Campione and Brown, 1984). Such generalization is also more probable where subjects know the general appropriateness of strategic behaviour and where they are given a clear explanation as to why a strategy should be used (Campione and Brown, 1977; Belmont, Butterfield and Borkowski, 1978; Kendall, Borkowski and Cavanaugh, 1980; Borkowski, Reid and Kurt, 1984).

Findings of limited generalization have suggested that training should be broadened beyond specific task-oriented strategies to more general problem-solving strategies (the higher order strategies discussed earlier). Brown, Campione and Barclay (1979) suggested the teaching of self-questioning or self-instructional routines such as stop-and-think, do I know what to do? Is there anything I already know that will help me? Is there anything more I need to know before beginning? Borkowski and Varnhagen (1984) looked at the effects of teaching these sorts of general self-instructional skills in addition to specific task strategies to children with learning disabilities functioning at around the eight-year development level, using memory tasks based upon picture lists and prose passages. While the specific strategies aided task performance, the general self-instruction strategies only appeared to give additional help with maintenance of performance over the longer term. However, the amount of training given was very limited so that even such restricted significance is noteworthy. It is also not clear how problem-solving skills develop in normal children and Butterfield and Ferretti (1984) have argued that further study of this would help to operationalize a more comprehensive 'curriculum' of underlying psychological processes and their application. Certainly the nature of higher order strategies is not at all clear and until these are better operationalized it will be difficult to know how to assess their development. However, a promising lead has been opened up, one that has gone some way to narrowing the gap between applied and experimental endeavours.

Conclusions

Despite all the difficulties and limitations acknowledged earlier, laboratory-based experimental research has both advanced the under-standing of the possible location of performance difficulties, and more recently has begun to explore the value of such knowledge for remediation. Much more needs to be known about the stuctural and processing aspects of the cognitive system and the higher order strategies which coordinate the functioning of this system. There is certainly a long way to go before useful devices will be available for assessing the performance of this system and for planning remedial action. Such developments will require greater dialogue between applied and experimental workers but there is at least an indication of the potential value of such dialogue. There is definitely every indication that understanding learning difficulties will require much more complex psychological models than those presently available.

The value of understanding cognitive functioning and of cognitive intervention is not just supported by laboratory-based experimental work. There are a range of applied endeavours for people with learning disabilities which either explicitly or implicitly acknowledge the role of cognitive factors in performance deficits.

APPLIED COGNITIVE STUDIES

More detail on remediation is provided in Parts 2 and 3 of this book. Nevertheless, it is worth looking at some of the more cognitively oriented work at this stage to illustrate how the nature of the difficulty facing the person with learning disabilities is defined. In two books describing his approach to work with adolescents who were socio-culturally deprived and had some degree of learning disability, Reuven Feuerstein (1979a, b) adopts a distinctively cognitive approach. He interprets their learning difficulties as lack of key generic problem-solving skills which are normally acquired through contact with competent adults. He identifies, in particular, difficulties with selecting relevant stimuli, impulsive responding, poor orientation in time and space, and poor interpersonal communicative skills as some of the core problems involved in learning disabilities. Although his work did not grow out of laboratory-based experimentation there is a clear overlap between his conceptions and some of those highlighted earlier, especially in relation to attentional processes and higher order strategies. In his books he details the methods for assessing these difficulties and programmes to remedy them. He targets particularly upon visual-perceptual problem solving and places strong emphasis in remediation on verbalizing problem solving strategies. Claims for the efficacy of this approach have yet to be substantiated by properly controlled research. Arbitman-Smith, Haywood and Bransford (1984) report on a programme based upon Feuerstein's work intended to occupy 300–350 hours of teaching over a two- to three-year period with children who are low achieving or experiencing a mild degree of learning disability. Brooks and McCauley (1984) have adapted this approach to pre-schoolers with mild to moderate degrees of learning disability. The outcome of these studies is not yet known; but irrespective of this, interest resides in Feuerstein's definition of the underlying difficulty in learning disabilities and the overlap with laboratory-based conceptualizations.

Similar considerations are germane to a second major area of applied cognitive work, that to do with self-control. Chapter 8 is devoted entirely to this topic which covers a wide range of techniques drawn from different theoretical backgrounds (see, for example, Mahoney and Mahoney, 1976; Kurtz and Neisworth, 1976; Shapiro, 1981, for useful discussions of this area). Much of the work stresses the importance of self-instruction and self-monitoring as a means of improving both skill acquisition and behavioural adjustment. By implication, this suggests that those with learning disabilities are failing in the natural course of events to acquire these skills. This, in turn, is seen to act as an inhibitory factor upon their development. It is, in fact, a key aspect of Russian theories about learning disability that there is a major deficit in language gaining control over behaviour (for example, Luria, 1961; Vygotsky, 1962). As with Feuerstein's work and some laboratory-based work on information storage and retrieval, the self-control literature draws attention to deficits in higher order strategies as relevant to the understanding of learning disability.

There thus exist disparate intellectual streams of thought with at least one common element seen as relevant to understanding the nature of learning disabilities. Other such common elements may emerge as experimental and applied endeavours proceed and further operationalize their conceptual frameworks. At the very least, it is encouraging to find some correspondence between ideas developed in the laboratory and those developed in applied work, especially given the very limited dialogue to date between the two areas.

MOTIVATION AND COGNITION

People with learning disabilities may show the same range of motivational and personality differences as those without such disabilities, and such factors may exert the same effect upon performance. Some people are more motivated by tangible incentives, others by the desire to be correct (information). Performance will be influenced according to whether the task provides pay-offs matched to the individual in this way (e.g. Byck, 1968). Claridge and O'Connor (1957) were able to show among people with severe disabilities that the more extroverted and outgoing were better motivated by material as opposed to informational incentives and that performance was clearly affected by whether the incentive offered suited the individual personality type. Likewise, Evans and Hogg (1975) found some evidence that independent of level of development, efficiency of discrimination learning related to whether their severely disabled subjects were regarded by others as generally excitable or inhibited. Claridge and O'Connor's work suggest such differences may have been mediated in part by motivational factors.

But in addition to the general motivational factors which influence everyone, the experience of disability itself may exert a distinctive effect upon the individual's motivational structure (see Zigler and Balla, 1982, for a useful overview of these issues). The experience of failure and social rejection would seem particularly significant. Such experiences might induce high expectations of failure, avoidance of new or difficult tasks, reliance upon cues from others for solving problems rather than seeking to find one's own solution (outerdirectedness), and either an excessive wish for social attention or a wariness or avoidance of social contacts. Zigler and Balla (1982) review their own and other people's work evidencing the influences of such factors upon performance in people with disabilities.

It is clear therefore that motivational and personality factors exert a significant influence upon cognitive functioning. They do not explain all the cognitive deficits involved in severe learning disabilities, but must be taken into account in any comprehensive understanding of the individual. As for cognitive variables there is a need to improve assessment methodologies, but much is already available from questionnaire and rating measures (e.g. Claridge and O'Connor, 1957) to systematic means of assessing reinforcer preferences (e.g. Kiernan and Jones, 1982). The remedial implications are also clear either in terms of incorporating individual preferences into learning tasks or of enhancing sensitivity to important but less favoured sources of motivation. When motivation is optimized it is possible to study the true nature of cognitive difficulties — but conversely motivation is itself greatly affected by the nature and experiences of such cognitive difficulties. Understanding the interactions between these domains represents a considerable challenge to researchers.

GENERAL CONCLUSIONS

The experimental literature and the theories developing out of it highlight the possibility of there being many different kinds of difficulty underlying the performance problems that are taken as evidence of learning disability. There is no need to believe in a single dysfunction. Diversity of dysfunctions seems most likely, given the diversity of performance difficulties and the diversity of aetiological factors. As improvement takes place in the understanding of the structures, processes and higher order strategies involved in cognitive functioning as well as motivational and personality factors, so develops a framework which permits more sensitive study of individual differences. Much work will need to be done in order to produce viable means of assessing the different aspects of cognitive functioning, and to produce remedial strategies for tackling problems so highlighted. Nevertheless, it has been the purpose of this chapter to suggest that there are 'windows' which give encouragement as to the potential of this area. In particular, the convergent information on the role of attentional processes in selecting relevant stimuli, and on the role of higher order strategies in solving problems, represents two such promising 'windows'. This, at least, suggests that it is worth while to pursue further the attempts to understand the cognitive psychological factors underlying learning disabilities; and that such understanding will not prove irrelevant for attempts to help people experiencing these difficulties. The discussion thus far has been confined to physical cognition but it is hoped that the next chapter will illustrate that similar potential exists in the study of social cognition.

REFERENCES

Anderson, N.B., and Rincover, A. (1982) The generality of overselctivity in developmentally disabled children. *Journal of Experimental Child Psychology*, **34**, 217–230.

Arbitman-Smith, R., Haywood, H.C., and Bransford, J.D. (1984) Assessing cognitive change. In P.H. Brooks, R. Sperber and C. McCauley (eds) *Learning and Cognition in the Mentally Retarded*. New Jersey: Laurence Erlbaum Associates.

Atkinson, R.C., and Schiffrin, R.M. (1968) Human memory: a proposed system and its control processes. In K.W. Spence and J.T. Spence (eds) *The Psychology of Learning and Motivation*, Vol. 2. New York: Academic Press.

Bailey, S.L. (1981) Stimulus overselectivity in learning disabled children. *Journal of Applied Behavior Analysis*, **14**, 239–249.

Baumeister, A.A. (1984) Some methodological and conceptual issues in the study of cognitive processes with retarded people. In P.H. Brooks, R. Sperber and C. McCauley (eds) *Learning and Cognition in the Mentally Retarded*. New Jersey: Laurence Erlbaum Associates

Belmont, J.M., Butterfield, E.C., and Borkowski, J.C. (1978) Training retarded people to generalize memorization methods across memory tasks. In M.M. Gruneberg, P.E. Morris and R.N. Sykes (eds) *Practical Aspects of Memory*. London: Acadmic Press.

Borkowski, J.G., Peck, V.A., and Damberg, P.R. (1983) Attention, memory and cognition. In J.L. Matson and J.A. Mulick (eds) *Handbook of Mental Retardation*. New York: Pergamon.

Borkowski, J.G., Reid, M.K., and Kurt, B.C. (1984) Metacognition and retardation: paradigmatic, theoretical, and applied perspectives. In P.H. Brooks, R. Sperber, and C. McCauley (eds) *Learning and Cognition in the Mentally Retarded*. New Jersey: Laurence Erlbaum Associates.

Borkowski, J.G., and Varnhagen, C.K. (1984) Transfer of learning strategies: contrast of self-instructional and traditional training formats. *American Journal of Mental Deficiency*, **88**, 363–379.

Broadbent, D.E. (1958) *Perception and Communication*. Oxford: Pergamon.

Brooks, P.H., and Baumeister, A.A. (1977) A plea for consideration of ecological validity in the experimental psychology of mental retardation: a guest editorial. *American Journal of Mental Deficiency*, **81**, 407–416.

Brooks, P.H., and McCauley, C. (1984) Cognitive research in mental retardation. *American Journal of Mental Deficiency*, **88**, 479–486.

Brown, B.L., Campione, J.C., and Barclay, C.R. (1979) Training self-checking routines for estimating test readiness: generalization from list learning to prose recall. *Child Development*, **50**, 501–512.

Butterfield, E.C., and Ferretti, R.P. (1984) Some extensions of the instructional approach to the study of cognitive development and a sufficient condition for transfer of training. In P.H. Brooks, R. Sperber and C. McCauley (eds) *Learning and Cognition in the Mentally Retarded*. New Jersey: Laurence Erlbaum Associates.

Byck, M. (1968) Cognitive differences among diagnostic groups of retardates. *American Journal of Mental Deficiency*, **73**, 97–101.

Campione, J.C., and Brown, A.L. (1977) Memory and metamemory development in educable retarded children. In R.V. Kail, Jr. and J.W. Hagen (eds) *Perspectives on the Development of Memory and Cognition*. New Jersey: Laurence Erlbaum Associates.

Campione, J.C., and Brown, A.L. (1984) Learning ability and transfer propensity as sources of individual differences in intelligence. In P.H. Brooks, R. Sperber and C. McCauley (eds) *Learning and Cognition in the Mentally Retarded*. New Jersey: Laurence Erlbaum Associates.

Claridge, G.S., and O'Connor, N (1957) The relationship between incentive, personality type and improvement in performance of imbeciles. *Journal of Mental Deficiency Research*, **1**, 16–25.

Detterman, D.K. (1979) Memory in the mentally retarded. In N.R. Ellis (ed.) *Handbook of Mental Deficiency. Psychological Theory and Research*. New Jersey: Laurence Erlbaum Associates.

Doran, J., Holland, J.G. (1979) Control by stimulus features during fading. *Journal of Experimental Analysis of Behavior*, **31**, 177–187.

Dunst, C.J. (1984) Toward a social-ecological perspective of sensorimotor development among the mentally retarded. In P.H. Brooks, R. Sperber and C. McCauley (eds) *Learning and Cognition in the Mentally Retarded*. New Jersey: Laurence Erlbaum Associates.

Easterbrook, J.A. (1959) The effect of emotion on cue utilization and the organization of behaviour. *Psychological Review*, **66**, 183–201.

Ellis, N.R. (1963) The stimulus trace and behavioural inadequacy. In N.R. Ellis (ed.) *Handbook of Mental Deficiency, Psychological Theory and Research*. New York: McGraw-Hill.

Ellis, N.R. (1970) Memory processes in retardates and normals. In N.R. Ellis (ed.) *International Review of Research in Mental Retardation*, Vol. 4. New York: Academic Press.

Etzel, B.C., and LeBlanc, J.M. (1979) The simplest treatment alternative: the law of parsimony applied to choosing appropriate instructional control and errorless-learning procedures for the difficult-to-teach child. *Journal of Autism and Developmental Disorders*, **9**, 361–382.

Evans, P.L.C., and Hogg, J. (1975) Individual differences in the severely retarded child in acquisition, stimulus generalization, and extinction in go-no go discrimination learning. *Journal of Experimental Child Psychology*, **20**, 377–390.

Feuerstein, R. (1979a) *The Dynamic Assessment of Retarded Performers: The Learning Potential Assessment Device, Theory, Instruments and Techniques*. Baltimore: University Park Press.

Feuerstein, R. (1979b) *Instrumental Enrichment: redevelopment of cognitive functions of retarded performers*. Baltimore: University Park Press.

Fisher, M.A., and Zeaman, D. (1973) An attention-retention theory of retardate discrimination learning. In N.R. Ellis (ed.) *International Review of Research in Mental Retardation*, Vol. 6. New York: Academic Press.

Gersten, R. (1983) Stimulus over-selectivity in autistic, trainable mentally retarded and non-handicapped children: comparative research controlling chronological (rather than mental) age. *Journal of Abnormal Child Psychology*, **11**, 61–76.

Glidden, L.M. (1979) Training of learning and memory in retarded persons: strategies, techniques and teaching tools. In N.R. Ellis (ed.) *Handbook of Mental*

Deficiency, Psychological Theory and Research. New Jersey: Laurence Erlbaum Associates.

Hermelin, B.M., and O'Connor, N. (1975) Seeing, speaking, ordering. In N. O'Connor (ed.) *Language, Cognitive Deficits, and Retardation.* London: Butterworths.

Herriot, P., Green, R., and McConkey, R. (1973) *Organization and Memory.* London: Methuen.

House, R.J. (1977) Scientific explanation and ecological validity: a reply to Brooks and Baumeister. *American Journal of Mental Deficiency,* **81**, 534–542.

Jeffree, D., and Skeffington, M. (1980) *Let Me Read.* London: Souvenir Press.

Kendall, C., Borkowski, J.G., and Cavanaugh, J.C. (1980) Maintenance and generalization of an interrogative strategy by EMR children. *Intelligence,* **4**, 255–270.

Kiernan, C., and Jones, M. (1982) *Behaviour Assessment Battery.* Windsor: NFER-Nelson.

Koegel, R.L., and Schreibman, L. (1977) Teaching autistic children to respond to simultaneous multiple cues. *Journal of Experimental Child Psychology,* **24**, 299–311.

Kurtz, P.D., and Neisworth, J.T. (1976) Self control possibilities for exceptional children. *Exceptional Children,* January, 212–216.

Lally, M., and Nettlebeck, T. (1977) Intelligence, reaction time and inspection time. *American Journal of Mental Deficiency,* **82**, 273–281.

Lovaas, O.I., Koegel, R.L., and Schreibman, L. (1979) Stimulus over-selectivity: a review of research. *Psychological Bulletin,* **86**, 1236–1254.

Luria, A.R. (1961) *The Role of Speech in Normal and Abnormal Behaviour.* Oxford: Pergamon Press.

McMillan, D.L., and Meyers, C.E. (1984) Molecular research and molar learning. In P.H. Brooks, R. Sperber and C. McCauley (eds) *Learning and Cognition in the Mentally Retarded.* New Jersey: Laurence Erlbaum Associates.

Mahoney, M.J. and Mahoney, K. (1976) Self control techniques with the mentally retarded. *Exceptional Children,* March, 338–339.

Maisto, A.A., and Baumeister, A.A. (1984) Dissection of component processes in rapid information processing tasks: comparison of retarded and non retarded people. In P.H. Brooks, R. Sperber and C. McCauley (eds) *Learning and Cognition in the Mentally Retarded.* New Jersey: Laurence Erlbaum Associates.

Meisel, C.J. (1981) Stimulus over-selectivity by mentally retarded adolescents: effects of pre-training on cue identification. *American Journal of Mental Deficiency,* **86**, 317–322.

Mosk, M.D., and Bucher, B. (1984) Prompting and stimulus shaping procedures for teaching visual-motor skills to retarded children. *Journal of Applied Behavior Analysis,* **17**, 23–24.

Nettlebeck, T., and Lally, M. (1979) Age, intelligence and inspection time. *American Journal of Mental Deficiency,* **83**, 398–401.

Rilling, M. (1977) Stimulus control and inhibition processes. In W.K. Honig and J.E.R. Staddon (eds) *Handbook of Operant Behaviour.* New Jersey: Prentice Hall.

Rincover, A. (1978) Variables affecting stimulus fading and discriminative responding in psychotic children. *Journal of Abnormal Psychology,* **87**, 1541–1553.

Schilmoeller, K.J., and Etzel, B.C. (1977) An experimental analysis of criterion-related and non-criterion-related cues in 'errorless' stimulus control procedures. In B.C. Etzel, J.M. LeBlanc, and D.M. Baer (eds) *New Developments in Behavioral Research – Theory, Method and Application.* New Jersey: Laurence Erlbaum Associates.

Schilmoeller, G.L., Schilmoeller, K.J., Etzel, B.C., and LeBlanc, J.A. (1979) Conditional discrimination after errorless and trial-and-error training. *Journal of the Experimental Analysis of Behavior,* **31**, 405–420.

Schover, L.R., and Newsom, C.D. (1976) Overselectivity, developmental level and overtraining in autistic and normal children. *Journal of Abnormal Child Psychology*, **4**, 289–298.

Shapiro, E.S. (1981) Self control procedures with the mentally retarded. In M. Hersen, R.M. Eisler, and P.A. Miller (eds) *Progress in Behavior Modification*, Volume 12. New York: Academic Press.

Terrace, H.S. (1966) Stimulus control. In W.K. Honig (ed.) *Operant Conditioning: Areas of Research and Application*. New Jersey: Prentice-Hall.

Venables, P. (1967) Selectivity of attention, withdrawal and cortical activation. *Archives of General Psychiatry*, **4**, 74–78.

Vygotsky, L.S. (1962) *Thought and Language*. Chichester: John Wiley.

Zawlocki, R.J., and Walls, R.T. (1983) Fading on the S+, the S−, both, or neither. *American Journal of Mental Deficiency*, **87**, 462–464.

Zeaman, D., and House, B.J. (1963) The role of attention in retardate discrimination learning. In N. Ellis (ed.) *Handbook of Mental Deficiency*. New York: McGraw-Hill.

Zeaman, D., and House, B.J. (1979) A review of attention theory. In N.R. Ellis (ed.) *Handbook of Mental Deficiency, Psychological Theory Theory and Research*. New Jersey: Laurence Erlbaum Associates.

Zigler, E., and Balla, D. (1982) Motivational and personality factors in the performance of the retarded. In E. Zigler and D. Balla (eds) *Mental Retardation: The Developmental Difference Controversy*. Hillsdale, NJ: Laurence Erlbaum Associates.

Chapter 4

Social Cognition

INTRODUCTION

Cognition in social situations involves analysis of information from other people concerning their thoughts and feelings and use of this analysis to generate expectancies about the inner states and overt behaviour of others. Extracting social meaning involves processing a wide range of information — for example, information about the general physical context, the general nature of the social situation, the speech, body postures and facial expressions of others. From the analysis of presenting information and from knowledge available in memory, inferences are made about the general requirements of the situation and about many essentially unobservable features of other people (their thoughts, emotions and general dispositions). Into this already complex picture the individual must integrate self-knowledge — the kind of person that he or she is, the 'messages' that are to be presented to others, the goals to be achieved from the specific social interaction. On the basis of all this information expectations will be generated about the behaviour of others and the individual will make plans for his or her own behaviour.

This can be understood as a general 'cognitive' enterprise involving the elements outlined in the previous chapter — structures, processes and higher order strategies. Nevertheless, the sheer complexity of social as opposed to physical problem solving would suggest that it merits separate consideration. There are, in addition, other grounds for giving such separate consideration. The study of normal child development does suggest that while there is some relationship between performance on physical and social problem solving tasks this relationship is not always very strong, so that social cognition does appear to represent a separable area of development (Schantz, 1975; Chandler, 1977; Dunst, 1984).

Such a view is further supported by evidence of the clear separability of social and non-social cognition in some pathological conditions. A particularly striking example is provided by early childhood autism which is marked by a major discrepancy between functioning in the physical and social spheres. Thus, while people with autism may have visual-perceptual abilities within the normal range, and special gifts or talents in such areas as mathematics, they will show gross difficulties in social situations and in general communicative functioning. At the earliest developmental levels this will be marked by absent or abnormal patterns of eye contact and body posture and unpredictable responses to the social behaviour of others. At higher developmental levels it will be marked by tactlessness in social interactions. In the population of people with severe degrees of learning disability Wing and her colleagues have clearly documented a range of social impairments, including those seen in 'classic' autism (Wing and Gould, 1975; Wing, 1981a). Some children are described as aloof or passive, others appear socially active but bizarre in their approaches. When all these social impairments were put together it was found that the children with these difficulties constituted more than half the total group of children with IQs under 50 in the sample. Social difficulties, therefore, constitute a very common problem for people with severe learning disabilities and often represent a specific area of difficulty over and above problems in other areas of functioning. This suggests that social behaviour difficulties merit careful consideration in their own right, and the study of social cognition may contribute to the understanding of these problems.

The need for such consideration is strengthened by the impact of social difficulties upon the affected persons and those around them. In Wing's sample social impairment was strongly associated with verbal communication problems, absence of symbolic play and a generally severe degree of intellectual impairment. It was also strongly associated with a range of extremely difficult behaviour problems such as tantrums, destructiveness and self-injurious behaviour. Children with this range of difficulties are far more likely to be admitted to residential care and to be excluded from day facilities. Even at the youngest ages Strain (1983) found that children without disabilities were more likely to think positively about disabled peers if the latter were affectionate, responded positively to peer interactions, shared materials and helped with tasks. In studies of the breakdown in community placements of people discharged from institutions, socially inappropriate behaviours are clearly implicated in the rejection of people from community settings (e.g. Schalock, Harper and Genung, 1981). Among adults with learning disabilities there is an association between depression and poor social skills, as perceived by others (Benson et al., 1985). Thus social difficulties are both common and 'costly' for people with learning disabilities.

As with other areas of cognitive function the interplay between cognition and motivation must be considered. Difficulties in social behaviour may be mediated by problems in social understanding and/or by motivational variables such as social anxiety, indifference to others or excessive need for attention; inevitably the two areas interact — difficulties in understanding people may generate indifference or anxiety and avoidance in social situations; anxiety or indifference may interfere with the processing of social information. There has been little explicit examination of these issues in the literature but it is clearly relevant to be aware of both motivational and cognitive factors when studying social behaviour.

However, before examining the literature comment is necessary upon some of the methodological issues involved in researching social cognition.

THE STUDY OF SOCIAL COGNITION

In the previous chapter considerable attention was devoted to the methodological problems which make it difficult to judge the relevance of experimental cognitive research for understanding the nature of an ·individual's learning difficulties. These same cautions apply to the present chapter, but additional points need to be made.

Although the experimental cognitive literature has many shortcomings, there is at least a sizeable body of research specifically aimed at trying to understand intellectual impairment and learning disabilities. There is no equivalent body of research aimed at understanding specific social impairments. It has already been indicated that there is a strong overlap and relationship between social and intellectual impairment. Many who are severely intellectually impaired are also socially impaired. The proportion of people with social impairments among those with severe intellectual impairments is far higher than that found in the population functioning intellectually within the normal range. Social impairments can certainly be found at all levels of ability, it is just that they are more common among those with marked intellectual difficulties, which suggests some relationship between the two areas.

However, unlike intellectual impairment there exists, as yet, no objective way of defining social impairment. For all its faults, the IQ test at least provides a relatively objective way of measuring an individual's intellectual performance in some areas. It enables a judgement of relative standing compared to others. No such equivalent assessment exists for social impairment. Many normative studies of child development do include items related to social functioning — smiling, mutual gaze, discrimination of strangers from familiar people, waving good-bye, motor imitation, cooperation with peers in play (e.g. Gesell, 1942; Griffiths, 1954, 1970). However, such items are not selected on any particular theoretical basis, are often intermingled with items concerning basic self-care skills (feeding, dressing, toileting), and provide no secure objective foundation for defining difficulties in social understanding and interaction. These kinds of social problems are often analysed in clinical settings and diagnosed as a form of psychiatric illness. Rutter has provided a number of clear guidelines about the signs and symptoms which justify the diagnosis of autism and these include social interactional abnormalities (Rutter, 1978). Wing (1981b) has developed an interview schedule which incorporates ratings of a number of social interactional behaviours. Such ratings can be used to categorize different kinds of social impairment — aloof, odd, withdrawn or passive. While each approach can produce reliable assignment to categories, it is not clear how psychologically meaningful such categories are. Based as they are upon presenting behaviours they do not offer any insight into the functional significance of particular behaviours. Lacking a normative base, it is difficult to know for any particular individual to what extent his or her social functioning is discrepant from other areas of functioning and to assess with any exactitude the degree of social difficulty. Thus, although psychiatric categorization offers many valuable insights, it cannot provide a secure anchor point for the experimental investigation of social development and social impairment.

The experimental base for the present chapter will, therefore, be rather different from that used in the previous chapter. There is literature on social cognition in both adults and children who function intellectually within the normal range. For present purposes, in order to gain an understanding of the social functioning of people with learning disabilities, use will be made of the literature on developmental aspects of social cognition. This literature provides the very few studies which seek to elucidate the problems of those with learning disabilities.

Such developmental research has studied social cognition in a number of ways. Tasks studied include role taking, where the individual must demonstrate how well another's point of view is understood. The accurate identification of others' emotions has been explored through tasks where the individual makes a judgement about the feelings of a character on the basis of a story told verbally or enacted, for example with puppets. A similar story-type approach has been used to explore moral judgements where the subject must judge the worth of an act from the character and the consequences of the act. Although such experimental tasks are perhaps closer to real-world situations than some of the tasks described in the previous chapter, it should still be noted that little is known about the relationship between performance in such situations and performance in real life.

There is a further issue regarding the generalizability of performance in experimental cognitive situations, that is, the relationship between cognition and overt behaviour. In reviewing the developmental literature

Schantz (1975) describes some studies with normal children which show a moderate relationship between ability on role-taking tasks and level and type of social behaviour. Denham (1986), likewise, found some relationship between the understanding of emotions shown in structured tasks and behaviour in free play with two- to three-year old normal children. However, other findings suggest that such a relationship is not always present. In reviewing the literature about the effects of cognitive training on overt social skills in normal children, Gresham (1985) could find little evidence that improving performance on the sort of cognitive tasks described above had any effect upon social interactions in everyday situations. Edmondson et al. (1967) produced similar findings when they trained adolescents with mild to moderate learning disabilities to improve their interpretation of social cues. Benson et al. (1985), in a study with adults who had a mild degree of learning disability, found a clear relationship between ratings of depression and how other people rated the social skills of the affected person in everyday situations. However, they found no relationship between depression and the individual's ability to describe appropriate responses to imaginary situations (a more 'cognitive' task). This argues that social performance is not purely determined by social understanding and that breakdowns in performance will not necessarily reflect cognitive dysfunctions.

There may be a number of reasons for this. The individual may be very poor at monitoring his or her own behaviour — he or she may not notice the discrepancy between interpretation and action. Alternatively, motivation may be involved. The person may be disinterested in social performance, in the reactions and judgements of others and simply not wish to be appropriate. Emotions such as anxiety may disrupt performance and prevent an individual displaying the behaviour known to be appropriate in a given situation. Caution is therefore needed in making any inference from social cognition to social performance and vice versa. The two areas are related but also have separate determinants which may be more or less evident in any given situation.

The relationship between cognition and performance is further complicated by the large cultural differences which affect both activities. In developed industrialized countries there may be some commonality in the types of physical problems which have to be understood and resolved. No such commonality exists in the social sphere. There are very large differences in what constitutes appropriate behaviour: what is appropriately assertive in one culture is rude in another; expressions of emotion acceptable in one culture are unacceptable in another. Such differences in standards must clearly affect the cognitive system in terms of what cues are processed and how they are interpreted. Thus social cognition and performance cannot be studied in isolation from characteristics of the external environment. In reaching any understanding of social impairment, the nature of the surrounding environment will need also to be understood as impairment may reside in the environment as well as within the individual.

The rest of this chapter, therefore, will look at what is involved in understanding social situations and how this understanding can break down. This is seen as relevant to the social performance difficulty experienced by some people with learning disabilities; but it is recognized that many other 'non-cognitive' factors may be involved in such performance problems. The role of the environment is clearly critical as in other areas of functioning and there will be some exploration of factors which may mediate or exacerbate 'cognitive' difficulties. Likewise motivation will receive some consideration.

EXPERIMENTAL STUDIES OF SOCIAL COGNITION

From very early in development infants appear sensitive to social information. Within weeks they are fixating upon the faces of others, particularly the eyes, and by five months they begin to show fixation preference for the mouth. By twelve months infants will use information from their mother's facial expression to determine whether or not they should proceed over a visual 'cliff' (Klinnert et al., 1982). As children begin to recognize that others are separate from themselves, they begin to move through a number of stages which are revealed in many different areas of performance (see Schantz, 1975; Chandler, 1977, for useful reviews). In role-taking situations they first assume that others see, think and feel exactly as they do. They then recognize that another's viewpoint may be different from their own but are not very accurate at knowing in what way it is different. Finally, they progress to becoming accurate at understanding exactly where the differences lie and what it is that others see, think and feel.

They are then also able to recognize that they themselves may be the objects of inferences by others, i.e. that their own thoughts and feelings are the object of other people's consideration. The exact ages at which these changes can be shown depend on the type of task and the means of assessment.

In person perception tasks which require a judgement about how another is feeling, the situation is described or enacted and the child must say, or indicate from a picture, how the character in the situation is feeling. At around two to four years of age (depending on the method of assessment) children are only accurate if the situations described are very familiar to them and they rely heavily upon general contextual cues. They identify only a limited range of emotions, the earliest being happiness, sadness, fear and anger. Over the period of four to seven years of age they gradually become more adept at judging less familiar situations, at differentiating a wider range of emotions and at using more specific cues such as facial expression, as well as general contextual information. Beyond this age children then begin to describe and interpret others' behaviour in terms of more abstract traits and states.

Another area that has been studied is that of evaluative judgement, where children have to evaluate an action when provided with information about its consequences and the intentions of the person carrying out the action. In ascribing praise or blame, children in the pre-school years rely mainly upon the consequences of action (for example, if something gets broken or damaged); but over the four- to six-year-old period they begin to weight intentions with increasing significance until these come to dominate in controlling their judgements. All the above processes continue into adolescence and adult life, but this is even less clearly documented than at ·the younger ages.

Likewise, documentation on development in people with severe learning difficulties is extremely sparse. Marcell and Jett (1985) showed that teenagers with mild to moderate degrees of learning disability would recognize emotions such as happiness, sadness and anger from tape-recorded vocal cues at above chance level. Simeonsson, Monson and Blacher (1984) suggest that performance on role-taking tasks is in line with level of mental development rather than chronological age. However, they do also suggest that slow learners show less insight into the feelings and motives of others than would be predicted from their mental age, which reinforces the earlier proposition that social development should be treated separately from other areas of intellectual functioning., Likewise, these authors suggest that in studies of evaluative judgement, although the weighting of consequences and intentions is often in line with mental development, again there may be a greater tendency for the person with slow development to persist in assigning greater importance to consequences. The studies these authors refer to are not concerned with people who are known to have major difficulties in social development in addition to their general learning disabilities.

A fascinating insight in to how social information processing may deviate in people with such particular disabilities is provided by the work of Hobson and his collaborators (Hobson, 1983, 1986; Weeks, 1983). These investigators have compared the performance of autistic children with other children who have learning difficulties matched for overall mental age, and with normal children also matched for mental age. In one series of experiments, situations were presented on videotape and the children had to match appropriate pictures to the situations presented. All groups were equally skilled when the basis for matching was in terms of shape, movement or noise.

When, however, they had to match facial expression of emotion to the presented situation, the autistic children did far worse than the other two groups. Likewise, when the task involved matching gestures to portrayed facial expressions, the autistic children also showed a clear deficit. In a photo-sorting task, where the photos differed in terms of sex, facial expression and hats worn, the autistic children were far less likely spontaneously to sort on the basis of facial expression, and indeed, found it difficult to do so even when constraints were placed upon their sorting. In a similar vein, Langdell (1981) found that when examining photographs autistic children were only able to identify accurately happiness and sadness whereas matched children, also with learning difficulties, could identify additionally joy, anger, fear and distress. The autistic children were also far worse at acting-out and demonstrating emotional expressions on request.

In a rather different experimental situation it has been shown that compared to children with and without disabilities, matched for mental age, autistic children have a specific difficulty in understanding what it is that other people might know (Baron-Cohen, Leslie and Frith, 1985). In viewing a story sequence played out with puppets they found it difficult to understand that one of the characters might not share his or her own knowledge (they but not the character had seen an object displaced from its original container and they assumed that the character would know this and know where to look). Lack of such insight would make it extremely difficult to predict accurately how others will behave. This would render the social world a very frightening place with people appearing to act quite 'arbitrarily' (i.e. unexpectedly).

These findings suggest how learning difficulties can be associated with specific problems in dealing with social information. There may be a number of groups who experience a variety of difficulties in this respect, but present research only establishes this clearly for autistic children. Even for this latter group it is not clear where the difficulty lies. It may be at the attentional level, i.e. they do not notice important social cues — as suggested by Hobson's work. Alternatively, the problem may lie further on in the processing system so that they may notice the cues but not know how to interpret them — as suggested by Baron-Cohen et al. Higher order strategies may also be implicated as these difficulties could be seen as reflecting a failure to assign any kind of priority to the processing of social information. It is interesting, in the light of the earlier discussion, that autistic children also show marked deficits and deviations in social performance which suggests, at least for this group, a very strong relationship between cognition and performance.

As yet, what is known about the processing of social information has had little direct impact upon attempts to remedy social difficulties. There are, however, some studies and a number of promising lines of enquiry. For example, there is some indication from the developmental literature that the environment can certainly influence social cognitive performance. The weighting of intentions in evaluating judgements seems to be enhanced in children whose parents use disciplinary tactics which rely upon reasoning and the stressing of inferences about what is going on inside a person rather than tactics which rely on the use of physical power or unqualified instructions (Sears, Maccoby and Levin, 1957; Schantz, 1975). Chandler (1973) reports on a more direct attempt to intervene with anti-social adolescents and found that training them in role-taking skills was associated with a significant decrease in the likelihood of their re-offending. Edmondson *et al.* (1967) described a curriculum for 'social signal decoding' involving 40 one-hour lessons which they field-tested on adolescents with learning disabilities of a mild to moderate degree. They were able to demonstrate significant gains for those who went through the programme on a test involving responses to pictures of social scenes. These gains were greater than for a control group who received no intervention, or one that received just extra attention but not related to social understanding. However, there was little impact of the programme shown upon teacher ratings of the young people's actual social performance in the classroom setting.

The literature on developmental aspects of social cognition and attempts at intervention is limited both in quantity and quality. However, the general developmental literature does offer a range of insights that could potentially be used to operationalize a social cognitive curriculum. This, in its turn, could be used to develop more comprehensive training efforts. Short-term, narrowly based, interventions, targeted upon social understanding, in the areas outlined above would seem to have limited impact upon social functioning in significant areas. This is true for those whose intellectual functioning falls within the normal range, and for those with mild to moderate degrees of impairment. There is little study of those with more severe degrees of learning difficulty, but the outcome is hardly likely to be more optimistic. However, given the complexity of what is being undertaken, more sustained and coherent interventions are clearly going to be required. This can be understood in purely rational terms as the developmental literature indicates that social understanding proceeds through a number of stages, and that such development takes place over many years. It is hardly credible that 20 or 30 hours' intervention is going to make a great deal of difference. This need for more sustained and comprehensive efforts is reinforced by the limitations which are apparent when examining some of the applied work which has targeted upon social understanding and performance; and it is to this area that the next section now turns.

APPLIED STUDIES OF SOCIAL COGNITION AND PERFORMANCE SKILLS

Zisfein and Rosen (1974) described a complex package which they called 'personal adjustment training'. This involved an element of direct teaching on how to interpret real-life social situations. The authors used this approach with adolescents and young adults who had a mild to moderate degree of learning disability and had been institutionalized for some years. Many other elements were contained in the treatment package which lasted for 12 hours. Unfortunately, little significant impact of this programme could be demonstrated on a range of outcome measures. Benson, Miranti and Johnson (1984) drew on the work of Novaco (1976a, b, 1977) to examine the value of stress management training with adults who had a mild degree of learning disability. The authors compared a group which received a whole package with other groups who received individual elements of the package — training in interpreting and solving social problem situations, training in the use of self-instructions and relaxation training. All groups showed some improvement. The relaxation only and self-instruction only groups did marginally better than the others with outcome being measured in terms of self-report, supervisor ratings and role-play performance. The training directed at interpreting social situations proved very difficult for the subjects to understand and seemed to have little impact upon their functioning. However, it should be noted that the total training time was only 12–18 hours. It should also be noted that in both these studies no evidence was presented as to whether the subjects involved actually experienced specific difficulties in interpreting social situations.

This failure to establish the nature of the difficulty to be changed is evident in another area of relevant applied work — that of cognitive behaviour therapy for teaching social skills to children without learning difficulties. This area has been critically reviewed by Gresham (1985). He cites a number of studies which have tried to teach social problem-solving skills such as how to judge feelings or select appropriate actions from a story context. These studies tend to show a significant effect upon their own measures of social problem solving; but these measures are usually of unknown reliability and it is not clear how well they relate to social problem-solving skills in everyday life. However, it is very clear that such cognitive effects as are achieved show little carry-over into social performance as assessed by peer or teacher rating.

Social performance skills are the focus of the largest body of applied research (see Robertson, Richardson and Youngson, 1984; Davies and Rogers, 1985, for useful recent reviews). A very wide range of skills have been taught from hand waving with people who have a profound degree of intellectual impairment to conversational skills for people with a mild degree of impairment. A similarly wide range of teaching methods have been used — direct behaviour shaping, modelling, instructions, coaching and rehearsal. Although this is a large research area it throws little light upon any of the processes which might underlie performance deficits. However, it does reinforce the need to consider more cognitive factors. As the above reviewers point out, aside from the methodological limitations of many studies, it is quite clear that there are serious difficulties in getting trained skills to maintain over time or generalize from the training situation into everyday life situations. This may reflect limitations in the type of skills taught or the methods of teaching; but it may also suggest the need to take a broader view of social functioning and to recognize the importance of social cognitive difficulties, at least for some people.

Such a broader view needs also to encompass the role of the environment. The environment sets the demands in terms of what skills are required for effective functioning. The environment also influences the way in which the cognitive system functions — which information is processed, how inferences are drawn, which responses are selected. The next section considers this role of the environment and some of the delicate interactions between environment, behaviour and understanding.

THE ENVIRONMENT AND SOCIAL COGNITION

The growth of social understanding and performance occurs through the complex interactions over time of an individual and the environment (see Dunst, 1985, for a useful review and theoretical model as applied to child development). The individual will analyse social information from the environment. On the basis of this analysis behaviours will be selected and performed. Feedback from the environment will validate or otherwise both the analysis made and the behaviours performed. Thus an impairment in social functioning may arise from a number of sources: the individual may not analyse correctly the information available, may not select the appropriate behaviour or may misinterpret the feedback. Alternatively, the environment may provide inappropriate feedback.

Evidence for difficulties in social information processing was presented earlier. The social skills training literature implies that people with learning disabilities may not have available (or may fail to select) appropriate social behaviours. They may not put out 'readable' social behaviours. The 'readability' of social behaviours put out by people with learning disabilities, however, has been more directly studied. Ricks (1972, 1975) studied the cries of autistic infants. Cries are an early form of social behaviour which can signal a number of needs in the infant and parents and others come rapidly to understand their significance. The cries of autistic children were quite different from those of normal children. They did convey as much information as the cries of other children and the parents of these children were able to interpret their meanings. However, such meanings were not understood by other parents, even of autistic children, whereas the cries of normal children proved to be interpreted more reliably by a wide range of people. This would suggest that these early social signals were not as easily read for autistic as compared with normal infants. Dunst (1985) studied early forms of communication in children with Down's syndrome compared to normal children. He found that the Down's infants were less able to combine gesture, vocalization and eye contact into a simultaneous communicative act (for example, to get a wanted object). They could manage the elements individually but tended to emit them in succession to one another. Parental response (to get the wanted object) was far more likely where such cues were performed simultaneously by the infant. Thus, again, the readability of the behaviour put out by the child with the learning disability was less than that of the normal child. The potential effects of this problem seem enormous. Lower readability means less experience of successful interaction with the social environment which is bound in its turn to distort social understanding as well as self-image. One might speculate how such failures to contact successfully the environment might lead the individual either to pay less and less attention to the social world (withdrawal) or to generate extraordinary behaviours which might extract clearer environmental feedback (acting out).

Readability may not be the only difficulty for those with severe learning disabilities. Another possibility is that the environment itself is limited in terms of the social contacts available, or because of the attitudes and expectations of significant others about the competence of people with a severe degree of intellectual impairment. If one does not expect a person to be able to perform in a certain way (for example, communicate) one may ignore or misinterpret the behaviours which are shown by that person. It is certainly the case that people with severe learning disabilities can be exposed to environments bereft of social contacts. Almost by definition institutional environments fail to provide adequate or meaningful social relationships and interactions. However, there is some evidence also for the second propositon — that of less than normal levels of responsivity even in enriched environments. Thus Dunst's studies (1979, 1980, 1985) indicated that even where infants put out equally competent communications combining gesture, visual and vocal behaviours, the mothers of Down's syndrome infants were less likely to respond than the mothers of normal infants. This was mainly due to the previously mentioned difficulty that Down's children have in combining these three elements into simultaneous transmission. Beveridge's studies in classroom settings for children with severe learning disabilities showed a very low level of initiation of social behaviour by the pupils, but also a high probability that teachers will act not to maintain such interaction attempts as do occur (Beveridge and Berry, 1977; Beveridge, Spence and Mittler, 1978; Beveridge and Hurrell, 1980). Unfortunately these studies lack normal controls so that it is not known to what extent such experience would be true for children without learning disabilities. Nevertheless, such findings raise the possibility that even in enriched environments with caring and/or professionally trained people, appropriate social behaviours by a person with disabilities may not achieve a normal response. The potential impact of this upon how a person with disabilities understands the world and what is learned about appropriate social behaviour is enormous.

MOTIVATION AND SOCIAL COGNITION

There has been little experimental study of the role of motivational factors in the social functioning of people with learning disabilities. As outlined earlier there are likely to be complex interactions between a range of motivational and cognitive variables and these in turn will interact with environmental variables. A number of important motivational factors have been suggested — anxiety, indifference, an excessive desire to please; but these have not been independently measured to assess their impact in research situations (experimental or applied) dealing with social performance. There is a need for improved assessment methodologies and at this stage all that can be said is that when seeking to understand social performance difficulties it will be important to consider the cognitive, motivational and environmental variables contributing to these difficulties in the individual case.

CONCLUSIONS

Social functioning is critical to the success of the many policy initiatives directed towards increasing the opportunities for people with learning disabilities to operate in a wide range of everyday environments. As this chapter indicates there has yet to be more than a very superficial analysis of the factors involved in social functioning and its impairment. It was indicated at the outset that many people with severe learning disabilities experience difficulties in their social relationships. There is no adequate framework for conceptualizing these difficulties, but at least four elements appear to be important.

The main purpose of this chapter has been to establish the importance of social cognition as a separable area from general cognition. There is no literature equivalent to that reviewed in chapter 3, to examine in depth the specific types of social cognitive dysfunction which can occur. Nevertheless it is clear that social cognition shows a recognizable developmental sequence, and that some studies have highlighted specific deficits in the social cognitive system for some people with learning disabilities (e.g. Hobson, 1983, 1986; Baron-Cohen et al., 1985). Attempts to apply knowledge of social cognitive functioning to remedial efforts have been few; but given the many limitations outlined earlier, the results are perhaps moderately encouraging.

By its very nature social cognition requires a close understanding of the social environment which interacts with the cognitive system of the individual. Once again research is scarce but there is at least enough to highlight the importance of very detailed study of the social environment. Cognition can only change and develop through interaction with the environment. If people are to understand the world 'normally' then the world must respond to them 'normally'. For people who carry such powerful labels as do those with severe learning disability (labels such as handicapped, retarded, autistic), ensuring normal responsivity in an environment is a major challenge yet to be tackled in any applied research.

The third element in any analysis of social functioning is the behavioural repertoire of the individual. People with severe learning disabilities may lack particular behaviours or have deviant social behaviours which are difficult to 'read'. It will be important to develop adequate means to describe the skills required in everyday environments and the degree to which these are available to the individual. While there is a considerable literature on training social skills, there is little to indicate the degree to which such skills are relevant to the individual's social encounters in life.

The fourth element which is relevant to social functioning is one which has received scant attention in this chapter. This is the issue of motivation. A person may fully understand a situation and be able to carry out the appropriate behaviours, but may fail to do so because of disinterest or anxiety. Such motivational characteristics are enshrined to some extent in many traditional personality traits (introversion-extraversion, neuroticism). Their role in the social functioning of people with severe learning disabilities has yet to be adequately recognized.

All formal attempts to define intellectual impairment refer both to generalized learning difficulties and level of social functioning. These are related but separable areas of performance. In seeking to understand the difficulties of this group of people and the reasons for such large individual differences as exist, a much better understanding is needed of the many different aspects of cognitive functioning. This chapter and the previous one have tried to draw together some of the disparate strands of knowledge about cognitive functioning in social and non-social situations. While the knowledge base is limited there are definite advances in understanding these issues, advances which are beginning to carry with them remedial implications. Such advances may be small, and the remedial implications often of unknown validity, but it is hoped that at the very least, the signs are encouraging.

What is lacking from formal definitions of intellectual impairment, is any reference to the fact that the more severe the degree of difficulty, the greater is the likelihood that there will be evidence of damage to the central nervous system. Severe intellectual impairment has a strong biological dimension. In order to understand fully the nature of this impairment and its resulting disabilities, it is important to look at how biological factors may be implicated in psychological functioning. It is to this topic that the next chapter turns.

REFERENCES

Baron-Cohen, S., Leslie, A.M., and Frith, U. (1985) Does the autistic child have a 'theory of mind'? *Cognition*, **7**, 37–46.

Benson, B., Miranti, S.V., and Johnson, C. (1984) Self control techniques for anger management with mentally retarded adults. Paper presented at the ABBT Convention, Philadelphia.

Benson, B., Reiss, S., Smith, D.S., and Laman, D.S. (1985) Psychosocial correlates of depression in mentally retarded adults: II. Poor social skills. *American Journal of Mental Deficiency*, **89**, 657–659.

Beveridge, M.C., and Berry, R. (1977) Observing interactions in severely mentally handicapped children. *Research in Education*, **17**, 13–22.

Beveridge, M., and Hurrell, P. (1980) Teacher's responses to severely mentally handicapped children's initiations in the classroom. *Journal of Child Psychology and Psychiatry*, **21**, 175–181.

Beveridge, M., Spencer, J., and Mittler, P. (1978) Language and social behaviour in severely educationally subnormal children. *British Journal of Social and Clinical Psychology*, **17**, 75–83.

Chandler, M.J. (1973) Egocentrism and anti-social behaviour: the assessment and training of social perspective taking skills. *Developmental Psychology*, **9**, 326–332.

Chandler, M.J. (1977) Social cognition: a selective review of current research. In W.F. Overton and J.M. Gallagher (eds) *Knowledge and Development*. Vol. 1: *Advances in Research and Theory*, pp. 93–148. New York: Plenum Press.

Davies, R.R., and Rogers, E.S. (1985) Social skills training with persons who are mentally retarded. *Mental Retardation*, **23**(4), 186–196.

Denham, S. (1986) Social cognition, prosocial behaviour and emotion in pre-schoolers: contextual validation. *Child Development*, **57**, 194–201.

Dunst, C.J. (1979) Cognitive-social aspects of communicative exchanges between mothers and their Down's syndrome infants and mothers and their nonretarded infants. Unpublished doctoral dissertation, Vanderbilt University, Nashville, Tennessee.

Dunst, C.J. (1980) Developmental characteristics of communicative acts among Down's syndrome infants and nonretarded infants. Paper presented at the biennial meeting of the South Eastern Conference on Human Development. Alexandria, VA, April.

Dunst, C.J. (1984) Toward a socio-ecological perspective of sensorimotor development among the mentally retarded. In P.H. Brooks, R. Sperber and C. McCauley (eds) *Learning and Cognition in the Mentally Retarded*, pp. 359–388. New Jersey: Laurence Erlbaum Associates.

Dunst, C.J. (1985) Communicative competence and deficits: effects on early social interactions. In E. McDonald and D. Gallagher (eds) *Facilitating Social Emotional Development in Multiply Handicapped Children*. Philadelphia: Home of the Merciful Saviour for Crippled Children.

Edmondson, B., Leland, H., De Jung, J.E., and Leach, E. (1967) Increasing social cue interpretations (visual decoding) by retarded adolescents through training. *American Journal of Mental Deficiency*, **71**, 1017–1024.

Gesell, A. (1942) *The First Five Years of Life*. London: Methuen.

Gresham, F. (1985) The utility of cognitive-behavioural procedures for social skills training with children: a critical review. *Journal of Abnormal Psychology*, **13**, 411–423.

Griffiths, R. (1954) *The Abilities of Babies. A Study in Mental Measurement*. Amersham: Association for Research in Infant and Child Development.

Griffiths, R. (1970) *The Abilities of Young Children. A comprehensive system of mental measurement for the first eight years of life*. London: Child Development Research Centre.

Hobson, R.P. (1983) The autistic child's perception of facial cues of gender and emotional state. Paper presented to September Conference of the Developmental Section of the British Psychological Society.

Hobson, R.P. (1986) The autistic child's appraisal of expressions of emotion. *Journal of Child Psychology and Psychiatry*, **27**(3), 321–342.

Klinnert, M.P., Lampos, J.J., Sorce, J.F., Emde, E.N., and Svejda, M. (1982) Emotions as behaviour regulators: social referencing in infancy. In R. Plutchik and H. Kellerman (eds) *The Emotions*. Vol. 2: *The Emotions in Early Development*. New York: Academic Press.

Langdell, T. (1981) Face perception: an approach to the study of autism. Unpublished Ph.D. thesis, University of London.

Marcell, M.M., and Jett, A.D. (1985) Identification of vocally expressed emotions by mentally retarded and non-retarded individuals. *American Journal of Mental Deficiency*, **89**, 537–545.

Novaco, R.W. (1976a) The functions and regulation of the arousal of anger. *American Journal of Psychiatry*, **133**, 1124–1128.

Novaco, R.W. (1976b) Treatment of chronic anger through cognitive and relaxation controls. *Journal of Consulting and Clinical Psychology*, **44**, 681.

Novaco, R.W. (1977) Stress inoculation: a cognitive therapy for anger and its application to a case of depression. *Journal of Consulting and Clinical Psychology*, **45**, 600–608.

Ricks, D.M. (1972) The beginning of verbal communication in normal and autistic children. Unpublished M.D. thesis, University of London.

Ricks, D.M. (1975) Vocal communication in pre-verbal normal and autistic children. In N. O'Connor (ed.) *Language, Cognitive Deficits and Retardation*. London: Butterworths.

Robertson, L., Richardson, A.M., and Youngson, S.C. (1984) Social skills training with mentally handicapped people: a review. *British Journal of Clinical Psychology*, **23**, 241–264.

Rutter, M. (1978) Diagnosis and definition. In M. Rutter and E. Schopler (eds) *Autism: A Reappraisal of Concepts and Treatment*. New York: Plenum.

Schalock, R.L., Harper, R.S., and Genung, T. (1981) Community integration of mentally retarded adults: community placement and program success. *American Journal of Mental Deficiency*, **85**, 478–488.

Schantz, C.V. (1975) The development of social cognition. In E.M. Hetherington (ed.) *Review of Child Development Research*, **5**, pp. 257–323. Chicago: University of Chicago Press.

Sears, R.R., Maccoby, E.E., and Levin, H. (1957) *Patterns of Child Rearing*. New York: Harper and Row.

Simeonsson, R.J., Monson, L.B. and Blacher, J. (1984) Social understanding and mental retardation in P.H. Brooks, R. Sperber, C. McAuley (eds.) Learning and Cognition in the Mentally Retarded. New Jersey: Lawrence Erlbaum Associates.

Strain, P.S. (1983) Identification of Social Skill curriculum targets for severely handicapped children in mainstreamed pre-schools. *Applied Research in Mental Retardation*, 4, 369–382.

Weeks, S.J. (1983) The salience and discriminability of facial qualities. Unpublished M. Phil. thesis, University of London.

Wing, L. (1981a) Language, social, and cognitive impairments in autism and severe mental retardation. *Journal of Autism and Developmental Disorders*, **11**, 31–43.

Wing, L. (1981b) A schedule for deriving profiles of handicap in mentally retarded children. In B. Cooper (ed.) *Assessing the Handicaps and Needs of Mentally Retarded Children*. London: Academic Press.

Wing, L., and Gould, J. (1975) Severe impairments of social interaction and associated abnormalities in children: epidemiology and classification. *Journal of Autism and Development Disorders*, **9**, 11–29.

Zisfein, L., and Rosen, M. (1974) Effects of a personal adjustment training group counselling program. *Mental Retardation*, **12**, June, 50–53.

Chapter 5

Biological Aspects of Severe Learning Disabilities

INTRODUCTION

The biological factors relevant to intellectual impairment can be of many kinds. There are a range of genetic anomalies which can be associated with learning difficulties — anomalies such as extra or damaged chromosomes or inborn errors of metabolism. Damage to the brain in the early period of development from conception onwards can also be associated with some degree of learning impairment. There are many ways in which such damage can occur — through infections such as rubella or encephalitis, poisons such as drugs or alcohol, loss of oxygen to the brain or physical trauma such as road traffic accidents. The extent of any such damage will vary from that affecting one small area to devastating damage covering most areas of the brain. There are other factors such as malnutrition which can interfere with the satisfactory development of the brain and, in turn, affect subsequent intellectual functioning.

Although increasing numbers of such biological factors are being identified there has been some reluctance in recent years to consider the possible psychological implications of these factors. An emphasis upon organic involvement in learning difficulties has had a number of adverse effects upon people who suffer these difficulties. Emphasizing such factors has tended to draw undue attention to the differences that exist between those who have serious learning problems and those who do not. This has drawn attention away from the many human needs which exist in common. Describing biological differences has also served to indicate that people so affected are in some way 'sick'. Diagnosing an illness is normally carried out in order to select treatment for that illness. Diagnosis of organic involvement in learning difficulties, however, has had no such positive implications as to what can be done to help. Given that the known biological factors are basically unalterable with our present technologies there has been a clear implication that nothing can be done to help people with these problems. There were few conditions (phenylketonuria being an exception) where 'diagnosis' had any positive implications for the individual. For the majority, it carried the implication of being untreatable — it was simply not possible to alter deviant genes, rearrange chromosomes or repair damaged brains. The social implications of indicating that people with intellectual difficulties were untreatable was disastrous. The response of ordinary people to those experiencing difficulties who apparently cannot be treated may at best be sympathetic, at worst indifferent or rejecting. The response of professionals whose *raison d'etre* is to 'treat' people is more than likely to be avoidance and rejection of those who are 'untreatable'. These social responses act to prevent anything being done to help such people and this creates a self-fulfilling prophesy. If it is thought that nothing can be done then nothing will be done; and if nothing is done to help people with learning disabilities then it is most unlikely that they will make progress. Such lack of progress in its turn is taken as evidence of basic untreatability. This cycle of events has exerted enormously detrimental effects upon people with severe learning problems — they have been excluded from society, deprived of basic human rights, deprived of stimulation and opportunities to learn. Services for them have been starved of professional interest and resources. Thus the original intellectual impairment becomes compounded by a secondary handicap of deprivation based upon the low expectations of 'normal' people. The emphasis upon organic factors has had a central role in creating low expectations and the ensuing secondary handicaps for people with intellectual impairment. It served to create and maintain an atmosphere of pessimism.

Two key developments challenged this prevailing pessimism. First was the growth of the human rights movement which stressed the perception of people with intellectual impairments as a deprived minority group. This movement sought to emphasize the commonalities between those affected and 'normal' people and the basic human rights common to us all. This in turn directly challenged the policies and services which emphasized differences and it asserted the rights of those with intellectual impairment to a fair share of resources and to as normal a life as possible.

The second development provided direct empirical support to the new philosophies. This was the development of new educational and therapeutic technologies founded upon behavioural principles which clearly demonstrated the potential for change in people at all levels of ability (see Chapters 6 and 7). Under the impact of these twin developments major changes in social policy have occurred, with institutional care beginning to give way to community care, segregation beginning to give way to integration and all services moving towards a developmental rather than a custodial approach. Both movements, for different reasons, saw reference to orgnic factors as at best of little interest and at worst as positively detrimental. This created a climate of opinion where study of such factors would not find encouragement. This was not helped by the fact that, until recently, there had been few interesting relationships found between biological factors and functioning in everyday life. Discussing the neuropsychology of intellectual impairment appeared both sterile and potentially damaging to the prospects of people with severe learning disabilities.

In such a climate of opinion, it becomes necessary to offer some justification for devoting attention to relationships between biology and psychology in a book such as this. While fully acknowledging that organic concepts have often proved unhelpful to those who experience a degree of intellectual impairment, it would be foolish to deny the existence of a biological dimension in severe learning disabilities. If such a dimension exists it would seem important to elucidate what it involves and what implications it might have. This is undoubtedly a very long-term enterprise but one which, nonetheless, must be undertaken. The second point to make is that the present social policies and the educational and therapeutic technologies available do not prevent or cure severe learning difficulties. They may well prevent secondary handicaps such as those resulting from institutionalization. They may well improve the number of skills that a person acquires or the ease with which a behavioural difficulty is overcome. They do not resolve the disability itself. Nor do present policies and intervention technologies necessarily produce personally and socially significant change in every case. It is important to recognize the limitations of the present knowledge base and to be prepared to explore every avenue which might potentially improve the ability to help those with severe intellectual impairment.

There are, at present, dramatic changes taking place in the fields of biological assessment and intervention. There is continuing growth in the number of specific biological factors being identified as associated with learning disabilities. In and of itself, knowledge about such factors may improve our ability to prevent impairment through genetic counselling, through the development of early screening in societies which offer the possibility of abortion for affected foetuses, and through public health and education programmes. An increasing range of biological interventions is becoming available for directly altering or managing some of the identified features and thus preventing or ameliorating their consequences for development. Such interventions may include diet (as in phenylketonuria), drugs (as in folic acid in Fragile-X syndrome) and surgery (as in bone marrow transplants for some of the mucopolysaccharidoses). In the near future there may be dramatic possibilities opened up through genetic engineering. A third potential benefit of this growth in knowledge will emerge if it becomes possible to explore more specific relationships between biological and psychological factors. This will help to refine psychological interventions and develop rational broad-spectrum interventions incorporating both biological and psychological components.

It is the promise of the last-named area which will primarily be explored in the following sections. These sections deal with four types of identified biological factors associated with learning and behavioural difficulties — infantile hypercalcaemia, Lesch-Nyhan disease, Fragile-X syndrome and Down's syndrome. Although these are just four examples, it is hoped that they will serve to justify the value of this general approach both in terms of improving our understanding of learning difficulties and in terms of improving the practical help that can be offered to those affected. Much exists at the level of possibility rather than proven reality, but it is hoped that sufficient justification will be made for the value of exploring the relationship of biology to psychology.

INFANTILE HYPERCALCAEMIA

First described in 1952, infantile hypercalcaemia is a disorder which is marked by increased intestinal absorption of calcium (see Martin, Snodgrass and Cohen, 1984, for a useful review). It is usually identified in the first year of life through such physical symptoms as failure to thrive, feeding difficulties, vomiting, constipation and irritability. The raised calcium levels are treatable by dietary intervention but this does not appear to have a dramatic effect upon the children's health or eliminate the other problems associated with the condition. Although varied in expression, infantile hypercalcaemia is thought to have a range of characteristic physical and psychological features. The children tend to be small and floppy with delayed motor milestones. Most have cardiovascular defects and a number suffer from hypertension. Many have elf-like facial characteristics which are particularly noticeable in the middle-school years.

Psychological aspects reported have included a degree of intellectual impairment, structurally sophisticated speech but more limited comprehension, problems with gross and fine motor skills and spatial orientation, poor peer relationships but excessive friendliness to adults, sleep difficulties, hypersensitivity to particular noises often amounting to clear noise phobias, and a generally high level of anxiety. These characteristics tend to be reported clinically, and Arnold, Yule and Martin (1985) attempted to quantify them in a more objective fashion through surveying a group of 23 children with infantile hypercalcaemia in the seven- to twelve-year-old age range. Udwin, Yule and Martin (in press) developed this work further in a survey of 44 such children, aged six to sixteen years old. All the children had some degree of intellectual impairment, with most having moderate to severe learning disabilities. Udwin *et al.* (in press) found that scores on the WISC-R Verbal Scale were significantly higher than those on the Performance Scale, which confirms anecdotal reports of verbal skills being superior to visual-spatial and motor abilities. However, there were considerable individual differences, and within the verbal sphere some evidence for specific difficulties with general knowledge and understanding, and numeracy skills. Although the children did tend to score higher on tests of expressive language compared to comprehension, in Arnold *et al.* (1985) this was not particularly marked and did not really confirm the clinical impressions reported in the literature. A considerable number of the children were able to read and spell. On the Rutter Scales concerned with behaviour difficulties, the children with infantile hypercalcaemia tended to be rated at home and school as generally more disturbed than normal children of a similar age, and than other children with an equivalent degree of learning difficulty (Udwin *et al.*, in press). In terms of specific behaviours, compared to other children with equivalent intellectual problems they were rated as more overactive, more solitary, had more worries, were more tearful, were more likely to have sleep problems and to be faddy about the food they would eat. This agrees with the anecdotal picture of these children as being overanxious and having poor relationships with peers. Many of the children with infantile hypercalcaemia were reported as hypersensitive to sound, particularly electrical and sudden noises (it should be noted that they have no recognizable hearing abnormality).

As yet, little is known about the causal mechanisms underlying this disorder. Although many of the features reported as part of the syndrome are present in other disorders, there do appear to be distinctive individual features and distinctive clusters of characteristics. These cover both physical and psychological aspects of the children's make-up and functioning. In terms of the psychological characteristics, what is already known does have implications for counselling of the parents of these children. It also has implications for direct work with the children themselves, particularly in relation to developing better peer interaction skills, enhancing academic achievement, developing satisfactory sleep patterns and helping them to manage environmental noise. There is no indication that such characteristics are not amenable to change. Knowing that the child suffers from infantile hypercalcaemia may enable one to intervene at an early stage to prevent some of these characteristics developing into additional handicaps. This is particularly true in terms of social relationships and noise phobias which both can hamper the child's day-to-day functioning. In this sense, therefore, identifying the syndrome can have important positive implications for the children affected and for their families.

LESCH-NYHAN DISEASE

This is a genetically based disorder found only in males and involving an abnormal gene on the X-chromosome (see Christie *et al.*, 1982; Watts *et al.*, 1982, for useful reviews). The abnormality is associated with the complete absence of activity of one particular enzyme which is involved in purine metabolism. While this metabolic defect can be corrected by drug administration, such correction exerts no influence over the highly distinctive physical and psychological characteristics of those affected. The children are initially identified because of excessive hypotonia, but as they develop their muscles become rigid, and they show uncontrolled writhing movements of the arms and body (choreoathetosis) and an uncontrolled twisting and arching of the back. This last named difficulty can cause lesions of the pyramidal tract with ensuing additional physical handicaps and this sometimes results in death. Most of those affected learn to speak but their speech is dysarthric and difficult to understand. No person with Lesch-Nyhan disease has yet learned to walk, and all require support in sitting as well. Physical development is generally retarded, particularly in terms of weight, and to a lesser degree, in terms of height and bone age. No very clear structural abnormalities of the brain have yet been detected but it has been suggested that there may be some imbalance in biogenic amines, and thus in the activities of the different neurotransmitter-mediated neuronal circuits.

To assess intellectual functioning in the presence of such major physical handicaps is a very difficult process. From clinical surveys it appears that the degree of intellectual impairment can vary with at least some people scoring within the normal range, although most will be impaired to some degree. The most obvious and distinctive behavioural characteristic is the marked and severe self-injurious behaviour found in all cases. All cases so far reported bite themselves, particularly on their hands or lips, and this results in clear tissue damage. They may also show a range of other self-injurious behaviour such as head banging. Many show aggressive behaviour towards others which, in some cases, involves spitting or vomiting on them. As language skills develop people with Lesch-Nyhan disease express awareness of their disabilities and behavioural difficulties. They often show ambivalence about their behaviours, but most are clearly afraid of their self-injury and become very anxious when not restrained. Most people with this disorder have some form of restraint on their limbs both day and night. While some of their behaviour difficulties are distinctive and appear to be part of a clearly identifiable organic syndrome, it does appear that such behaviours are susceptible to environmental control in the same way as the behaviour problems of other people. Thus Bull and Lavecchio (1978) reported on the successful management of self-injury in a single case study involving a person with Lesch-Nyhan disease. They used a combination of desensitization to the removal of restraint (which was very anxiety provoking), ignoring and time-out. It is interesting to note that Anderson *et al.* (1977), and Anderson, Dancis and Alpert (1978) found that children with this disorder could not learn from punishment techniques but were able to learn via positive reinforcement and time-out. This suggests a distinctive learning characteristic which might relate to abnormalities in the neurotransmitter systems in the brain. If confirmed, it certainly has clear implications particularly as to how behavioural difficulties should be tackled, and perhaps more generally, for how skill development should be promoted.

Once again there are many unknowns about Lesch-Nyhan disease and the exact causal mechanisms involved. However, it does seem to constitute a clear syndrome at both the biological and psychological levels. What is known already has implications for family counselling and individual management; and the future may hold many possibilities for combined biological and psychological interventions.

FRAGILE-X SYNDROME

The study of human chromosomes has revealed at least twelve sites where fragility may occur, that is where the chromosome appears to be constricted and sometimes shows clear breakage (Sutherland, 1979; August and Lockhart, 1984). The exact incidence and prevalence of fragile sites in the general population is not known. In general, there appear to be few adverse outcomes associated with this anomaly except where fragility is present on the X-chromosome in males, in which case there appears to be a strong association with some degree of intellectual impairment. The discovery of this association may be highly significant as it is estimated that the incidence of Fragile-X syndrome may be as high as 0.92 per 1000 male births, and this would make it the second most common factor after Down's syndrome associated with serious learning difficulties.

The physical and psychological characteristics of people with Fragile-X syndrome are not as distinctive as those for infantile hypercalcaemia and Lesch-Nyhan disease. None of the associated characteristics is unique to Fragile-X. Those affected tend to have a long narrow face with a high forehead and long low set ears. They have a high arched palate. They show poor muscle tone with delay in fine and gross motor development and, after puberty, have large testes and a long penis (August and Lockhart, 1984; De La Cruz, 1985).

The degree of intellectual impairment associated with Fragile-X varies, and intelligence can be within the normal range. It has been suggested that those affected have specific difficulties with speech and language. However, the degree of retardation may be equal in all areas and, conversely, speech and language problems can be found in forms of X-linked impairment other than Fragile-X (Howard-Peebles, Stoddard and Mims, 1979). There does appear to be a significant link between Fragile-X syndrome and autistic features (Brown et al., 1982; August and Lockhart, 1984; De La Cruz, 1985; Gillberg and Wahlstrom, 1985). The association is much stronger than would be expected by chance even though most of those with Fragile-X chromosomes are not autistic, and most people with autistic difficulties do not have fragility of their X-chromosomes. It certainly seems that, in general, there is a link between X-chromosome anomalies and specific difficulties in language and social development. However, such difficulties are not an inevitable consequence and details of causal mechanisms are, as yet, unclear. There is certainly no simple relationship between the biological and psychological features as, for example, between the proportion of cells showing the Fragile-X feature and the level of intellectual functioning.

Fragile-X was only discovered when the medium used to culture chromosomes was deficient in folic acid — that is, in the presence of folic acid the chromosomes do not appear fragile or broken. This led to speculation that administration of folic acid might 'repair' the chromosomes and improve general functioning. Lejeune (1982) reported behavioural improvements in seven out of eight people with Fragile-X syndrome and psychotic-like behaviours who were given folic acid. Gustavson et al. (1985) reported on nine people with Fragile-X syndrome ranging in age from 3 to 50 years who showed a positive effect from administration of folic acid in terms of improvement in autistic-like behaviours but not in overall level of intellectual functioning. These improvements in behavioural difficulties but not general functioning were confirmed in a controlled trial of folic acid and placebo (Carpenter et al., 1983). In the Gustavson study it was the older people who showed no benefit from folic acid and, indeed, one adult in the study was adversely affected. All these studies confirm that oral administration of folic acid does lead to marked reduction or complete elimination of chromosome fragility.

As with all the conditions so far discussed, the details of the causal mechanisms are poorly understood. However, even at the present level of knowledge exciting possibilities are suggested. For example, if screening for Fragile-X became part of routine diagnostic procedures then an early intervention programme combining folic acid administration with intensive work on language and social skills might yield important dividends in terms of behavioural adjustment and level of functioning. Whether such dividends could be confirmed, of course, requires careful scientific research but it does illustrate the potential value of integrating biological and psychological approaches. It should also be noted that all the advances discussed here which are helping to tease out the factors involved in a child's intellectual impairment are of great benefit when it comes to counselling work with families.

DOWN'S SYNDROME

Down's syndrome is the largest single contributor to the population who experience severe intellectual impairment. It has long been identified because of the physical features of those affected, but it was not until the 1950s that an associated chromosomal anomaly was discovered — extra chromosome material, usually a complete extra chromosome, at the 21st pair of chromosomes. The physical features include short stature with a small round head, a small nose lacking a bridge, epicanthic skin folds around the eyes, a fissured tongue which tends to protrude because of structural abnormalities of the mouth and jaw, and a single palmar crease. Muscle tone is very poor early in life. Although the brain itself shows no major structural abnormalities the frontal lobes, brain-stem and cerebellum tend to be relatively small (Penrose, 1966). Many people with Down's syndrome have heart defects and they are also at risk for a range of visual difficulties (squints, cataracts and short-sightedness). As a group, they are also more at risk for leukaemia, late onset epilepsy and the development of Alzheimer's disease (a form of pre-senile dementia).

Recent investigations have indicated a number of other abnormalities in brain functioning which may offer some insight into the causal mechanisms involved in Down's syndrome (e.g. Balazs and Brooksbank, 1984; Blair and Leeming, 1984). The brain cells tend to show a lower degree of dendritic elaboration than normal. There are also enzyme dysfunctions which tend to influence the working of the brain cells. There is a general increase in oxidative processes because of raised levels of intracellular superoxide dismutase. This, in its turn, affects other enzymes and, in particular, leads to a loss at cell level of the enzyme tetrahydrobiopterin (THB). THB is involved in the formation of neurotransmitters in the central nervous system so that any alteration in it will tend to affect the general functioning of these transmitter systems, particularly the cholinergic systems. It has been noted that THB levels do correlate with intellectual performance in a number of different conditions, not just Down's syndrome. It is also of interest that the activity of superoxide dismutase is controlled by a specific gene on the 21st chromosome and it is argued that one of the effects of the extra chromosome material is to increase the concentration of gene products with the secondary effects illustrated above. Although these findings are new and there is a degree of speculation, it certainly produces a more detailed picture of biological functioning in Down's syndrome. It also offers a potential insight into the association between Down's syndrome and Alzheimer's disease as the effect of excessive oxidation on the brain cells is essentially an ageing one.

There are, therefore, a wide range of biological factors involved in Down's syndrome. It may be possible to link some of these to certain aspects of psychological functioning. The general intellectual functioning of people with Down's syndrome does vary to some extent, although nearly all will be impaired to some degree and most to a moderate or severe degree. One universally reported phenomenon is that the gap between chronological and mental development increases with age. That is, there seems to be a progressive decline in relative intellectual functioning particularly noticeable in the first two years of life (Cowie, 1970; Carr, 1975; Clements, Bates and Hafer, 1976; Cunningham, 1984). It is also often remarked that the development of children with Down's syndrome is marked by spurts with long plateaux in between times, during which there appears to be little progress being made and indeed there seems a greater frequency of regression to earlier levels of development than found in non-affected infants (e.g. Dunst, 1986). The reported decline may be an artefact of testing procedures as the abilities tapped by tests do become more specific and discriminative with increasing age and development. However, it is also possible that the decline represents the net outcome of two conflicting processes: relatively normal maturational developmental processes and the abnormal cellular processes outlined earlier. This is obviously a vast oversimplification, but at least produces some kind of theoretical explanation capable of experimental investigation. It should, of course, be stressed that, although the rate of development for people with Down's syndrome shows a progressive slowing, development itself does continue throughout childhood and even into adult life (Cunningham, 1984).

However, in later adult life people with Down's syndrome appear to be seriously at risk for the development of Alzheimer's disease and a true deterioration in functioning. It appears extremely likely, possibly inevitable, that as people with Down's syndrome grow older (particularly beyond the age of 35) their brains will show increasing evidence of the signs of Alzheimer's disease — neurofibrillary tangles, senile plaques and granulovacular deterioration (see Miniszek, 1983; Oliver and Holland, 1986, for a general discussion of Down's syndrome and Alzheimer's disease). Plaques, in particular, appear early in adult life (in the 20s and 30s) and the frontal lobes and hippocampus appear to be the brain areas most affected. People with Down's syndrome often show overt signs of premature ageing (such as greying of the hair) and some show clear loss of skills and the general deterioration associated with dementia, in their 40s and 50s. However, early onset dementia is by no means inevitable, nor is there any clear association between the degree of neurological involvement and interference with day-to-day functioning. It has been suggested that there might be a closer association between the neurological involvement and subtler aspects of psychological functioning, particularly in terms of memory. Dalton, Crapper and Schlotterer (1974) and Dalton and Crapper (1977) found some evidence for specific short-term memory difficulties in older people with Down's syndrome who were showing no overt signs of deterioration. However, this finding was not confirmed by Crawley (1984). Thus the relationship between neurological and psychological functioning in adult life for people with Down's syndrome is, at this stage, uncertain although it seems likely that there will be major advances in our understanding of this area in the coming few years.

The review of biological functioning in Down's syndrome indicates a number of other ways in which psychological functioning might be affected. The poor dendritic elaboration and the possible neurotransmitter depletion might indicate that there would be some differences in overall speed of information processing. While at the gross level children with Down's syndrome go through the same stages of development as normal children but at a slower rate (see, for example, Serafica and Cicchetti, 1976; Cicchetti and Sroufe 1976; Mahoney, Glover and Finger, 1981; Dunst, 1986), there is some evidence that they do analyse information at a much slower rate even compared to those at an apparently equivalent level of development. Lincoln et al. (1985) review a number of studies and report an original study of their own using evoked brain potentials. These studies do tend to indicate that people with Down's syndrome respond more slowly to both auditory and visual stimulation compared to others matched for overall level of development. Likewise, Cicchetti and Sroufe (1976), who studied situations which make children smile and laugh, found that although the children with Down's syndrome went through the same stages as normal children, their latency of response to test items was much slower. They were also very much delayed in the onset of laughter, being much more likely to smile than laugh. Cicchetti and Sroufe speculate that the tendency to smile rather than laugh reflects difficulty in processing the incongruity of stimuli quickly enough to produce the arousal level necessary for laughter. There is need of much more research both to confirm the hypotheses about speed of information processing and to understand its implications if confirmed. In practical terms it might suggest a specific need to take care over rate of presentation of information and over allowing sufficient time to respond. In this respect it is interesting that mothers of young Down's syndrome children do tend to show more initiation of speech towards their child with correspondingly less initiation from the child compared to mothers of normal children (Buium, Rynders and Turnure, 1974; Peterson and Sherrod, 1982; Cardoso-Martins and Mervis, 1985).

There might be many explanations for this but one possibility is that the slowness of the Down's child to respond produces pauses which the adult tends to fill. The long-term consequences of this could possibly be very serious. (See also Chapter 4).

The relatively small size of the cerebellum is one of the more notable structural characteristics of the brain in people with Down's syndrome. Given that the cerebellum plays a key role in motor functioning it might be expected that people with Down's syndrome might show difficulties in this area. Certainly most Down's syndrome infants are markedly hypotonic; and there appears to be a specific delay in motor milestones experienced by these children (see, for example, Carr, 1975). But even when all major motor milestones have been achieved there still appears to remain a difficulty in motor functioning. Motor reaction times are excessively slow in people with Down's syndrome compared to others of similar levels of ability (e.g. Hermelin and Venables, 1964; Lincoln et al., 1985). Frith and Frith (1974) have suggested that people with Down's syndrome have a general difficulty in learning and executing programmed sequences of motor movements. In a test of this theory Henderson, Morris and Frith (1981) looked at performance on a visual tracking task where subjects had to follow with a pencil a rolling track of predictable shape. They compared people with Down's symdrome to others at an equivalent level of development, both normally developing and those with learning disabilities. While all subjects showed some knowledge of the shape of the track to be followed, people with Down's syndrome had much greater difficulty in accurate tracking because they were slower to adjust their pencil movements to the predicted changes in track direction. Such a central motor difficulty has also been invoked by Dodd (1975, 1976) to explain some of the speech difficulties experienced by people with Down's syndrome. It has long been known that people with Down's syndrome have a range of speech problems — poor articulation, stuttering, and voicing difficulties (Bilovsky and Share, 1965; Zisk and Bialer, 1967; Evans, 1976). Such problems are not as common among others equally delayed in development and they are not explicable in terms of a general language delay as syntax, understanding and imitation may be at a considerably higher level than quality of expression. No peripheral motor disability would explain these difficulties either. The possibility of a central motor difficulty was highlighted in Dodd's studies where she demonstrated that Down's syndrome children made far more phonological errors when items had to be spontaneously named, or words spontaneously generated compared to when the same words had to be uttered in imitation. Such a difference between imitation and naming is not found in normal children and children with learning disabilities matched for overall level of development. Dodd suggests that her imitation task in some way by-passed the motor control centre whereas naming tasks require active motor initiation. Whether such motor difficulties could be overcome if children with Down's syndrome were exposed to a curriculum more heavily weighted towards motor development is an interesting speculation. Likewise, such a difficulty might indicate the use of augmentative systems of communication which make lesser demands on motor skills — for example, symbol systems.

Such motor difficulties might also underly some of the reported anomalies shown by Down's syndrome children in visual functioning. Thus these children are reported as showing less systematic visual scanning of their environment, make less use of eye gazing to effect communication and make less use of eye and hand coordination when developing the reach-and-grasp response (Miranda and Fantz, 1973; Jones, 1977, 1979, 1980; Gunn, Berry and Andrews, 1982; Cunningham, 1984).

Down's syndrome exemplifies a range of possible links between biology and psychology. Many of these links are rather speculative but a coherent picture is beginning to emerge and a range of practical outcomes seems likely. Thus through genetic engineering or replacement therapy it may prove possible to correct some of the enzyme dysfunctions. More active monitoring of older people with Down's syndrome may detect early signs of functional difficulty and stimulate active rehabilitation efforts to mitigate the effects of any neurological dysfunction. The concepts of slowed information transmission and executive motor problems have important implications for parents and educators in terms of rate of input and permitting adequate response time. It also suggests the need for greater priority to motor-based learning in educational endeavours. A role for augmentative systems of communication with a minimal motor involvement seems indicated if Dodd's speculation on the link between motor and speech difficulties can be confirmed. Thus, using knowledge from biological and psychological spheres it becomes possible to construct more specific and rational intervention strategies geared to the particular needs of people with Down's syndrome.

CONCLUSIONS

The four areas discussed above are just some examples of the ways in which biological aspects of severe learning disabilities are being linked to psychological aspects. These developments are very much 'driven' by advances in biological assessment techniques, with the field of psychological assessment remaining relatively static. These developments might be capitalized upon further if there were more sophisticated approaches to psychological assessment — for example, in terms of being able to assess specific task learning strengths and weaknesses, information processing strategies and motivational preferences.

At present, there is considerable speculation involved in interpreting much of the information available. The understanding of causal mechanisms is often very limited. Nevertheless, it is clear from what is already known that there can be no single unidimensional theory of intellectual impairment, a fact obvious to anyone who works with the very different people who experience these learning disabilities. There will be a need to develop more specific theories which will account for the learning and behavioural difficulties of individuals or more clearly delineated groups.

However, it is not the purpose of this book simply to deal with theoretical issues and developments, important though these are. Rather, it was the purpose of this chapter to illustrate that real-world practical advantages can be derived from the attempts to integrate biological and psychological knowledge. This is not just in terms of prevention of disability and/or active treatment through biological interventions. Rather, such an integrated approach will bring improvements both in family counselling and in the education and management of the individual experiencing severe learning disabilities. It is hoped that the present chapter has gone some way to vindicate this optimism and to allay fears that any reference to organic factors is inevitably detrimental to people with severe intellectual impairment.

REFERENCES

Anderson, L., Dancis, J., and Alpert, M. (1978) Behavioural contingencies and self mutilation in Lesch-Nyhan disease. *Journal of Consulting and Clinical Psychology*, **46**,(3), 529–536.

Anderson, L.T., Dancis, J., Herrman, L., and Alpert, M. (1977) Punishment learning and self mutilation in Lesch-Nyhan disease. *Nature*, **265**, 461–463.

Arnold, R., Yule, W., and Martin, N. (1985) The psychological characteristics of infantile hypercalcaemia: a preliminary investigation. *Developmental Medicine and Child Neurology*, **27**, 49–59.

August, G.J., and Lockhart, L.H. (1984) Familial autism and the Fragile-X chromosome. *Journal of Autism and Developmental Disorders*, **14**, 197–204.

Balazs, R., and Brooksbank, B.W.L. (1984) Development of the brain in Down's Syndrome. Paper presented at the Royal Society of Medicine, Mental Handicap Forum.

Bilovsky, D., and Share, J. (1965) The ITPA and Down's Syndrome: an exploratory study. *American Journal of Mental Deficiency*, **70**, 78–82.

Blair, J.A., and Leeming, R.J. (1984) Tetrahydrobiopterin metabolism, neurological disease and mental retardation. In J. Dobbing with A.D.B. Clarke, J.A. Corbett, J.

Hogg and R.O. Robinson (eds) *Scientific Studies in Mental Retardation*. London: Royal Society of Medicine and Macmillan Press.

Brown, W.T., Jenkins, E.C., Friedman, E., Brooks, J., Wisniewski, K., Raguthus, S., and French, J. (1982) Autism is associated with the Fragile-X Syndrome. *Journal of Autism and Developmental Disorders*, **12**, 303–308.

Buium, N., Rynders, J., and Turnure, J. (1974) Early maternal linguistic environment of normal and Down's Syndrome language-learning children. *American Journal of Mental Deficiency*, **79**, 52–58.

Bull, M., and Lavecchio, F. (1978) Behavior therapy for a child with Lesch-Nyhan Syndrome. *Developmental Medicine and Child Neurology*, **20**, 368–375.

Carpenter, N.J., Barber, D.H., Jones, A., Lindley, W., and Carr, C. (1983) Controlled six month study of oral folic acid therapy in boys with Fragile X-linked mental retardation. Paper presented at the 34th Annual Meeting of the American Society of Human Genetics, Norfolk, Virginia, November.

Cardoso-Martins, C., and Mervis, C.R. (1985) Maternal speech to pre-linguistic children with Down's Syndrome. *American Journal of Mental Deficiency*, **89**, 451–458.

Carr, J., (1975) *Young Children with Down's Syndrome*. London: Butterworths.

Christie, R., Bay, L., Kaufman, I.A., Bakay, B., Burden, M., and Nyhan, W.L. (1982) Lesch-Nyhan Disease: Clinical experience with nineteen patients. *Development Medicine and Child Neurology*, **24**, 293–306.

Cicchetti, D. and Sroufe, L.A. (1976) The relationship between affective and cognitive development in Down's Syndrome infants. *Child Development*, **47**, 920–929.

Clements, P.R., Bates, M.V., and Hafer, M. (1976) Variability within Down's Syndrome (Trisomy-21): empirically observed sex differences in IQs. *Mental Retardation*, February, 30–31.

Cowie, V. (1970) *A Study of the Early Development of Mongols*. Oxford: Pergamon Press.

Crawley, B. (1984) The relationship between Alzheimer's disease and Down's Syndrome. Unpublished M. Phil thesis, Institute of Psychiatry, University of London.

Cunningham, C. (1984) Patterns of development in infancy and childhood: Down's Syndrome. Paper Presented at the Royal Society of Medicine, Mental Handicap Forum.

Dalton, A.J., and Crapper, D.R. (1977) Down's syndrome and ageing of the brain. In P. Mittler (ed.) *Research To Practice in Mental Retardation: Biomedical Aspects*. Baltimore: University Park Press.

Dalton, A.J., Crapper, D.R., and Schlotterer, G.R. (1974) Alzheimer's disease in Down's Syndrome: visual retention deficits. *Cortex*, **10**, 366–377.

De La Cruz, F. (1985) Fragile X Syndrome. *American Journal of Mental Defiency*, **90**, 114–123.

Dodd, B. (1975) Recognition and reproduction of words by Down's syndrome and non-Down's syndrome retarded children. *American Journal of Mental Deficiency*, **80**, 306–311.

Dodd, B. (1976) A comparison of the phonological systems of mental age matched, normal, severely subnormal and Down's syndrome children. *British Journal of Disorders in Communication*, **11**, 27–42.

Dunst, C. (1986) Sensorimotor development of infants with Down's Syndrome. In D. Cicchetti and M. Beeghley (eds) *Down's Syndrome: The Developmental Perspective*. New York: Cambridge University Press.

Evans, D. (1976) Language development in Down's Syndrome retardation: a factorial study. *Contemporary Educational Psychology*, **1**, 319–328.

Frith, U., and Frith, C.D. (1974) Specific motor disablties in Down's Syndrome. *Journal of Child Psychology and Psychiatry,* **15,** 293–301.

Gillberg, C., and Wahlstrom, J. (1985) Chromosome abnormalities in infantile autism and other childhood psychoses: a population study of 66 cases. *Developmental Medicine and Child Neurology,* **27,** 293–306.

Gunn, P., Berry, P., and Andrews, R.J. (1982) Looking behaviour of Down's Syndrome infants. *American Journal of Mental Deficiency,* **87,** 344–347.

Gustavson, K.H., Dahlbom, K., Flood, A., Holmgren, G., Blomquist, H.K., and Sanner, G. (1985) Effect of folic acid treatment in the fragile X syndrome. *Clinical Genetics,* **27,** 463–467.

Henderson, S.E., Morris, J., and Frith, U. (1981) The motor deficit in Down's Syndrome children: a problem of timing? *Journal of Child Psychology and Psychiatry,* **22,** 233–245.

Hermelin, B.M., and Venables, P.M. (1964) Reaction time and alpha blocking in normal and severely subnormal subjects. *Journal of Experimental Psychology,* **67,** 365–372.

Howard-Peebles, P., Stoddard, G.R., and Mims, M.G. (1979) Familial X-linked mental retardation, verbal disability and Marker-X chromosomes. *American Journal of Human Genetics,* **31,** 214–222.

Jones, O.H.M. (1977) Mother-child communication with pre-linguistic Down's syndrome and normal infants. In H.R. Shaffer (ed.) *Studies in Mother-Infant Interaction,* pp. 370–401. New York: Academic press.

Jones, O.H.M. (1979) A comparative study of mother-child communication with Down's syndrome and normal infants. In H.R. Shaffer and J. Dunn (eds) *The First Year of Life: Psychological and Medical Implications of Early Experience,* pp. 175–195. New York: Wiley.

Jones, O.H.M. (1980) Prelinguistic communication skills in Down's Syndrome and normal infants. In T.M. Field (ed.) *High-Risk Infants and Children: Adult and Peer Interactions,* pp. 205–225. New York: Academic Press.

LeJeune, J. (1982) Is the Fragile X Syndrome amenable to treatment? *Lancet,* 30 January, 273–274.

Lincoln, A.J., Courchesne, E., Kilman, B.A., and Galambos, F. (1985) Neuropsychological correlates of information processing by children with Down's Syndrome. *American Journal of Mental Deficiency,* **89,** 403–414.

Mahoney, G., Glover, A., and Finger, I. (1981) Relationship between language and sensorimotor development of Down's Syndrome and non-retarded children. *American Journal of Mental Deficiency,* **86,** 21–27.

Martin, N.D.T., Snodgrass, G.J.A.I. and Cohen, R.D. (1984) Idiopathic infantile hypercalcaemia — a continuing enigma. *Archives of Disease in Childhood,* **59,** 605–613.

Miniszek, N.A. (1983) Development of Alzheimer's Disease in Down's Syndrome individuals. *American Journal of Mental Deficiency,* **87,** 377–389.

Miranda, S.B., and Fantz, R.L. (1973) Visual preferences of Down's Syndrome and normal infants. *Child Development,* **44,** 555–561.

Oliver, C., and Holland, A.J. (1986) Down's syndrome and Alzheimer's Disease: a review. *Psychological Medicine,* **16,** 307–322.

Penrose, L.S. (1966) *The Biology of Mental Defect.* London: Sidgwick and Jackson.

Peterson, G.A., and Sherrod, K.G. (1982) Relationship of maternal language to language development and language delay of children. *American Journal of Mental Deficiency,* **86,** 391–398.

Pueschel, S., Hays, R.M., and Mendoza, T. (1983) Familial X-linked mental retardation Syndrome associated with minor congenital anomalies, macroorchidism and Fragile X-chromosome. *American Journal of Mental Deficiency*, **87**, 372–376.

Serafica, F.C., and Cicchetti, D. (1976) Down's Syndrome children in a strange situation: attachment and exploration behaviours. *Merrill-Palmer Quarterly*, **22**, 137–150.

Sutherland, D.G.R. (1979) Heritable fragile sites on human chromosomes: II. Distribution, phenotypic effects, and cytogenetics. *American Journal of Human Genetics*, **31**, 136–148.

Udwin, O., Yule, W., and Martin, N. (in press). Cognitive abilities and behavioural characteristics of children with idiopathic infantile hypercalcaemia. *Journal of Child Psychology and Psychiatry*,

Watts, R.W.E., Spellacy, E., Gibbs, D.A., Allsop, J., McKern, R.O., and Slavin, R.E. (1982) Clinical, post-mortem, biochemical and therapeutic observations on the Lesch-Nyhan syndrome with particular reference to neurological manifestations. *Quarterly Journal of Medicine*, **51**, 43–78.

Zisk, P.K., and Bialer, I. (1967) Speech and language problems in mongolism: a review of the literature. *Journal of Speech and Hearing Disorders*, **32**, 228–241.

CONCLUSIONS TO PART 1

It has been the purpose of Part 1 to look at some of the factors that may be involved in severe intellectual impairment. An outline has been given of some of the possible reasons why those affected experience such serious difficulties in learning and development. Focus has been upon factors which operate within the individual and less attention has been paid to environmental factors. This inevitably creates something of an artifical distinction — individuals do not operate in isolation from the environment or from history and in order to understand individual behaviour at any given moment in time weight must be given to environmental and historical factors. Nevertheless, the individual is not a *tabula rasa* and inevitably brings personal characteristics of many kinds to any given situation. These serve to mediate the impact of history and the external environment, and the resulting behaviour is a synthesis derived from the interaction of individual and environmental characteristics.

The present review has attempted to highlight some of the possible characteristics relevant to the experience of serious learning disabilities. Given the amount and quality of research and the many methodological difficulties any of these 'characteristics' is rather speculative in nature — they are more in the way of pointers, indications of where to look rather than proven matters of fact. In understanding learning disabilities it seems important to examine how an individual handles and stores information and how problems are tackled; and to look at those factors in relation to different types of problems and demands. It also seems important to know more about the structural and functional characteristics of the nervous system involved in these psychological activities. With more insight into these factors it becomes possible to construct a framework for understanding learning difficulties and from this will come a rational development of strategies to deal with these difficulties. It is hoped that the previous chapters at least suggest that this is a worthwhile enterprise.

However, the knowledge base is very limited and not yet adequate for generating wide-ranging valid strategies for helping people overcome their disabilities. It is also unlikely that a secure knowledge base can be constructed in isolation from direct efforts to intervene with and change the functioning of people with severe learning disabilities. There must be a very close dialogue between experimental and applied endeavours.

Part 2 goes on to review applied work directed at improving the level of functioning and adjustment of people with severe learning disabilities. A major foundation for these efforts has been the approach known as applied behaviour analysis. This has brought in to use the concepts, methods and principles developed through the laboratory study of the environmental determinants of behaviour established by the American behaviourist, B.F. Skinner. This is an 'atheoretical' approach to behaviour change. Those who work within this tradition deliberately avoid elaborate theories about how to change behaviour. They are concerned with establishing general rules about the way the environment can influence behaviour not with explanations as to why, or exactly how such influences occur. The problem for people with severe learning disabilities is defined in terms of the absence of some behaviours (skills) and excesses of other behaviours (problems). The aim of intervention is to increase the frequency of some behaviours and to decrease that of others; the methods to be used are those which have been shown in laboratory situations to influence behaviour frequency (primarily methods of stimulus control and contingency management). Individual differences are seen primarily as reflecting differences in learning history rather than any 'in-built' individual characteristics.

While this is a considerable oversimplification of the behavioural approach it does help to explain the apparent disjunction between the experimental and applied psychologies of severe learning disability — their foundations lie in quite different scientific traditions which have developed in relative isolation from each other. While both traditions can claim significant advances in understanding the difficulties experienced by people with severe intellectual impairment, both also have significant limitations. These limitations can only be overcome if dialogue is opened between these traditions as well as between experimental and applied approaches in general. In this way will grow more systematically a comprehensive understanding of severe learning disabilities and how to overcome them.

Part Two

Remediating Severe Learning and Behavioural Disabilities: General Overview

INTRODUCTION TO PART 2

Part 2 is concerned with what can be done to overcome learning and behavioural disabilities so that the individuals affected experience the minimum degree of handicap in their everyday lives. As discussed in the conclusions to Part 1, the literature on remediation has developed relatively independently of the experimental literature. It was pointed out that one of the most powerful and positive influences upon remedial work has been the behaviour change techniques derived from the work of American behaviourists. Those who have worked within this tradition have developed wide-ranging methods for improving skill levels, managing behaviour problems and designing service systems which will deliver these techniques to those with severe learning disabilities. An extensive research literature exists to document these techniques and their value for many different skills and behavioural problems with people experiencing all degrees of learning difficulty. The existence of such a data base is one reason for focusing the chapters in Part 2 upon behavioural approaches to development and adjustment. The second major reason is that it is the approach with which the author is most familiar.

This attention to behavioural approaches should not be taken to imply that this is the only useful way of tackling skill development and behavioural adjustment. There are many alternative approaches to education. People with severe learning disabilities *do* learn through the same methods as other people — through discovery, imitation and instruction. They do, of course, need more than this, some special additional help, and many educationists have contributed valuable insights into how this should be provided. The writings of Itard, Seguin, Montessori, Steiner and Kephart and many others would repay closer research attention in this respect. When tackling the issues of adjustment there *are* alternatives to a behavioural approach. A range of individual psychotherapy and coun-selling approaches can be applied (see, for example, Sternlicht, 1965;

Szymanski, 1980; Szymanski and Rosefsky, 1980; Nuffield, 1983). Judicious use of drugs can be of positive benefit to some who experience emotional and behavioural disturbance. With the limited understanding that there is of severe learning disabilities, ideas should not be rejected out of hand. The way forward is clearly through research and it is in this area that behavioural approaches lead the way. It remains the case, however, that a plurality of approaches will be needed if, as suggested in Part 1, severe learning disabilities involve many diverse individual problems. The long-term aim must be to match teaching and treatment strategies on an individual basis to the needs of the person affected. Progress in this direction is only likely through an open-minded, evaluative approach which will encourage the expression of ideas and their careful validation through research.

The focus of the present chapters will, however, be upon operant-behavioural work. The definition of a behavioural approach adopted in this part will be a broad one. The main thrust of such work is to establish lawful relationships between observable features of the environment and observable behaviours of the individual. The term 'environment' may refer to features that are external to the individual such as other people, places, times, events and interactions. Alternatively, it may refer to observable features within the individual such as hormone levels, heart rate, body temperature, verbal expressions of mood or emotion. Within this analysis of behaviour three aspects of the environment have attracted particular interest. The first is the immediate consequence of behaviour. Much work has been devoted to studying the effects of a range of immediate consequences which may increase (reinforcers) or decrease (punishers) the probability of a behaviour occurring. The second aspect of the environment is closely linked to the first and concerns the controlling effects of events which precede a behaviour. Through the association of such antecedent events with particular consequences, these antecedents come to signal the likely consequences and thereby trigger an increase or decrease in the probability of a behaviour (discriminative stimulus control). Thus behaviour comes under 'stimulus control' and a considerable literature exists on the techniques for establishing control by one set of events and transferring this control to another set of events. Broadly speaking contingency management will influence whether behaviour occurs; stimulus control when and where it occurs. Both such procedures are clearly relevant to the establishment and utilization of skills and the understanding and management of behaviour difficulties.

Setting events constitute the third aspect of the environment that will be considered in the present model of behavioural analysis. Setting events are much broader features of the environment which determine the likelihood of specific discriminative stimuli and contingencies occurring. They may be represented in both quantitative and qualitative aspects of the environment. For example, level of environmental stimulation, noise, illumination, temperature, state variables in the individual such as mood, aspects of social systems such as harmony and clarity — all these may be regarded as setting factors. These more global and diffuse aspects of the environment may exert considerable control over behaviour and may indeed control the occurrence of a very wide range of behaviours. Hence, altering setting events may be a route to wide-ranging behaviour change and represent an alternative to changing each item of behaviour individually or at least may prove a way of maximizing the success of individual stimulus control and contingency management programmes.

The first two chapters in this part use this three-fold conception of the way that the environment influences behaviour to look at skills development (Chapter 6) and behaviour management (Chapter 7). Chapter 8 then goes on to consider the implications of these approaches for the design and delivery of service systems. The oft lamented gap between research and practice reflects in part the difficulty in translating knowledge about effective help into long-term everyday practice. This translation is essential if those with long-term disabilities are to be effectively helped. Short-term demonstrations show what *can* be done — however, long-term implementation is a requirement for significant impact to be made upon the development and adjustment of people with severe learning disabilities. Knowledge of how to do this is limited and Chapter 8 will focus mainly upon some of the issues which need to be addressed rather than upon offering solutions.

REFERENCES

Nuffield, E.J. (1983) Psychotherapy. In J.L. Matson and J.A. Mulick (eds) *Handbook of Mental Retardation*. New York: Pergamon.

Sternlicht, M. (1965) Psychotherapeutic techniques useful with the mentally retarded: a review and critique. *Psychiatric Quarterly*, **39**, 84–90.

Szymanski, L.S. (1980) Individual psychotherapy with retarded persons. In L.S. Szymanski and P.E. Tanguay (eds) *Emotional Disorders of Mentally Retarded Persons*. Baltimore: University Park Press.

Szymanski, L.S., and Rosefsky, Q.B. (1980) Group psychotherapy with retarded persons. In L.S. Szymanski and P.E. Tanguay (eds) *Emotional Disorders of Mentally Retarded Persons*. Baltimore: University Park Press.

Chapter 6

Developing New Skills

A lack of the skills expected at a given age is an important factor which leads to the identification of people as having a learning disability. The more skills that an individual acquires, the less likely that he or she will be identified as disabled. Improving the level of skill functioning widens the choice for the individual, generates a more positive image and enables the person to participate more fully in the everyday life of the community. Quality of life may, therefore, be raised through skill acquisition. People who have severe behaviour problems in addition to severe learning disabilities often experience the poorest quality of life. As the next chapter will illustrate, a key element in resolving behaviour difficulties is to provide the individual with a wider range of options for influencing the environment — that is, to improve the number of skills the person has and the use that is made of those skills already available. Thus it is for many reasons that services aimed at helping people with severe learning disabilities, may have as a major purpose the improvement of skill functioning. Effecting these improvements requires an understanding of the general developmental aspects of living environments as well as the specific educational technologies which can be applied within these environments.

DEVELOPMENTAL ASPECTS OF LIVING ENVIRONMENTS (SETTING CONDITIONS)

There are a number of features of living environments which influence the development of people with severe learning disabilities. Many of these features are exactly those which influence the development of people without such disabilities. However, it is worth reiterating these as society has tended to provide specialized and/or abnormal environments for people with disabilities and careful judgement is always required when trying to meet both normal and special needs. It is well recognized that socio-economic standing of the family and parental level of education are strongly related to verbal intelligence and general attainment of children in Western culture. Quite how such variables operate is not clear but they are certainly setting factors for individual development. In a longitudinal study with children who have Down's syndrome, Cunningham has found that parent education indices do predict developmental level of these children with the children from parents with higher educational levels scoring better on normative tests of development (Cunningham, 1984). Conversely, various types of environments appear to retard the development of those with learning disabilities. In early studies it was shown that removal of adults with mild learning disabilities from adverse family backgrounds to hospital settings was followed by marked gains in measured intelligence, with a greater gain shown for those with more adverse backgrounds (Clarke and Clarke, 1954, 1959; Clarke, Clarke and Reiman, 1958). More commonly it is large institutional environments which have themselves been implicated as adversely affecting development. People with Down's syndrome have been shown to achieve higher developmental levels when they are brought up at home, compared to when they are brought up in institutions (Centerwall and Centerwall, 1960; Ludlow and Allen, 1979). A number of studies have shown how removal from institutional care can be followed by marked gains in development, gains which exceed those made by similar people who remain institutionalized. Skeels and Dye (1939) took children with learning disabilities from a barren orphanage environment and placed them in a school for those with learning disabilities but with a high degree of personal care from staff and older residents of the school. This group showed marked gains in skills compared to others who remained in the original orphanage. Children with severe learning disabilities taken from a hospital ward and put in a house providing nursery level stimulation with a house mother care system, showed a marked improvement in verbal skills and behavioural adjustment, compared to those who remained in hospital (The Brooklands experiment, e.g. Lyle, 1960; Tizard, 1964). In the Wessex experiment children with very severe degrees of disability brought up in small local residential units were more likely to gain skills and less likely to lose skills compared to similar children brought up in large remote hospital settings (Smith, Glossop and Kushlick, 1980).

Thus the sorts of environments that advantage or disadvantage normal children do likewise for those with learning disaiblities. Concepts such as class, institutional care, socio-economic deprivation are at best crude quantitative indices of unknown factors which are influencing development. A number of studies have sought to define in more detail the exact nature of the setting conditions encompassed in such notions. King, Raynes and Tizard (1971) developed schedules for measuring child-oriented as opposed to institution-oriented residential environments. Child-oriented environments were marked by generally higher levels of social interaction, more varied types of verbal interaction, less role differentiation among staff with senior staff engaging more in direct child care tasks, and less regimentation and block treatment of children. Such qualitative aspects of the environment bore no relation to unit size but were related to the background training of staff (child care as opposed to nursing) and the degree of autonomy staff had in decision making (Raynes, Pratt and Roses, 1979). King, Raynes and Tizard (1971) were able to produce some evidence that children with severe learning disabilities brought up in more child-oriented environments were able to do more for themselves than similarly disabled children in institution-oriented settings.

In cross-sectional and longitudinal studies of families with children who had moderate degrees of learning disabilities, Nihira and colleagues were able to find a number of variables that predicted attainment and adjustment in the children (Nihira, Meyers and Mink, 1983; Nihira, Mink and Meyers, 1984). These included positive parental attitudes and expectations about attainment in the children, warmth and harmony in the home, and level of educational and cognitive stimulation provided. Studies reviewed in Nihira *et al.* (1984) suggest that a degree of structure in family settings acts to the developmental advantage of children with learning disabilities. Such findings are echoed for educational settings in the studies of Rutter and Bartak (1973) who compared a variety of facilities for autistic children. They found that autistic children exposed to structured settings which emphasized more direct attempts at education and intrusion into the self-stimulatory activities of the children, showed higher attainment, better task orientation and better behavioural adjustment.

All this body of literature suggests that setting conditions for personal development in people with severe learning disabilities are very similar to those for ordinary people. Stimulation, personal care and attention, warmth, interest, positive expectations — environments which incorporate these features facilitate development. Clarity, cohesion and structure also seem important. While these factors provide the broad framework within which development proceeds, specific educational technologies will also have a role to play in determining whether or not particular skills are acquired.

BEHAVIOURAL TEACHING TECHNIQUES (STIMULUS CONTROL AND CONTINGENCY MANAGEMENT)

The behavioural procedures of stimulus control and contingency management have shaped an approach to skill development known as precision teaching. Such an approach incorporates a number of elements:

1. Any teaching programme must have a clear objective specified in terms of observable student behaviour.
2. Skills must be broken down into small steps. The size of step will be determined by the learner and the rate of progress. Steps should be mastered one at a time in sequence, and it may be advantageous to begin by working on the last step in the sequence and moving backwards through the task. As well as breaking individual skills into small steps, all complex behaviours can be broken down into individual component skills, each of which can be taught separately. The components are then chained together to make up the complex sequence. Table 1 gives an example of a task analysis.
3. Learning can and should proceed with the minimum of errors. Such 'errorless' learning can be effected in a number of ways. It is assisted by careful task analysis and can also be ensured by providing extra help (prompts) to aid correct performance. Common forms of prompt are instructions, modelling and physical guidance. Such extra help is gradually reduced while performance is maintained. There are also a number of other techniques of graded environmental change which help learning to proceed without error — for example, reinforcing the student at first for very crude approximations to the desired behaviour

TABLE 1   ILLUSTRATIVE TASK ANALYSIS

Long-term goal:	Know the difference between big and little.
Component skills:	Match big and little objects. Select big and little objects when asked. Name big and little objects.
Short-term goal:	Match big and little objects.

Task analysis
1. Student hands object on table when teacher holds up a matching object.
2. Student hands large object from choice of two when teacher holds up large object (same objects).
3. Student hands small object from choice of two when teacher holds up small object (same objects).
4. Student hands large or small object from choice of two to match sample (same object) held up by teacher.
5. Student hands large or small object from choice of two to match sample held up when objects are different, i.e. matches only by size.

Note   There could be many more steps and there are many other ways in which the task could be analysed and taught — there is no 'right' task analysis.

and then gradually raising standards so that the behaviour becomes more and more like the desired end performance. Thus a student might be reinforced at first for making any sound to indicate that someting is wanted. As the general frequency of sound making is increased, only sounds which are more like the correct word are reinforced with other sounds not followed by any meaningful consequence.

4. The procedure of reinforcement is essential to skilled performance. Behaviours should be immediately followed by a consequence which will increase the likelihood of these behaviours being emitted again in the future. Thus an important part of the teaching process is to select a reinforcement procedure — to find a consequence that works for the learner and schedule it to maximize performance. Early in learning it is best achieved by reinforcing behaviour at a high frequency which is then steadily reduced as mastery of the behaviour is attained.

5. Learning is likely to be specific to the situation in which teaching takes place. If it is necessary for a skill to be used in situations other than those in which it is taught, then such generalization needs to be planned and not left to chance (see Stokes and Baer, 1977).

6. Generalization problems are less likely to occur if teaching takes place in the natural situation where the behaviour is actually used. Doing up buttons may most relevantly be taught when a shirt or coat is being put on before breakfast or going out. However, such natural teaching may prove difficult to implement (for example not enough time in the morning); or the natural opportunities may occur too infrequently for effective learning. Thus many examples of behavioural teaching follow a discrete trials format where a student is taught on a sessional basis with repeated trials of the required behaviour within a session. This may speed up the initial acquisition of the skill but inevitably requires careful planning to generalize the behaviour from the teaching sessions to the real-world situation where the behaviour must be used.

This describes the general approach labelled *precision teaching*. Not all behavioural teaching programmes reported in the literature incorporate all these elements. In particular, programmes have varied in the level of errors permitted, in whether punishment is used for any errors in training, and in the type and schedule of reinforcement used. Many published studies use the discrete trials training format without any indication as to whether and how generalization outside the specific teaching sessions was effected. Nevertheless, most studies incorporate many of the precision teaching elements described above.

In reviewing the literature a number of general methodological shortcomings become apparent. These include a lack of detailed information about the students involved, their level and pattern of functioning and the skills already in their repertoire. There is extensive reliance upon students who are resident in large, long-stay institutions so that it is unclear how generalizable results might be to other populations. Authors often give insufficient detail of the teaching techniques used so that replication becomes difficult; and few studies actually check on whether the stated techniques were implemented accurately by those carrying out the teaching. There is a lack of controlled research comparing precision teaching approaches with a rational alternative; and a lack of longitudinal research to see whether gains effected through teaching last over time. In published studies there is a high reliance upon special research staff and equipment so that it remains uncertain as to whether the same results might be achievable by people operating in more ordinary settings.

Allowing for these limitations, however, some conclusions can be drawn (see Yule and Carr, 1980; Matson and McCartney, 1981, for more detailed reviews of precision teaching applied to specific skill areas). A very wide range of skills have been reported as successfully taught using precision teaching approaches. These include basic motor and self-help skills, social relationship and communication skills, play and leisure skills and vocational skills. As well as evaluative research there are many publications describing in-depth specific teaching programmes for single content areas such as language (for example, Kent, 1974) or even for a wide-ranging curriculum covering disparate content areas (e.g. Baker et al., 1976, 1977). Such 'cookbooks' provide extensive 'recipes' on what to teach and how to teach it, although there is usually little well-controlled research underpinning the recommendations.

There is some evidence from early intervention programmes that those with less severe degrees of intellectual impairment, who are exposed to behaviourally oriented programmes, may not only gain specific skills but also show, at least in the short-term, some acceleration in overall rate of development (see, for example, studies reported in Begab, Haywood, and Garber, 1981; Revill and Blunden, 1979; Sandow et al., 1981). It is not clear that such accelerated rates (equivalent to a decrease in level of learning disability) are maintained in the longer term or can be demonstrated with older people (see Cunningham, 1985).

The literature, therefore, demonstrates the wide-ranging applicability of precision teaching. Not only has it been shown that such skills can be taught to people with severe learning disabilities; but there is some evidence that the rate at which skills are acquired is to some extent dependent upon how teaching is carried out (rather than upon the inbuilt capacities of the learner). Thus Azrin and his colleagues have developed a number of 'intensive' programmes for teaching toileting, self-feeding and dressing which condense teaching time from months and years into days and weeks (Azrin and Foxx, 1971; Azrin and Armstrong, 1973; Azrin, Schaeffer and

Wesolowski, 1976). These programmes rely mainly upon increasing the number of opportunities and trials for learning over and above those which might be available naturally (for example, by increasing fluid intake to encourage extra toileting).

Precision teaching has been successfully applied at all levels of ability, even with learners who have multiple disabilities and a profound degree of intellectual impairment. However, it is equally clear that rate of progress is to some extent dependent upon level of disability and some people make slow and variable progress even when exposed to precision teaching approaches (see, for example, Callias and Carr, 1975; Whiteley and Krenn, 1986).

Most studies on precision teaching use experimental designs of the time series type with subjects acting as their own controls. These demonstrate that precision teaching may lead to greater progress than might be expected from the simple passage of time. However, some studies have attempted to use control group designs, which compare a precision teaching approach with some alternative form of intervention. Azrin and Armstrong (1973) found that their mini-meals system was more effective when teaching a wide range of self-feeding skills than simply encouraging staff to use their own best efforts, although it should be noted that both interventions achieved significant results. Ney, Palvesky and Markely (1971) found that behavioural techniques were more effective at teaching expressive language to autistic children than play therapy. The home-based study with autistic children (Hemsley et al., 1978) showed that children exposed to systematic behavioural techniques progressed better in a number of areas such as use of language and behavioural adjustment, compared to those exposed to the more usual techniques available in services for autistic children. In social skills training with adults a behavioural approach proved superior to psychotherapy in effecting change in social skills in a study by Matson and Senatore (1981).

Reaching a balanced view about the value of precision teaching becomes difficult given the reluctance of authors and journals to publish failures and the generally greater interest in new studies rather than attempts to replicate earlier findings. Nevertheless, enough information exists to sound a cautionary note. It has already been mentioned that there have been difficulties in effecting socially significant progress with some people. For example, Smith et al. (1975) reported an attempt to replicate Azrin's work on rapid toilet training with adults whose level of disability was profound. While progress was made it was not as rapid, reliable or extensive as that reported in the original studies. While the Hemsley et al. (1978) study showed some significant gains for autistic children exposed to precision teaching approaches, this was not reflected in any long-term superiority in scores on norm-referenced tests of language structure. Indeed, the whole area of language training is controversial and is more fully reviewed in Chapter 9.

The controlled study by Matson, Marchetti and Adkins (1980) on training adults in self-care skills is notable for two reasons. It shows the superiority of a training package involving self-monitoring and evaluation combined with direct behavioural training when compared to direct behavioural training alone. It also shows that direct behavioural training was *ineffective* in changing skill levels compared to no intervention at all. The early intervention programme described by Revill and Blunden (1979) shows that a home-based precision training programme led to greater gains in skills acquired than no programme at all. It shows that skills targeted for training were more likely to be acquired than those not subject to specific programmes. It also shows that many skills were acquired for which **no** programming occurred. The exact value of precision teaching has, therefore, yet to be established.

The whole behavioural approach has undoubtedly been of immense significance in shifting expectations about what can be achieved for people with severe learning disabilities. It has clearly established that change can be effected with people at all ages and all levels of ability. It has shown that behavioural approaches can be used to teach a very wide range of skills and an extensive research literature has been established to support practitioners. Concern has been expressed about the difficulties in generalizing gains made (see Stokes and Baer, 1977, for a review of these issues). Related to this are the difficulties in sustaining programming — that is, in getting those who carry out teaching to maintain precision approaches over time (see Chapter 8). There are also few comparative studies to establish the relative efficacy of precision teaching and alternative approaches. As many of the people involved in precision teaching research have previously been regarded as 'ineducable', there have been few rational alternatives from which to choose. However, people with learning disabilities do learn by a variety of means, both formal and informal. It will be an important task for the future to establish more precisely the interactions between teaching techniques, skills to be taught, the stage of development of the learner and the precise nature of the learning disability.

CONCLUSIONS

There are an increasing number of demonstrable relationships between environmental factors and the functioning of people with severe learning disabilities. Not surprisingly, most of the factors so far identified are very much the same as those which influence the functioning of people without such disabilities. The general settings which favour development are those which provide adequate levels of stimulation, good quality personal relationships with clear positive expectations of progress. It stands as a serious indictment that so many of the services that society has provided for people with learning disabilities have failed to provide these very ordinary setting conditions, and have further handicapped those already disadvantaged by their learning difficulties.

The role of specific teaching techniques has also been established as contributing to the personal development of those with learning disabilities. The principles of learning so far validated are very much those which are relevant to normal education. Precision teaching is the application of programmed learning to early developmental and social independence skills. It has helped to radicalize expectations for people with severe learning disabilities and has indicated that if progress fails to occur then the teaching method should be examined rather than some inherent limitation in the learner. In that sense a failure to learn becomes a failure to teach.

Although the environment exerts a powerful influence upon personal development, none of the factors so far identified constitutes a 'cure' for learning disabilities. Rather, by optimizing environmental influence the degree of handicap accruing from the learning disability will be limited. The disability itself will not be removed. The next important stage is to understand more of the complex interactions between type of disability, level of development and environmental factors. Given the large individual differences between people with severe learning disabilities, it is likely that to maximize personal functioning a more individual approach will be required. The environmental influences so far established perhaps represent the common ground — the factors that are relevant to all human development. Yet to be established is a grasp of the differences and how to respond sensitively to those. There is considerable folklore and some research findings to give direction to this area of study. Some workers feel that people who have autistic features function better in environments which have a lot of outdoor space. Uncertainty exists about the degree of intrusion which should take place into the repetitive, stereotyped behaviours of people with these difficulties; and how to blend respect for privacy with promotion and development. The work of Romer and Berkson has helped to highlight the setting factors which contribute to social inter-action, factors which need to be recognized in any attempt to improve 'social skills' (e.g. Romer and Berkson, 1980a, b, 1981). There is some evidence from research upon language training (see Chapter 10) that behavioural speech programmes are only likely to be effective if the individual already has a considerable vocal repertoire. Cunningham's (1982) work with Down's syndrome infants also illustrates interaction between type of disability and type of programme. Having established that Down's syndrome infants have a specific difficulty in coordinating visual attention and motor movements (see also Chapter 5) he was able to show that a group given a more routine early intervention programme. These are just illustrative of the sorts of issues that can be tackled now that it is clearly established that the environment has a key role in determining the functioning of people with severe learning disabilities. The next chapter will go on to illustrate that similar conclusions emerge from the growing understanding of the factors that influence behavioural adjustment.

REFERENCES

Azrin, N.H., and Armstrong, P.M. (1973) The 'Mini-Meal': a method for teaching skills to the profoundly retarded. *Mental Retardation*, **11**, 9–11.

Azrin, N.H., and Foxx, R.M. (1971) A rapid method of toilet training the institutionalized retarded. *Journal of Applied Behaviour Analysis*, **4**, 89–99.

Azrin, N.H., Schaeffer, R.M., and Wesolowski, M.D. (1976) A rapid method of teaching profoundly retarded persons to dress. *Mental Retardation*, **14**, 29–33.

Baker, B.L., Brightman, A.J., Heifetz, L.J.D., and Murphy, T. (1976, 1977) *Steps to Independence: Behaviour Problems, Early self help skills, Intermediate self help skills, Advanced self help skills*. Series published at Champaign, Ill.: Research Press.

Begab, J., Haywood, H.C., and Garber, H.L. (eds) (1981) *Psychosocial Influences in Retarded Performance*. Vol. I: *Issues and Theories in Development*. Vol. II: *Strategies for Improving Competence*. Baltimore: University Park Press.

Callias, M., and Carr, J. (1975) Behaviour modification programmes in a community setting. In C.C. Kiernan and F.P. Woodford (eds) *Behaviour Modification with the Severely Retarded*. Amsterdam: Associated Scientific Publishers.

Centerwall, S.A., and Centerwall, W.R. (1960) A study of children with mongolism reared at home compared to those reared away from home. *Paediatrics*, **47**, 678–686.

Clarke, A.D.B., and Clarke, A.M. (1954) Cognitive changes in the feeble-minded. *British Journal of Psychology*, **45**, 173–179.

Clarke, A.D.B., and Clarke, A.M. (1959) Recovery from the effects of deprivation. *Acta Psychologica*, **16**, 137–144.

Clarke, A.D.B., Clarke, A.M., and Reiman, S. (1958) Cognitive and social changes in the feeble-minded — three further studies. *British Journal of Psychology*, **49**, 144–157.

Cunningham, C. (1982) Psychological and educational aspects of handicap. In F. Cockburn and R. Gitzelman (eds) *Inborn Errors of Metabolism in Humans*. Lancaster: MTP Press.

Cunningham, C. (1984) Early intervention: Some findings from the Manchester cohort of children with Down's Syndrome. Paper presented at the National Portage Conference, England.

Cunningham, C. (1985) Training and education approaches for parents of children with special needs. *British Journal of Medical Psychology*, **58**, 285–305.

Hemsley, R., Howlin, P., Berger, M., Hersov, L., Holbrook, D., Rutter M. and Yule,

W. (1978) Treating autistic children in a family context. In M. Rutter and E. Schopler (eds) *Autism: A Reappraisal of Concepts of Treatment*. New York: Plenum Press.

Kent, L.R. (1974) *Language Acquisition Program for the Retarded or Multiply Handicapped*. Champaign, Ill.: Research Press.

King, R.D., Raynes, N.V., and Tizard, J. (1971) *Patterns of Residential Care: Sociological Studies in Institutions for Handicapped Children*. London: Routledge and Kegan Paul.

Ludlow, J.R., and Allen, L.M. (1979) The effects of early intervention and pre-school stimulus on the development of the Down's Syndrome child. *Journal of Mental Deficiency Research*, **23**, 29–44.

Lyle, J.G. (1960) The effect of an institution environment upon the verbal development of imbecile children: III. The Brooklands residential unit. *Journal of Mental Deficiency*, **4**, 14–22.

Matson, J.L., Marchetti, A., and Adkins, J.W. (1980) Comparison of operant and independence-training procedures for mentally retarded adults. *American Journal of Mental Deficiency*, **84**, 487–494.

Matson, J.L., and McCartney, J.R. (eds) (1981) *Handbook of Behaviour Modification with the Mentally Retarded*. New York: Plenum.

Matson, J.L., and Senatore, V. (1981) Comparison of traditional psychotherapy and social skills training for improving interpersonal functioning of mentally retarded adults. *Behaviour Therapy*, **12**, 369–382.

Ney, P.G., Palvesky, A.E., and Markely, J. (1971) Relative effectiveness of operant conditioning and play therapy in childhood schizophrenia. *Journal of Autism and Childhood Schizophrenia*, **1**, 337–349.

Nihira, K., Meyers, E.C., and Mink, I.T. (1983) Reciprocal relationships between home environment and development of TMR adolescents. *American Journal of Mental Deficiency*, **88**, 139–149.

Nihira, K., Mink, I.T., and Meyers, C.E. (1984) Salient dimensions of home environment relevant to child development. In N.R. Ellis and N.W. Bray (eds) *International Review of Research in Mental Retardation*, Vol. 12. Orlando: Academic Press.

Raynes, N.V., Pratt, M.W., and Roses, S.S. (1979) *Organizational Structure and the Care of the Mentally Retarded*. London: Croom Helm.

Revill, S., and Blunden, R.B. (1979) A home training service for pre-school developmentally handicapped children. *Behaviour: Research and Therapy*, **17**, 207–214.

Romer, D., and Berkson, G. (1980a) Social ecology of supervised community facilities for mentally disabled adults: II. Predictors of affiliation. *American Journal of Mental Deficiency*, **85**(3), 229–242.

Romer, D., and Berkson, G. (1980b) Social ecology of supervised communal facilities for mentally disabled adults: III. Predictors of social choice. *American Journal of Mental Deficiency*, **85**(3), 243–252.

Romer, D., and Berkson, G. (1981) Social ecology of supervised communal facilities for mentally disabled adults: IV. Characteristics of social behaviour. *American Journal of Mental Deficiency*, **86**(1), 28–38.

Rutter, M., and Bartak, L. (1973) Special educational treatment of autistic children: a comparative study. II. Follow-up findings and implications for services. *Journal of Child Psychology and Psychiatry*, **14**, 241–270.

Sandow, S.A., Clarke, A.D.B., Cox, M.V., and Stewart, F.L. (1981) Home intervention with parents of severely subnormal pre-school children: a final report. *Child: Care, Health and Development*, **7**, 135–144.

Skeels, H.M., and Dye, H.B. (1939) A study of the effects of differential stimulation on mentally retarded children. *Proceedings of the American Association on Mental Deficiency*, **44**, 114–136.

Smith, J., Glossop, C., and Kushlick, A. (1980) Evaluation of alternative residential facilities for the severely mentally handicapped in Wessex: client progress. *Advances in Behaviour Research and Therapy*, **3**, 5–11.

Smith, R.S., Britton, P.G., Johnson, M., and Thomas, D. (1975) Problems involved in toilet-training of institutionalized mentally retarded individuals. *Behaviour Research and Therapy*, **13**, 301–307.

Stokes, T.F., and Baer, D.M. (1977) An implicit technology of generalization. *Journal of Applied Behaviour Analysis*, **10**, 349–367.

Tizard, J. (1964) *Community Services for the Mentally Handicapped*. See particularly Part IV, The Brooklands Residential Unit. London: Oxford University Press.

Whiteley, H.H., and Krenn, M.J. (1986) Use of the Bayley Mental Scale with non-ambulatory profoundly mentally retarded children. *American Journal of Mental Deficiency*, **90**(4), 425–431.

Yule, W., Carr, J. (eds) (1980) *Behaviour Modification with the Mentally Handicapped*. London: Croom Helm.

Chapter 7

Managing Problem Behaviours

The last chapter illustrated how the environment can influence the degree of handicap that follows from an initial intellectual impairment. Handicaps, however, do not arise only through lack of skill. A person who exhibits socially unacceptable behaviour is also likely to be additionally handicapped over and above any difficulties that there might be with skill development. People with behavioural difficulties may be disliked and rejected by those around them, they are likely to be excluded from many learning opportunities, and are much more likely to be segregated from the mainstream of society, often into the most deprived of institutional settings (Raynes, Pratt and Roses, 1979; Schalock, Harper and Genung, 1981; Favell, 1983). To suffer from a severe learning disability and to exhibit socially unacceptable behaviour is, therefore, to be doubly exposed to handicap.

There are many kinds of difficulties which may be shown by people with learning disabilities, none of them unique to this population. Some people may show the tantrums, destructiveness and non-compliance which occur with considerable frequency in the normal pre-school population. There may be those who exhibit the sort of conduct problems which affect the non-handicapped child, adolescent and young adult population (problems such as aggression, impulsiveness, poor frustration tolerance). The high activity levels and poor concentration span characteristic of hyperactive children whose intelligence is within the normal range may be found among those with serious learning difficulties. Impaired social relationships and ritualistic, stereotyped behaviours are characteristic of autistic children at all levels of ability. Even problems such as self-induced vomiting, eating inedible substances and self-injurious behaviour may be found at some point in development at all levels of intellectual ability. In addition to these behavioural difficulties there are psychiatric syndromes such as schizophrenia, depression and manic depression which can be identified across a wide ability range.

It is not that people with severe learning disabilities have unique behavioural difficulties. There are, however, both qualitative and quantitative differences which do have to be considered. The problems which are characteristic of younger normal children may appear at older ages, last for much longer and exhibit a greater degree of intensity in a severely disabled population. Above all, behavioural difficulties occur much more frequently among people with a severe degree of intellectual impairment. Epidemiological surveys have suggested that 20 per cent or more of the child and adolescent population may exhibit some form of severe behaviour disorder (Wing, 1971; Kushlick and Cox, 1973; Cunningham, 1986). Corbett (1977) applied psychiatric classifications to the severely disabled child population in Camberwell and found that 47 per cent could be ascribed a psychiatric diagnosis. The rate of behavioural difficulties in an adult population may be a little lower but would still appear to be around the 15 per cent level (Kushlick and Cox, 1973). Surveys of psychiatric problems in hospital populations have suggested that up to 10 per cent of adults in such populations may be suffering from a definable psychiatric disorder (Heaton-Ward, 1977). Care must be taken in interpreting these figures. Studies vary in their definitions of behaviour disorder, in the populations that they survey and in case-finding techniques. It makes no sense to ascribe any exact figure to the level of difficulties in a severely impaired population. What is abundantly clear, however, is that these problems occur at a far higher frequency at all ages compared to the people whose intelligence falls within the normal range. At any point in time, therefore, a considerable proportion of people with learning disabilities are suffering from an additional disorder in behaviour. Some problems may improve just with age but there are new problems arising at any age, and there are some people who suffer chronic and recurring behavioural difficulties which may last for many years (Koller, Richardson and Katz, 1983; Foxx and Livesay, 1984). In seeking to understand intellectual impairment and its ramifications, it is important to consider the factors that might be involved in the genesis and maintenance of the behavioural difficulties to which this population seems so vulnerable.

As outlined in the Introduction to Part 2, this chapter will examine environmental influences upon behaviour difficulties from an operant-behavioural perspective. This perspective sees problem behaviours as lawfully related to the environment and thus modifiable by changes within that environment. Problem behaviours are equivalent to skills, learned and shaped in the same ways as other behaviours — they are built up by reinforcement and will become discriminated to stimuli which are reliably associated with such reinforcement. This approach sees problem behaviours as meaningful and as achieving significant goals for the individual. From a broad perspective these behaviours may well be maladaptive, but they can be recognized as successful at some level for the individual. A number of writers have stressed this point and emphasized that many of the goals attained by problem behaviours may well be 'legitimate' goals, but achieved by what are in the long run unsatisfactory means (see Goldiamond, 1974; Carr and Durand, 1984). In particular, Carr and Durand (1984) have stressed the communicative nature of problem behaviours, drawing attention to the similarities of many of the goals attained by such behaviours to those attained by other forms of communication. The authors have drawn attention to goals such as attention, assistance and choice. Viewed in this way the aim of intervention is to provide the individual with alternative means of attaining desired goals.

However, problem behaviours have also been viewed as 'surplus' behaviours, built up accidentally by reinforcement processes. Such a view de-emphasizes the significance of the reinforcement attained by the problem behaviours and emphasizes suppression as the main aim of intervention. This is to be achieved particularly through the application of punishment procedures, which have been extensively documented in the experimental behavioural research literature (e.g. Azrin and Holz, 1966).

The applied research literature varies in the emphasis placed upon understanding the significance of the problem behaviour as opposed to finding a means of suppressing it. This is particularly true of the literature dealing with stimulus control and contingency management aspects of environment-behaviour relationships. However, the occurrence of problem behaviour is also influenced by broader aspects of the environment, encompassed within the term *setting conditions*; and these are considered in the next section.

THE LIVING ENVIRONMENT AND BEHAVIOUR ADJUSTMENT (SETTING CONDITIONS)

The literature on normal child development and child psychiatry offers insights into the sorts of environmental factors which might be relevant to behavioural adjustment. Thus, Baumrind (1973) proposed that firm control by parents was an important factor in the socialization process, enhancing responsibility and self-control. The concept of firm control encompasses clear limit setting and consistent discipline by the parents but also involves granting the child a role in the decision-making process. Lewis (1981) examined further the concept of firm control and emphasized the importance of harmony as opposed to powerful external controls. Harmony in this sense refers to high levels of acceptance of the child, encouragement of individuality and participation by the child in formulating disciplinary rules. Such a concept is echoed by the work of Rutter (e.g. 1978) illustrating powerful relationships between parental conflict and disharmony in the home and problem behaviours in the child (particularly aggressive, non-compliant behaviour).

The studies by Nihira's group suggest that such qualitative aspects of the environment are equally significant for the adjustment of children with learning disabilities (Nihira, Meyers and Mink, 1983; Nihira, Mink and Meyers, 1984). They were able to show that level of stimulation, pride in the child, affection, cohesion and warmth in the home related positively to adjustment while a control-oriented atmosphere and conflict were associated with more negative outcomes. The Brooklands experiment, referred to in Chapter 6, illustrated how removal from a deprived hospital setting to a more stimulating and personalized environment, not only improved level of functioning, but also the degree of behavioural disturbance (Tizard, 1964).

Consistent associations between levels of stimulation available and problem behaviours have been demonstrated in a number of studies. Berkson and Mason (1963, 1964) showed how stereotyped rocking behaviours in people with severe learning disabilities, living in an institution, were far less likely when occupational materials were available. This effect of external stimulation was less noticeable upon stereotyped behaviours which involved complex movements of the hands. A number of studies have replicated these findings and shown how behavioural difficulties are far less likely when adequate occupational or leisure materials are available, particularly if social encouragement is offered for the use of these materials (Porterfield, Blunden and Blewitt, 1980; Horner, 1980; Favell, McGimsey and Schell, 1982). Level of stimulation may affect not only the likelihood of problem behaviours occurring but also determine how easy it is to manage these behaviours when they do occur. Thus time-out (see later) may prove to be an effective method of management only in environments which offer adequate levels of stimulation and social interaction (Solnick, Rincover and Peterson, 1977; Williams et al., 1983).

The effect of environmental space has also received some attention and Paluck and Esser (1971a, b) suggested that aggression can be related to territoriality, with individuals defining and defending a 'personal' space. Hereford, Cleland and Fellner (1973) applied the same sort of analysis to the occurrence of bedwetting, but were unable to demonstrate conclusively this relationship. Nevertheless, as a setting condition for problem behaviours, overcrowding and lack of personal space remain plausible.

Although not a part of the living environment, level and type of disability may be regarded as setting conditions for behaviour problems. It is known that brain damage, irrespective of level of intellectual functioning, makes the affected individual more likely to develop problem behaviours (e.g. Chadwick, 1985). Level of disability is also significant, with behaviour problems more prevalent among those with a greater degree of intellectual impairment. Independent of overall level of disability, specific difficulties with communication skills and social relationships are very strongly associated with behavioural difficulties (Wing and Gould, 1979; Wing, 1981). This is particularly interesting in view of Carr and Durand's (1984) formulation of problem behaviour as primarily communicative.

Thus broad features of the external and internal environment can be clearly related to the occurrence of a wide range of problem behaviours. In addition to these setting conditions, more specific and immediate transactions between the environment and behaviour can be shown to be of critical significance.

BEHAVIOURAL TREATMENT TECHNIQUES (STIMULUS CONTROL AND CONTINGENCY MANAGEMENT)

The behavioural treatment literature contains two major types of study. The first type includes studies which demonstrate functional relationships between events which take place in the natural environment (the antecedents and consequences of behaviour) and the probability of occurrence of the particular behaviour problem. The probability of the behaviour can be increased or decreased by manipulating these antecedents and consequences. Such studies often, but not always, include a treatment phase where the demonstrated relationship is systematically exploited to produce a socially significant decrease in the problem behaviour.

Other types of study are less analytic and more directly targeted upon socially significant change. These studies tend to monitor the occurrence of the behaviour problem, introduce an intervention, altering the antecedents or consequences of the behaviour, and demonstrate a decrease in the problem following intervention. Such studies use interventions which are conventionally accepted as reinforcers or punishers (for example, attention or time-out) and selection of these interventions is based upon previous usage in the management of problem behaviours. That is, the selection of intervention tactics is not based upon a functional analysis of the individual's own problem behaviour. It is based upon some judgement of the value of the technique itself and an empirical 'try it and see' attitude.

The more analytic studies have been important in establishing the meaningful nature of problem behaviours and the general value of viewing these from an operant behavioural perspective. Lovaas and his colleagues were pioneers in this field and were able to demonstrate the relationship of self-injurious behaviour to social attention with increases or decreases in the behaviour being controlled by whether social attention was provided or withheld, contingent upon the occurrence of self-injury (Lovaas et al., 1965; Lovaas and Simmons, 1969). Martin and Foxx (1973) likewise showed that aggressive responses could be increased or decreased according to whether they were followed by warning and comment from the victim or whether the victim completely ignored the assaults. A very exact relationship between number of comments and number of self-injurious responses was demonstrated in the study by Carr and McDowell (1980), who were also able to demonstrate a dramatic decrease in responses when the self-injury was completely ignored. A relationship of demand characteristics to behavioural difficulties was shown in a study by Carr, Newsom and Binkoff (1980). When the child was allowed to leave the demand situation following an aggressive response this led to a high rate of aggression, which dropped dramatically if the child was not permitted to leave the situation following an outburst.

In a slightly different type of study, Edelson, Taubman and Lovaas (1983) examined the relationship between self-injurious behaviour and social interaction in a hospital setting. They found that for 19 out of the 20 people observed that there was an increase in self-injurious behaviour if staff made a demand upon the client, refused to let the client have something that was wanted or reprimanded the client in some way. Such a range of functional relationships was confirmed by Iwata *et al.* (1982) who looked at the effects of different kinds of standardized environmental situations upon the frequency of self-injury. They were able to highlight individual differences by this means and showed that for some people there were clear differences between the conditions. Some showed raised frequencies when left on their own, others when demands were made directly upon them, others still when they were given attention following an occurrence of self-injury. It should also be noted that there were a group whose behaviour appeared uninfluenced by the particular kinds of environmental conditions manipulated in this study.

Such studies demonstrate with considerable elegance very close relationships between naturally occurring environmental events and severe behaviour problems (see Carr and Durand, 1984, for a more comprehensive overview). They indicate functional significance for even the most bizarre and serious behaviour difficulties. They illustrate some common functions expressed through behaviour and the sort of environmental conditions likely to trigger these behaviours. Such functions include seeking for attention, seeking to be left alone, seeking not to have demands made upon one and seeking sensory stimulation. As Carr and Durand (1984) point out, many other forms of communication achieve just such functions.

However, the applied research literature has also demonstrated that, irrespective of the reinforcement which has built and maintained the behaviour (its functional significance), suppression can be achieved by the application of punishing stimuli following a behaviour. Given that a major aim in settings where problem behaviour occurs is to decrease this behaviour, it is not surprising that a considerable amount of research has gone into detailing suppressive techniques. There were early and spectacular demonstrations of the suppression of self-injuriuous behaviour using contingent electric shock to various parts of the body, usually the upper arm or leg (e.g. Bucher and Lovaas, 1968; Lovaas and Simmons, 1969; Romanczyk and Goren, 1975; Richmond and Martin, 1977). Although the early results were impressive there were difficulties both practically and ethically (Corbett, 1975; Harris and Ersner-Hershfield, 1978). Equipment often proved unreliable, and its presence was so discriminable as to make generalization beyond treatment sessions difficult. In the case of self-injurious behaviour, intial suppression often seemed to be followed by relapse which could not always be successfully retreated using the same method (Romanczyk and Goren, 1975; Murphy and Wilson, 1981). Although laboratory studies of punishment relationships indicated the possibility of negative side-effects, such as increases in aggression, there were suprisingly few reports of any such effects in clinical practice.

There were, however, powerful ethical objections as well as practical difficulties. These included the stigmatizing and dehumanizing effect of such treatment on both the client and therapist, the potential for abuse, and the failure of such an approach to encompass the development of alternative skills (see Stolz, 1978). The controversy surrounding the use of these techniques served to stimulate long overdue consideration of how best to protect the human rights of vulnerable people. This, in turn, generated pressure on clinicians to seek more humane and imaginative ways of dealing with such difficulties.

Although this has meant that there are now very few published studies on the use of pain-shock, it is interesting to note that there has been no diminution of interest in the use of the punishment relationship. Indeed, the range of punishers exemplified in the literature has grown astronomically. For example, ammonia inhalation has been successfully used in the control of aggression and self-injury (e.g. Baumeister and Baumeister, 1978), taste aversion in the treatment of regurgitation and vomiting (e.g. Sajwaj, Leibert and Agras, 1974), water spray for self-injury (e.g. Dorsey et al., 1980), physical restraint for self-injurious and other stereotypic behaviours (e.g. Ollendick, Shapiro and Barrett, 1981; Singh, Dawson and Manning, 1981), and brief screening of the face for a range of behaviour difficulties (see Lutzker and Wesch, 1983). Even tickling and running have been used as effective punishers to decrease problem behaviours (e.g. Greene and Hoats, 1971). These techniques may appear rather less dramatic than the use of pain-shock but it is difficult to see how they are any different from a general ethical standpoint. They may also suffer from the very same practical problems as were raised for the use of shock, e.g. their discriminability.

In addition to these very obvious examples of punishment, there are a number of other techniques which involve a punishing element although they probably also incorporate a number of other elements as well. The two best known of these are time-out and over-correction. Time-out procedures make a period of time when reinforcement is not available contingent upon the problem behaviour. This may be effected by withdrawal of materials (for example, a meal), by withdrawal of social attention (for example, looking or moving away from the individual), by removing a stimulus which, when available, signals that the person can be reinforced (for example, removal of a card, badge or ribbon), by exclusion of the person from all ongoing activities (for example, being sat away from the group) or by seclusion of the person in a separate area (for example, special room, bedroom, bathroom). Thus, time-out can be effected in a number of ways and has been used for time periods ranging in duration from a few seconds up to many hours. Time-out does appear to function like a punishing stimulus, i.e. when it is effective it leads to a rapid decrease in the problem behaviour. However, it is a complex procedure and may incorporate a number of elements in any one case (see MacDonough and Forehand, 1973, Hobbs and Forehand, 1977; Williams et al., 1983, for more comprehensive reviews of time-out). As well as loss of reinforcement opportunity it may involve physical restraint, social isolation, extinction and escape learning where termination of the time-out is dependent upon a period of time when no problem behaviour has occurred.

In its many forms time-out has been used successfully at all ages, at all levels of ability and for a very wide range of behaviour difficulties — aggression (Pendergrass, 1971), self-injury (Lucero et al., 1976), destructiveness (Burchard and Barrera, 1972), and inappropriate mealtime behaviours (Barton et al., 1970). It can be effective at short durations (10 minutes or less) providing that the person has not had previous experience of longer durations. It can even be effective when not applied every time the problem behaviour occurs. It has not always been reported as successful (e.g. Doleys et al., 1976) and there are also reports of emotional responding and increases in other disruptive behaviours (e.g. Pendergrass, 1971).

Time-out has its own practical and ethical difficulties. Clients may resist removal or refuse to remain excluded, there may be no satisfactory exclusion area in normal everyday environments; and it can be difficult to ensure consistent application where a large number of people are involved in a programme. Some clients may also find implementation of the procedure, or the social isolation itself, positively reinforcing and this will obviously increase rather than decrease the problem behaviour. Ethical problems mainly arise in connection with the use of seclusion procedures, or lengthy exclusion procedures, as the client may be removed from important learning time and opportunities. Such procedures may also inadvertently encourage self-stimulatory behaviours, and there may be physical risks to both client and staff, or family, if physical manhandling is required, and inadequate observational facilities are available.

An alternative proposal for practicable and acceptable punishment is over-correction. This term refers to a varied and complex set of procedures. The rationale, developed by Foxx and Azrin (1972), is that, following a disruptive behaviour, the client should first restore the environment to the state that it was in prior to the disruption (restitution — for example, pick up thrown furniture). Following restitution, the client should carry out alternative, appropriate behaviours relevant to the disruption caused (positive practice—for example, clean and tidy all the furniture in the living area).

From this rationale specific procedures have been developed for a wide range of behaviour problems — aggression and destructiveness (Foxx and Azrin, 1972), pica (Foxx and Martin, 1975), stripping (Foxx, 1976), self-injury and stereotyped behaviours (Azrin et al., 1975). These procedures appear to act functionally as punishment, i.e. when applied consistently following a behaviour, that behaviour decreases. Reported procedures have varied in duration from 10 seconds up to 102 minutes and in whether one or both of the two elements, restitution and positive practice, are included. The procedures are complex, probably involving elements of extinction, time-out, response interruption, physical restraint and effort requirements. Nothing is known about the necessary or sufficient elements required, although the initial suggestion that the procedure used should closely match the type of problem behaviour has not been supported (see Epstein et al., 1974).

Although of demonstrated value with a wide range of behaviour difficulties, there are again both practical and ethical issues to be considered (see Murphy, 1978; Ollendick and Matson, 1978, for reviews). These procedures require a considerable amount of time and effort to implement, and such resources may not be available in many everyday settings. The degree of attention involved may also prove positively reinforcing for some people. Although the term 'educative punishment' has been used to describe over-correction techniques, there is little evidence of any new skill learning. Indeed, a number of studies report concurrent increases in other problem behaviours as target behaviours are reduced (e.g. Rollings, Baumeister and Baumeister, 1977). As with all other procedures, over-correction is potentially aversive and open to abuse if its implementation is not closely supervised.

The literature on punishment has been important in confirming belief in the controllability of a wide range of behavioural difficulties. The interventions described are often relatively brief and sometimes simple compared to the difficulties that exist in managing some of the problem behaviours themselves if they continue to occur. This literature is a reminder of the lawful nature of even chronic and bizarre behaviours. However, a number of factors suggest that emphasis upon behavioural suppression can be only one element in a comprehensive approach to helping people with serious behaviour problems. As already mentioned, the techniques described have a range of practical and ethical difficulties and these have, in turn, produced pressure for a more positive approach.

The very success of such contingency management techniques has also encouraged a rather lop-sided approach to behaviour problems, de-emphasizing analysis and understanding, and stressing effect on the target behaviour as the only relevant dependent variable. This rather unbalanced conceptual framework was pointed out by Goldiamond (1974). He stressed that behaviour analysis of socially unacceptable behaviours shows often that they are unacceptable means to acceptable ends. To receive attention from another person is perfectly legitimate, although spitting at them to gain it is perhaps unacceptable in many circumstances. Such a basically simple and obvious point as this suggests that an important focus of any intervention should be on building up more acceptable means to the ends desired by the client rather than just on eliminating behaviours. Goldiamond was writing in general about social problem behaviour, but his emphasis seems particularly important for people with severe learning disabilities who, by definition, lack many of the skills needed for satisfactory social adjustment. Thus practical, ethical and intellectual pressures have combined to urge a degree of re-orientation towards problem behaviours. Such re-orientation is expressed in the emphasis on the importance of educational strategies and techniques outlined in the previous chapter, and the increasingly expressed requirement that any attempt to decrease a behaviour must be accompanied by specific programmes to teach relevant, alternative skills. Such pressures have also encouraged the development of alternative contingency management approaches based upon the use of positive reinforcement, and a number of specific techniques are now available.

One such technique is differential reinforcement of other behaviour (DRO). This procedure makes positive reinforcement dependent upon the passing of a specified time period during which the problem behaviour does not occur, i.e. it reinforces any behaviour other than the problem behaviour. It has been used on its own, and in combination with other techniques, for such problems as stereotyped and self-injurious behaviours (e.g. Repp and Deitz, 1974; Foxx and Shapiro, 1978). It has not always proved effective (e.g. Luiselli, 1975; Johnson et al., 1982) and difficulties can arise in finding powerful, easily administered reinforcers. Care must also be taken to ensure that inappropriate behaviours, other than the target behaviour, are not accidentally reinforced. It certainly appears a useful approach but probably needs to be combined with other techniques.

Four other positive reinforcement procedures have been reported in the literature. Raising the density of positive reinforcement by providing it, independent of client responses, has been shown to decrease aggression in a residential setting (Boe, 1972). Johnson and Baumeister (1981) report on a schedule that they call 'differential reinforcement of compatible behaviour'. This refers to positive reinforcement for a specific behaviour, irrespective of the occurrence of the problem behaviour (the reinforced behaviour is, therefore, compatible with the occurrence of the problem behaviour which could, therefore, continue to be reinforced). They report a few case studies, but its main value appears to lie in strengthening the skill repertoires of clients and raising the overall density of positive reinforcement. Differential reinforcement of low rates of behaviour refers to a schedule whereby reinforcement is dependent upon achieving a rate of problem behaviour which is below a pre-set criterion. The criterion is then gradually lowered so that the behaviours become less and less frequent. As yet, there are few reports of its use with clinically significant problem behaviours. Finally, differential reinforcement of incompatible behaviour is a rather more specific and better documented approach. This reinforces behaviour which is incompatible with the problem behaviour. Such incompatability may be physical (reinforcing table-top toy play to prevent self-hitting, as both cannot be carried out together); or the incompatibility may be functional (reinforcing toy play only when it occurs in the absence of regurgitation). Such schedules have been used successfully to decrease a range of problem behaviours, such as self-injury (Tarpley and Schroeder, 1979), hyperactivity (Twardosz and Sajwaj, 1972), echolalia (Carr, Schreibman and Lovaas, 1975), and regurgitation (Mulick, Schroeder and Rojahn, 1980). There are a few reports of ineffectiveness (e.g. Risley, 1968) but it appears a potentially powerful positive-based approach.

The above-mentioned pressures for a more positive approach have also resulted in a return to considering variables other than the consequences of behaviour. There has been a revival of interest in the examination and manipulation of the immediate antecedents of problem behaviours, and the more general environmental characteristics which may raise or lower the probability of occurrence of such behaviours. The analysis and manipulation of antecedents is often referred to as 'stimulus control'. This approach focuses upon finding or creating situations where the problem behaviour does not occur and then extending these situations and/or gradually altering them so that the stimuli which previously 'triggered' the problem behaviour no longer do so. For example, in the study by Carr, Newson and Binkoff (1976) it was shown that instructions elicited self-injurious behaviour. However, if these instructions were embedded into a situation where the child was enjoying himself — in between entertaining stories — then self-injury was no longer elicited. Although not a part of the study, one could envisage how the child's tolerance for instructions could be built up by increasing the number of such 'embedded' instructions and gradually reducing the elaboration of the embedding context. In the management of self-injurious behaviour frequent use is made of physical restraints, such as splints. The presence of restraints is thus sometimes a discriminative stimulus for the non-occurrence of self-injury. This can be exploited therapeutically in a number of ways. One way is to look for a form of restraint which may minimize the interruption of normal functioning and use this continously. Rojahn et al., (1978) showed how adapted clothing (a smock with deep pockets) was helpful in controlling self-injury but permitted the client free use of his hands when necessary. An alternative or supplementary approach is to develop a situation where the problem cannot occur and then gradually alter this situation towards normality while keeping the behaviour at a low level in what is essentially an errorless learning paradigm. Thus, for a client who hits hands to head, rigid arm splints could be provided initially to control the behaviour. These could then be gradually reduced in size, rigidity, tightness and visibility, ensuring at every step in the fading sequence that the behaviour does not re-occur (see Foxx and Dufrense, 1984, for use of this approach among others in the treatment of severe self-injury). Another example might be where a client throws equipment in situations where materials are readily visible and accessible. One could start by removing all materials. As the behaviour is controlled materials could be gradually re-introduced in number, visibility and accessibility. Combining this sort of approach with a skill teaching intervention, targeted upon appropriate alternative skills, would provide a viable alternative strategy to the more traditional punishment contingencies used in the management of these kinds of disruption. There are, as yet, few examples in the published literature of these approaches with clinically significant problems.

Although stimulus control techniques represent a valuable and interesting supplement to contingency management approaches, the underlying analytic framework is still one that focuses upon single behaviours in relation to single stimuli occurring close in time to the target behavioural event. Others have suggested a need to re-examine this underlying analytic framework, to recognize the complexity of interactions between a wide range of behavioural and environmental events. This has often been termed as developing an ecological approach to behaviour analysis (see Rogers-Warren and Warren, 1977; Schroeder et al., 1981). A number of directions for improvement in analysis have been suggested. One such direction is to pay more attention to the organization of behaviour within the individual. It is clear that responses tend to be organized into classes and hierarchies which co-vary in a number of ways. Thus, intervention with one behaviour may have a number of effects upon other behavioural responses; and it has already been demonstrated in the clinical literature that there can be increases in other problem behaviours as a single target behaviour decreases (e.g. Rollings *et al.*, 1977). Studying multiple response systems may aid understanding of the significance of the problem behaviour, redefine the necessary target of any intervention and enable one to predict more satisfactorily the outcome of any particular intervention (see Rojahn and Schroeder, 1983).

A second example of analytic expansion is the recognition that changes in any one contingency will take place against the background of multiply operative contingencies for the individual in question. Gross and Drabman (1981) have discussed the possible significance of the phenomenon of behavioural contrast in clinical contexts. Where an individual is subject to multiple reinforcement and punishment schedules, then a shift in one schedule can have significant effects upon other behaviours controlled by other cues and consequences. Thus, for example, if a person has temper tantrums which are maintained by the social attention that they receive, then a programme to ignore these in one setting (for example, the home) may decrease the problems in this setting but lead to an increase of the behaviour in another setting (for example, the classroom) where the programme is not used. Such complex interrelationships between environment and behaviour are also illustrated in studies which have shown that the effectiveness of time-out procedures varies according to the quality of the environment within which they are applied (Solnick *et al.*, 1977; Williams *et al.*, 1983). These studies have shown that time-out is only effective where there is 'time-in', i.e. in situations which deliver adequate physical stimulation and social interaction. In impoverished custodial situations time-out will not be effective. This in itself is, of course, not surprising but is illustrative of the way in which analysis of behaviour–environment interactions is going to have to increase in complexity if a greater degree of precision in outcome is to be achieved (see Favell, 1983, for a very useful discussion of such broad spectrum behavioural approaches to the management of aggression).

A third direction in which the analysis is going to have to expand is to incorporate the role of temporary or permanent psychological and biological states of the individual. Functional and structural aspects of brain functioning, stable personality traits and transient states, such as anxiety or depression, undoubtedly contribute to the occurrence of problem behaviours.

Such an expansion in the analysis of the relationships between the environment and the individual not only multiplies the number of variables that need to be measured but challenges the whole notion of simple causation which underlies many earlier models, i.e. the notion that a single behaviour has a single cause which can be dealt with by a single intervention. It is clear that the interactions between individuals and the environment are complex and delicate, and the practical and methodological problems in moving towards an ecological perspective are somewhat daunting. It should not be forgotten that the simpler analysis of behaviour as a function of its immediate antecedents and consequences has proved of considerable value for people with severe learning disabilities. It has enabled the development of techniques for treating every kind of behavioural problem at all levels of ability and has, in a relatively short space of time, transformed the perception of these problems from being untreatable to being such as to demand treatment. The fact that the interventions do not always work, that they sometimes have unexpected side-effects or that their implementation cannot be sustained over long periods of time, is in no way an indictment of the approach but a spur to further research.

CONCLUSIONS

An extensive data base now exists to document the meaningful nature of problem behaviours presented by some people with severe learning disabilities. The literature emphasizes the key role of the external environment in determining the occurrence of such behaviours; and a range of intervention tactics have been derived from this understanding of the relationship between environment and behaviour. There are studies demonstrating successful change with virtually any problem which might occur, at all ages and at all levels of ability. As with the skill teaching literature such findings have helped to radicalize expectations for people with severe learning and behavioural disabilities.

However, a number of concerns remain. For some problems (for example, some kinds of self-injurious behaviour) it has proved difficult to effect long-term change. Interventions have sometimes had unexpected negative side-effects. There has been difficulty experienced in generalizing the effects of behaviour change in one environment to other settings. Some of the tactics described in the literature are impractical given the resources available in real-world situations as opposed to laboratory research settings. Others are controversial to the point of being socially unacceptable. There are, therefore, both technical and ethical limitations on our ability to resolve satisfactorily some behavioural difficulties; and a clear need to expand the conceptual framework for analysing these difficulties.

There are other concerns to which reference was made in the previous chapter. There can be difficulties in both implementing and sustaining long term the kinds of interventions described in the behavioural literature. A considerable gap exists between what can be done to help people with behavioural disturbances and what is actually done in everyday practice. Attention should be directed to the factors responsible for this gap. More broadly defined the task becomes not how to change behaviour itself, but how to create environments that will facilitate the delivery of effective help to those in need. The target for change moves from being the behaviour of the person with learning disabilities, to the behaviour of those responsible for helping the person with such difficulties. Some consideration of the tactics available for managing this task is the subject matter for the next chapter.

REFERENCES

Azrin, N.H., Gottlieb, L., Hughart, L., Wesolowski, M.D., and Rahn, T. (1975) Eliminating self-injurious behaviour by educative procedures. *Behaviour Research and Therapy*, **13**, 101–111.

Azrin, N.H., and Holz, W.C. (1966) Punishment. In W.K. Honig (ed.) *Operant Behavior: areas of research and application*. New York: Appleton-Century-Crofts.

Barton, E.S., Guess, D., Garcia, A.E., and Baer, D.M. (1970) Improvement of retardates' meal-time behaviours by time-out procedures using multiple baseline techniques. *Journal of Applied Behaviour Analysis*, **3**, 77–84.

Baumeister, A.A., and Baumeister, A.A. (1978) Suppression of repetitive self-injurious behaviour by contingent inhalation of aromatic ammonia. *Journal of Autism and Childhood Schizophrenia*, **8**, 71–77.

Baumrind, D. (1973) The development of instrumental competence through socialization. In A.D. Pick (ed.) *Minnesota Symposia on Child Psychology*, Vol. 7. Minneapolis: University of Minnesota Press.

Berkson, G., and Mason, W.A. (1963) Stereotyped movements of mental defectives: III. Situation effects. *American Journal of Mental Deficiency*, **68**, 409–412.

Berkson, G., and Mason, W.A. (1964) Stereotyped movements of mental defectives: IV. The effects of toys and the character of the acts. *American Journal of Mental Deficiency*, **68**, 511–524.

Boe, R.B. (1972) Economical procedures for the reduction of aggression in a residential setting. *Mental Retardation*, **15**, 25–28.

Bucher, B., and Lovaas, O.I. (1968) Use of aversive stimulation in behaviour modification. In M.R. Jones (ed.) *Miami Symposium on the Prediction of Behaviour: Aversive Stimulation*. Florida: University of Miami Press.

Burchard, J.D., and Barrera, F. (1972) Analysis of time-out and response cost in a programmed environment. *Journal of Applied Behaviour Analysis*, **5**, 271–282.

Carr, E.G., and Durand, V.M. (1984) The social-communicative basis of severe behaviour problems in children. In S. Reiss and R. Bootzin (eds) *Theoretical Issues in Behaviour Therapy*. New York: Academic Press.

Carr, E.G., and McDowell, J.J. (1980) Social control of self-injurious behaviour of organic etiology. *Behaviour Therapy*, **11**, 102–109.

Carr, E.G., Newsom, C.D., and Binkoff, J.A. (1976) Stimulus control of self destructive behaviour in a psychotic child. *Journal of Child Psychology*, **4**, 139–153.

Carr, E.G., Newsom, C.D., and Binkoff, J.A. (1980) Escape as a factor in the aggressive behaviour of the retarded child. *Journal of Applied Behaviour Analysis*, **13**, 101–117.

Carr, E.G., Schreibman, L., and Lovaas, O.I. (1975) Control of echolalic speech in psychotic children. *Journal of Abnormal Child Psychology*, **3**, 331–351.

Chadwick, O. (1985) Psychological sequelae of head injury in children. *Developmental Medicine and Child Neurology*, **27**(1), 72–75.

Corbett, J. (1975) Aversion for the treatment of self-injurious behaviour. *Journal of Mental Deficiency Research*, **19**, 79–95.

Corbett, J. (1977) Population studies in mental retardation. In P. Graham (ed.) *Epidemiological Approaches in Child Psychiatry*. London: Academic Press.

Cunningham, C. (1986) The effects of early intervention on the occurrence and nature of behaviour problems in children with Down's Syndrome. Abstract summary of final report to DHSS, London.

Doleys, D.M., Wells, K.C., Hobbs, S.A., Roberts, M.W., and Cartelli, L.M. (1976) The effects of social punishment on non-compliance: a comparison of time-out and positive practice. *Journal of Applied Behaviour Analysis*, **9**, 471–482.

Dorsey, M.F., Iwata, B.A., Ong, P., and McSween, T. (1980) Treatment of self-injurious behaviour using a water mist: initial response suppression and generalization. *Journal of Applied Behaviour Analysis*, **13**, 343–353.

Edelson, S.M., Taubman, M.T., and Lovaas, O.I. (1983) Some social contexts of self destructive behaviour. *Journal of Abnormal Child Psychology*, **11**, 299–312.

Epstein, L.H., Doke, L.A., Sajwaj, T.E., Sorrell, S., and Rimmer, B. (1974) Generality and side effects of over-correction. *Journal of Applied Behaviour Analysis*, **7**, 385–390.

Favell, J.E. (1983) The management of aggressive behavior. In E. Schopler and G.B. Mesibov (eds) *Autism in Adolescents and Adults*. New York: Plenum.

Favell, J.E., McGimsey, J.F., and Schell, R.M. (1982) Treatment of self-injury by providing alternative sensory activities. *Analysis and Intervention in Developmental Disabilities*, **2**, 83–104.

Foxx, R.M. (1976) The use of overcorrection to eliminate the public disrobing (stripping) of retarded women. *Behaviour Research and Therapy*, **14**, 53–61.

Foxx, R.M., and Azrin, N.H. (1972) Restitution: a method of eliminating aggressive disruptive behaviour in retarded brain damaged patients. *Behaviour Research and Therapy*, **10**, 15–27.

Foxx, R.M., and Dufrense, D. (1984) 'Harry': the use of physical restraint as a reinforcer, time-out from restraint and fading restraint in treating a self-injurious man. *Analysis and Intervention in Developmental Disabilities*, **4**, 1–13.

Foxx, R.M., and Livesay, J. (1984) Maintenance of response suppression following overcorrection: a 10 year retrospective examination of eight cases. *Analysis and Intervention in Developmental Disabilties*, **4**, 65–79.

Foxx, R.M., and Martin, E.D. (1975) Treatment of scavenging behaviour (coprophagy and pica) by overcorrection. *Behaviour Research and Therapy*, **13**, 153–162.

Foxx, R.M., and Shapiro, S.T. (1978) The timeout ribbon: a nonexclusionary time-out procedure. *Journal of Applied Behaviour Analysis*, **11**, 125–136.

Goldiamond, I.E. (1974) Toward a constructional approach to social problems. *Behaviourism*, **2**, 1–84.

Green, R., and Hoats, D. (1971) Aversive tickling: a simple conditioning technique. *Behaviour Therapy*, **2**, 389–393.

Gross, A.M., and Drabman, R.S. (1981) Behavioural contrast and behaviour therapy. *Behaviour Therapy*, **12**, 231–246.

Harris, S.L., and Ersner-Hershfield, B. (1978) Behavioural suppression of seriously disruptive behaviour in psychotic and retarded patients: a review of punishment and its alternatives. *Psychological Bulletin,* **85,** 1352–1375.

Heaton-Ward, A. (1977) Psychosis in mental handicap. *British Journal of Psychiatry,* **130,** 525–533.

Hereford, S.M., Cleland, C.C., and Fellner, M. (1973) Territoriality and scent-marking: a study of profoundly retarded enuretics and encopretics. *American Journal of Mental Deficiency,* **77,** 426–430.

Hobbs, S.A., and Forehand, R. (1977) Important parameters in the use of time-out with children: a re-examination. *Journal of Behaviour Therapy and Experimental Psychiatry,* **8,** 365–370.

Horner, R.D. (1980) The effects of an environmental 'enrichment' program on the behaviour of institutionalized profoundly retarded children. *Journal of Applied Behaviour Analysis,* **13,** 473–491.

Iwata, B.A., Dorsey, M.F., Slifer, K.J., Bauman, K.E., and Richman, G.S. (1982) Toward a functional analysis of self-injury. *Analysis and Intervention in Developmental Disabilities,* **2,** 3–20.

Johnson, W.L., and Baumeister, A.A. (1981) Behavioural techniques for decreasing aberrant behaviours of retarded and autistic persons. In R.M. Eisler and P.M. Miller (eds) *Progress in Behaviour Modification,* Vol. 12. New York: Academic Press.

Johnson, W.L., Baumeister, A.A., Penland, M.J., and Inwald, C. (1982) Experimental analysis of self-injurious, stereotypic and collateral behaviours of retarded persons: effects of over-correction and reinforcement of alternative responding. *Analysis and Intervention in Developmental Disabilities,* **2,** 41–66.

Koller, H., Richardson, S.A., and Katz, M. (1983) Behaviour disturbance since childhood among a five year birth cohort of all mentally retarded young adults in a city. *American Journal of Mental Deficiency,* **87,** 386–395.

Kushlick, A., and Cox, G.R. (1973) The epidemiology of mental handicap. *Developmental Medicine and Child Neurology,* **15,** 748–759.

Lewis, C.C. (1981) The effects of parental firm control: a reinterpretation of findings. *Psychological Bulletin,* **90,** 547–561.

Lovaas, O.I., and Simmons, J.Q. (1969) Manipulation of self destruction in three retarded children. *Journal of Applied Behaviour Analysis,* **2,** 143–157.

Lovaas, O.I., Freitag, G., Gold, V.J., and Kassorla, I. (1965) Experimental studies in childhood schizophrenia: analysis of self-destructive behaviour. *Journal of Experimental Child Psychology,* **2,** 67–84.

Lucero, W.J., Frieman, J., Spoering, K., and Fehrenbacher, J. (1976) Comparison of three procedures in reducing self-injurious behaviour. *American Journal of Mental Deficiency,* **80,** 548–554.

Luiselli, J.K. (1975) The effects of multiple contingencies on the rocking behaviour of a retarded child. *Psychological Record,* **25,** 559–565.

Lutzker, J.R., and Wesch, D. (1983) Facial screening: history and critical review. *Australia and New Zealand Journal of Developmental Disabilities,* **9,** 209–223.

MacDonough, T.S., and Forehand, R. (1973) Response contingent time out: important parameters in behaviour modification with children. *Journal of Behaviour Therapy and Experimental Psychiatry,* **4,** 231–236.

Martin, P.L., and Foxx, R.M. (1973) Victim control of the aggression of an institutionalized retardate. *Journal of Behaviour Therapy and Experimental Psychiatry,* **4,** 161–165.

Mulick, J.A., Schroeder, S.R., and Rojahn, J. (1980) Chronic ruminative vomiting: A comparison of four treatment procedures. *Journal of Autism and Developmental Disorders*, **10**, 203–213.

Murphy, G.M. (1978) Overcorrection: a critique. *Journal of Mental Deficiency Research*, **22**, 161–174.

Murphy, G.M., and Wilson, B. (1981) Long term outcome of contingent shock treatment for self-injurious behaviour. In P. Mittler (ed.) *Frontiers of Knowledge in Mental Retardation*, Vol. II. Baltimore: University Park Press.

Nihira, K., Meyers, E.C., and Mink, I.T. (1983) Reciprocal relationships between home environment and development of TMR adolescents. *American Journal of Mental Deficiency*, **88**, 139–149.

Nihira, K., Mink, I.T., and Meyers, C.E. (1984) Salient dimensions of home environment relevant to child development. In N.R. Ellis and N.W. Bray (eds) *International Review of Research in Mental Retardation*, Vol. 12. Orlando: Academic Press.

Ollendick, T.H., and Matson, J.L. (1978) Overcorrection: an overview. *Behaviour Therapy*, **4**, 830–842.

Ollendick, T.H., Shapiro, E.S., and Barrett, R.P. (1981) Reducing stereotypic behaviours: an analysis of treatment procedures utilizing an alternating treatments design. *Behaviour Therapy*, **12**, 570–577.

Paluck, R.J., and Esser, A.H. (1971a) Controlled experimental modification of aggressive behaviour in territories of severely retarded boys. *American Journal of Mental Deficiency*, **76**, 23–29.

Paluck, R.J., and Esser, A.H. (1971b) Territorial behaviour as an indicator of changes in clinical behavioural conditioning of severely retarded boys. *American Journal of Mental Deficiency*, **76**, 284–290.

Pendergrass, V.E. (1971) Effects of length of time-out from positive reinforcement and schedule of application in suppression of aggressive behaviour. *Psychological Record*, **21**, 75–80.

Porterfield, J., Blunden, R., and Blewitt, E. (1980) Improving environments for profoundly handicapped adults: establishing staff routines for high client engagement. *Behaviour Modification*, **4**, 225–241.

Raynes, N.V., Pratt, M.W., and Roses, S.S. (1979) *Organizational Structure and the Care of the Mentally Retarded*. London: Croom Helm.

Repp, A.C., and Deitz, S.M. (1974) Reducing aggressive and self-injurious behaviour of institutionalized retarded children through reinforcement of other behaviours. *Journal of Applied Behaviour Analysis*, **7**, 313–315.

Richmond, G., and Martin, P. (1977) Punishment as a therapeutic method with institutionalized retarded persons. In T. Thompson and J. Grabowski (eds) *Behaviour Modification of the Mentally Retarded*. London: Oxford University Press.

Risley, T.R. (1968) The effects and side-effects of punishing the autistic behaviours of a deviant child. *Journal of Applied Behaviour Analysis*, **1**, 21–34.

Rogers-Warren, A., and Warren, S. (1977) *Ecological Perspectives in Behaviour Analysis*. Baltimore: University Park Press.

Rojahn, J., and Schroeder, S.R. (1983) Behavioural Assessment. In J.L. Matson and J.A. Mulick (eds) *Handbook of Mental Retardation*. New York: Pergamon.

Rojahn, J., Mulick, J.A., McCoy, D., and Schroeder, S.R. (1978) Setting effects, adaptive clothing, and the modification of head banging and self restraint in two profoundly retarded adults. *Behavioural Analysis and Modification*, **2**, 185–196.

Rollings, J.P., Baumeister, A., and Baumeister, A. (1977) The use of over-correction procedures to eliminate stereotyped behaviours in retarded individuals. *Behaviour Modificaton*, **1**, 24–46.

Romanczyk, A.G., and Goren, E.R. (1975) Severe self-injurious behaviour:

the problem of clinical control. *Journal of Consulting and Clinical Psychology*, **43**, 730–739.

Rutter, M. (1978) Family, area and school influences in the genesis of conduct disorder. In L. Hersov, M. Berger and D. Shaffer (eds) *Aggression and Anti-Social Behaviour in Childhood and Adolescence*. Oxford: Pergamon.

Sajwaj, T., Libet, J. and Agras, S. (1974) Lemon juice therapy: the control of life threatening rumination in a six month old infant. *Journal of Applied Behaviour Analysis*, **7**, 557–563.

Schalock, R.L., Harper, R.S., and Genung, T. (1981) Community integration of mentally retarded adults: community placement and program success. *American Journal of Mental Deficiency*, **85**, 478–488.

Schroeder, S.R., Schroeder, S.S., Rojahn, J., and Mulick, J.A. (1981) Self-injurious behavior: an analysis of behavior management techniques. In J.L. Matson and J.R. McCartney (eds) *Handbook of Behavior Modification with the Mentally Retarded*. New York: Plenum.

Singh, N.N., Dawson, M.J., and Manning, P.J. (1981) The effects of physical restraint on self-injurious behaviour. *Journal of Mental Deficiency Research*, **25**, 207–216.

Solnick, J.V., Rincover, A., and Peterson, C.R. (1977) Some determinants of the reinforcing and punishing effects of time-out. *Journal of Applied Behaviour Analysis*, **10**, 415–424.

Stolz, S.B. (1978) *Ethical Issues of Behaviour Modification*. San Francisco: Jossey-Bass.

Tarpley, H.D., and Schroeder, S.E. (1979) Comparison of DRO and DRI on rate of suppression of self injurious behaviour. *American Journal of Mental Deficiency*, **84**, 188–194.

Tizard, J. (1964) *Community Services for the Mentally Handicapped* (see particularly Part IV. The Brooklands Residential Unit). London: Oxford University Press.

Twardosz, S., and Sajwaj, T. (1972) Multiple effects of a procedure to increase sitting in a hyperactive retarded boy. *Journal of Applied Behaviour Analysis*, **5**, 73–78.

Williams, J.L., Schroeder, S.R., Eckerman, D.A. and Rojahn, J. (1983) Time-out from positive reinforcement procedures with mentally retarded persons: an ecological review and analysis. In S.E. Breuning, J.L. Matson and R.P. Barrett (eds) *Advances in Mental Retardation and Developmental Disabilities*, Vol. I, pp. 199–236. Greenwich, Connecticut: JAI Press.

Wing, L. (1971) Severely retarded children in a London area: prevalence and provision of services. *Psychological Medicine*, **1**, 405–415.

Wing, L. (1981) Language, social and cognitive impairments in autism and severe mental retardation. *Journal of Autism and Developmental Disorders*, **11**, 31–44.

Wing, L., and Gould, J. (1979) Severe impairments of social interaction and associated abnormalities in children: epidemiology and classification. *Journal of Autism and Developmental Disorders*, **9**, 11–29.

Chapter 8

Implementing and Generalizing Programmes of Behaviour Change

Chapters 6 and 7 discussed a number of technical limitations in the research literature on ways of helping people acquire new skills and overcome behavioural problems. One problem that is frequently mentioned is described as the problem of generalization (Stokes and Baer, 1977). This refers to the fact that gains made in one time or setting sometimes do not generalize to other times and settings. The causal mechanisms involved in this difficulty can be conceptualized in three ways. One is to see the problem as inherent in the learner — it is seen as a characteristic of people with severe learning disabilities that they do not readily generalize their learning. Thus it becomes necessary to plan interventions which will need to be carried out at all the times and in all the settings where the behaviour change being sought is important. A skill taught at one place and time will need to be taught specifically in all other situations where it will have to be used. The techniques used to decrease a problem behaviour in one setting will have to be applied in other settings if the reduction is to be generalized. This is seen as the way of overcoming the learner's problem of generalization.

A second way of viewing this difficulty is to see generalization as related to the way in which intervention is carried out. Thus, if the behaviour change technique is very discriminable (uses discriminable materials or is only carried out in particular places and times with particular people), then it is not surprising that the learning itself remains under very specific stimulus control. The answer in this case is to use less discriminable behaviour change procedures — less specific materials, less specific techniques, with implementation in naturalistic contexts.

The third way of looking at the problem of generalization is to see it as reflecting the failure of those working with the individual to generalize effective strategies over time and settings. It is clear that in some cases effective strategies do not continue to be used and thus behaviour reverts to its pre-intervention level (see, for example, Lovaas *et al.*, 1973; Foxx and Dufrense, 1984). The training literature, which will be reviewed briefly in the next section, provides further evidence of this kind of difficulty. Given the wide range of difficulties experienced by people who have severe learning disabilities and the fact that progress will inevitably be slow, significant behaviour change will be best effected by those who have extensive face-to-face contact with the person (parents, friends, teachers, residential care staff). These people spend the most time with the individual and constitute a significant part of the natural context within which behaviour change is necessary. It is easy to recognize that the long-term outcome for people with severe learning disabilities is very much influenced by how those around them behave — these are the key 'teachers' and 'therapists' irrespective of whether that is their formally constituted role. If the gap between knowledge and practice is to be bridged then these are the key intermediaries.

Recognition of this has led to the growth of a large behavioural literature on how to influence the functioning of those in extensive immediate contact with people who have severe learning disabilities. It is one of the problems of much applied behavioural work that it tends to view behaviour influences as unidirectional, from the non-disabled to the disabled person. The focus is almost exclusively upon the dyadic interaction of the person with learning disabilities and the immediate caretakers with the main direction of influence from the latter to the former. With this perspective the problem of effecting widespread long-lasting behavioural change was seen to be resolved by making the non-disabled partner in the dyad an effective precision teacher and behaviour modifier. The key intervention became defined as training parents, teachers and residential care staff in behavioural skills which they could then practise *ad infinitum* on the person with learning disabilities for whom they were responsible. Much very useful research was done upon the feasibility and practicability of such training and this is reviewed in the next section.

EFFECTING GENERALIZED CHANGE — TRAINING INTERVENTIONS

The research literature demonstrates quite clearly that parents and staff at many levels of ability can successfully be taught how to implement precision teaching and behaviour modification programmes. As well as being able to implement such programmes, parents and staff can readily learn how to design programmes for themselves and master the basic behavioural principles which underlie these programmes (Mira, 1970; Berkowitz and Graziano, 1972; Martin, 1972; Gardner, 1972; O'Dell, 1974; Heifetz, 1977; Schinke and Wong, 1977; Cunningham, 1979, 1985; Callias,

1980; Brightman *et al.*, 1982). Being able to understand the principles and actually carrying out programmes appear rather separate skill domains, with the former encouraged by didactic training (such as lectures and reading) and the latter better taught by enactive methods such as modelling, role-play, feedback and assignments. However, in some cases, such as in Heifetz's (1977) study with parents, even reading a manual may prove an effective practicum training intervention.

Although there are many methodological difficulties in the experimental literature, the reported achievements are considerable, especially in view of the fact that most training programmes are relatively short (20–30 hours) and are carried out in a group format. This demonstrates the feasibility of providing powerful teaching and management techniques to those in the greatest position of influence over people with severe learning disabilities. This greatly improves the probability of significantly enhancing the development and adjustment of those with disabilities and at first sight training would seem a promising vehicle for closing the gap between knowledge and practice.

However, it is now clear that parent and staff training may not always fulfil the potential ascribed to it. Even if behavioural skills are mastered by caretakers, this is not always followed by measurable gains in the person with severe learning difficulties (Tavormina, 1975; Heifetz, 1977; Brightman *et al.*, 1982; Feldman, Manella and Varni, 1983; Sandler, Goren and Thurman, 1983; Hornby and Singh, 1984). There is little evidence that people make use of their training to generate programmes for tackling new problems which arise after the training period; and certainly parents do not sustain over time use of the highly structured practices taught to them (Cunningham and Jeffree, 1971; Martin, 1972; Callias and Jenkins, 1973; Baker, Heifetz and Murphy, 1980; Sloper, Cunningham and Arnljotsdottir, 1983; Cunningham, 1985).

Perhaps this should not be surprising. Severe learning difficulties are a long-term problem and such brief interventions should not really be expected to show sustained effects over many years. The high expectations for training are also based on a limited analysis of the nature of the job to be tackled. This can be seen in the two ways mentioned earlier. The first is a tendency to view influence unidirectionally, from the non-disabled to the disabled person. This neglects the powerful influences flowing in the other direction. Dunst (1985) reviews the early child development literature demonstrating the influence of infant behaviour upon the caretaker. He discusses the importance of the infant's behaviour being 'readable' so that the mother is able to adjust her own behaviour in the light of recognizable feedback from the infant. He then goes on to show that the feedback from some disabled children (he uses studies of Down's syndrome infants) is not always salient or recognizable and can fail to influence the mother in the same way as a normal baby might. This analysis stresses the mutuality of influence in any dyadic situation and the important role of mutual feedback in directing and sustaining interaction.

Working with people who have severe learning disabilities is a long-term process. Progress may be slow and erratic, and responses to intervention may not always be immediately recognizable or positive. Thus, in some cases the response of the person with disabilities may be such as to extinguish or punish attempts by others at behaviour change. If such efforts at teaching and treatment are to be sustained, parents and staff may have to be helped at interpreting the response of the person they are working with, and may need some other form of support to encourage their efforts and substitute for the response of the individual. Alternatively, those with disabilities may need to be taught to put out more recognizable or reinforcing signals to those seeking to aid their development and adjustment. As yet these issues have received scant attention in the research literature.

There is, however, an additional factor to be considered when seeking to effect lasting change. Even if the importance of mutual influence within dyadic interaction is recognized, most dyads are part of a larger system (family, school, staff groups, hospital, department) and each member is subject to other forms of influence upon their behaviour. If the behaviour of individuals is to be understood, then full account must be taken of the many influences that may be controlling this behaviour, not just those coming from their partner in the present interaction. Woods and Cullen (1983) provide an example of this, paradoxical in the light of the previous paragraphs. They describe a number of cases in a hospital setting where staff sustained programmes over long periods of time even though it was clear that the programmes were having no effect — that is, they illustrated that the control of staff behaviour lay outside of the response of the person for whom the programme existed. Researchers have tried to characterize broader system influences and their effect upon behaviour. The work of Moos (for example 1974, 1976) has been very important in this respect. He has tried to characterize psychosocial climate variables as a key dimension of system influence upon behaviour.

He has looked at these influences in a range of therapeutic settings and the work of Nihira's group reported in previous chapters has applied these concepts in studying family factors which influence the development and adjustment of children with learning disabilities (Nihira, Meyers and Mink, 1983; Nihira, Mink and Meyers, 1984). They have shown the predictive value of such general features as family cohesion and lack of conflict, expressiveness, positive attitudes to intellectual and cultural activities and a lack of emphasis upon authoritarian control. Likewise Raynes, Pratt and Roses (1979), developing the work of King, Raynes and Tizard (1971), have shown how quality of care, and hence indirectly development and adjustment, may be affected in large institutions by such general organizational characteristics as staff autonomy.

The theories and research on the nature of social influence argue the need for a more systems-oriented approach to tackling the problem of effecting lasting change. In behavioural language this is reflected in the shift of interest from immediate antecedents and consequences of behaviour to setting conditions and ecological variables. Whatever language is used it is clear that if the potential for helping people with severe learning disabilities is to be realized, attention will have to be paid to the influence of the disabled persons themselves and the influences exerted by families, schools, hospitals and other systems upon all members of that system. This shift in orientation can be seen in two further areas of literature.

EFFECTING LASTING CHANGE — DEMONSTRATION SERVICES

The literature contains a number of examples of complete service systems designed to deliver high quality sustained behavioural interventions to people with severe learning disabilities. Such service systems encompass both the interventions to be carried out with the service consumers, and the management arrangements (job descriptions, supervisory procedures, service evaluation components) which would ensure that the interventions are carried out. By and large no particular rationale is offered for the management arrangements adopted and there is no comparative literature looking at different ways of managing similar services. The services are presented as a complete 'package' which might serve as a model for imitation. Risley and Favell (1979) describe procedures for running a hospital ward for very disabled people in such a way as to ensure high quality physical and developmental care. Their approach to management used close supervision of direct care staff, allowing them little autonomy, providing clear job descriptions and a range of standardized operating procedures, time-tabling of all activities and good quality physical aids and equipment. They emphasized careful objective monitoring of general system functioning. Whether the system described lasted and the long-term results it achieved are unknown. It provides an interesting example of how to use tight hierarchical line management procedures to raise quality of care in institutional settings. However, the methods themselves are somewhat institutional and permit little autonomy and initiative to those caring for the clients. Autonomy is often held to be an important factor in quality of care (see Raynes et al., 1979) although this probably depends upon the overall system characteristics and individual staff characteristics. For example, the more competent the staff the more likely it is that there will be beneficial outcomes from increased autonomy. The system described by Risley and Favell (1979) had a very strong emphasis upon control, particularly of staff behaviours; and this again might be contrasted with the literature on family settings which suggests that a low emphasis upon authoritarian control has positive relationships with development and adjustment in the child with learning disabilities.

Other demonstration services described in the literature are also noticeable for their emphasis upon traditional bureaucratic management techniques for making the system work, techniques such as tight job specification, a multiplicity of written operational procedures and hierarchical supervisory arrangements to control staff performance. The Portage system (Shearer and Shearer, 1972; Bluma *et al.*, 1976) is an approach to providing a home-based teaching service for families who have a pre-school child with learning disabilities. In addition to providing a range of assessment and teaching materials, the system specifies in considerable detail how the home teacher is to behave and describes a management system based upon group staff meetings and individual supervision of home teachers, with a clear role division between supervisors and home teachers. The system has proved very popular and has spread particularly quickly in the United Kingdom (see, for example, Cameron, 1982). There has even been a book detailing how such a service can be established (Revill and Blunden, 1980). It is a structured system in terms of the service it provides to the families and in terms of how staff are managed. Such approaches certainly find favour with families (Revill and Blunden, 1979; Sloper *et al.*, 1983) and appear helpful to the children, at least in the short term (Revill and Blunden, 1979). It is not known which aspects of the system are related to its success but it is clear that some Portage services survive longer than others and that there is almost certainly variation in the quality of such services (Bendall, Smith and Kushlick, 1983). Felce *et al.*, (1984) describe an adaptation of this approach to provide structured individual teaching in a residential care setting with adults having a severe or profound degree of learning disability. The assessment and teaching materials were adapted for this client group but the staff management procedures were essentially those outlined above, with the exception that all programmes were written by the line supervisor. As yet the long-term achievements of this system are unknown (see also Mansell *et al.*, 1983).

The existence of such demonstration services provides much useful information about the factors to be considered in planning for lasting change. Most of those described in the literature draw inspiration for their management systems from basic behavioural principles — that is, they apply to staff management the principles and techniques used in behavioural teaching for people with learning disabilities. Again the view of behavioural influence tends to be rather narrow and unidirectional. The solutions in practice derived from these principles often appear as rather traditional line management practices with a strong bureaucratic component. There are no examples comparing different management systems aimed at achieving similar service goals. There is little discussion of alternative approaches to management of staff and how to match a management system to the nature of the services provided and the nature of the people who will provide and consume those services.

Model services have one other serious limitation from the practitioner's viewpoint. Most practitioners are not in the position of setting up services where none exists. Rather, they work in systems already operating, often with a long history. The nature of the work is to change the goals and/or working methods of already existing systems. This provides a lot of common ground for those working with families, with schools, with vocational or residential care systems. The nature of the work is to help the system achieve optimal functioning — to produce its outcomes in the most effective and efficient way possible. In the context of this book, and this part in particular, the problem is how to help families, schools, workshops and residential care settings to deliver effective teaching and behaviour management to people with severe learning disabilities. Such work might be broadly described as organizational development.

EFFECTING LASTING CHANGE — ORGANIZATIONAL DEVELOPMENT

While there are a number of theories about the nature of family and organizational systems and how to change them, these have yet to be applied in a systematic fashion to services for those with severe learning disabilities. However, a number of writers drawing upon personal experience have highlighted some of the setting factors which determine whether or not behavioural approaches are adopted by a system (for example, Sajwaj, 1973; Reppucci and Saunders, 1974; Reppucci, 1977). These writings have produced some rules of thumb for those who wish to implement organizational change and Georgiades and Phillimore (1975) have produced a useful summary of these. It is interesting how much common ground emerges from people working quite independently in a range of different settings. All draw attention to the need for selective focus and to work in a system with people who are already functioning well and are positively oriented towards change. In general, importance is attached to team building with the change agent being prepared to listen and to compromise rather than imposing ready-made solutions. Commitment of those involved is seen as best obtained through participation in decision making and through permitting staff a high degree of autonomy. The recognition of external constraints (for example, finances, union practices, public opinion) is stressed and thus the need to ensure wide-ranging support for proposed changes. This 'bottom up' approach to change stands in marked contrast to the 'top down' methods described in the demonstration services literature. Without specific reference, the writings on organizational change emphasize many of the climate variables which have been found of significance in other areas of research — variables such as cohesion, autonomy, expressiveness and a positive attitude to development.

Others writers in this area have used more formal social psychological concepts to understand and promote service functioning (for example, Watts and Bennett, 1983). Attention is drawn to group decision-making processes, the nature of leadership and role functioning. Problems in these areas are seen as sources of stress which, in turn, affect the ability of people to work constructively. Such stress would be in addition to that which already derives from living and working with people who have severe learning disabilities. Having a child with severe learning disabilities in a family introduces a range of stress factors, both physical and emotional, upon family members. Likewise for staff working with people who have such disabilities, there can be a range of stresses. There are, therefore, two sources of stress in this analysis. One derives from the nature of the person's disability and the type of working relationships expected with this person. The second derives from the social system within which people operate, which can compound the primary stress through such factors as lack of support, poor leadership, allowing conflicts to remain unresolved, failing to deal with role conflict and role ambiguity and other factors relevant to the functioning of working groups in many settings. Dealing with these issues becomes critical to the long-term viability of any service innovation.

From this rather brief overview of what is a fragmented literature it becomes possible to see some of the setting factors which are important determinants of staff and family functioning. This literature also offers insights as to how such factors can be dealt with and thus how change can be facilitated and innovation sustained. A vivid example of this kind of work in action is provided in a book by Towell and Harries (1979) who described consultancy work with staff of a psychiatric hospital. The aim of this work was to help staff effect for themselves changes in working practices that they desired. The book provides many useful insights into how such organizational change works and is one of the few detailed descriptions of such work and its potential in human service settings.

CONCLUSIONS

Any new method of help for people with severe learning disabilities will only be of benefit if its implementation can be effected in the long term. As long as such implementation is dependent upon people (as opposed to machines, chemical implants or other such mechanisms) then the psychology of such people, be they family members or professional staff, is as important as the psychology of severe learning disability itself. Behavioural approaches to help have been of enormous significance for two reasons. In the first place, techniques have been developed for effectively teaching skills and overcoming behavioural problems with people who were previously regarded as ineducable and untreatable. In the second place, these techniques are readily communicated to those in extensive face-to-face contact with those who experience the learning disabilities. This has opened up the potential for widespread and long-lasting change.

It is clear that if such potential is to be realized then consideration must be given to the broader settings in which intervention takes place. Training is not a sufficient intervention to guarantee implementation and thus attention has shifted to a more systems-oriented approach — to studying the variables which affect the day-to-day performance of those living and working with people who have severe learning disabilities. There is no one generally accepted analysis of social systems and no set of well-validated techniques of system change. Nevertheless, a number of themes begin to emerge as significant. There appear to be some general system characteristics which are supportive of positive and constructive efforts to help people with disabilities. Factors such as cohesion, autonomy, expressiveness emerge as important, as do general philosophies and attitudes oriented towards attainment rather than control. A degree of organization and structure appears useful. Promoting such conditions requires attention to social psychological factors such as role functioning, leadership and decision-making processes. These illustrate some of the goals that a system must attain if constructive work is to be possible. Within such appropriate contexts training becomes an important means for making help more effective. Without such system support training is unlikely to prove of any long-term value.

While the type of system which will be most capable of handling change is becoming clearer, there is rather less information about how systems can be changed if their present state is not optimal. Some techniques form part of the rules of thumb described earlier — for example, listening and ensuring support at all levels of a system. However, no coherent guide to practice yet exists and quite often systems seek to effect changes by the very kinds of intervention that have proven weak — for example, by investing heavily in staff training. A more coherent approach to attitude and behaviour change in a systems framework will be needed if significant headway is to be made in helping family and service systems incorporate readily new ways of helping people with severe learning disabilities.

REFERENCES

Baker, B.L., Heifetz, L.J., and Murphy, D.M. (1980) Behavioural training for parents of mentally retarded children: one year follow up. *American Journal of Mental Deficiency*, **85**, 31–38.

Bendall, S.A., Smith, J., and Kushlick, A. (1983) National Study of Portage Type Home Teaching Services. Vol 1, 2 and 3. Report 162, Health Care Evaluation Research Team: University of Southampton.

Berkowitz, B.P., and Graziano, A.M. (1972) Training parents as behaviour therapists: a review. *Behaviour Research and Therapy*, **10**, 297–317.

Bluma, S.M., Shearer, M.S., Frohman, A.H., and Hilliard, J.N. (1976) *Portage Guide to Early Education*. Portage, Wisconsin: CESA, 12.

Brightman, R.P., Baker, B.L., Clark, D.B., and Ambrose, S.A. (1982) Effectiveness of alternative parent training formats. *Journal of Behaviour Therapy and Experimental Psychiatry*, **13**, 113–117.

Callias, M. (1980) Teaching parents, teachers and nurses. In W. Yule and J. Carr (eds) *Behaviour Modification for the Mentally Handicapped*. London: Croom Helm.

Callias, M., and Jenkins, J.A. (1973) Group training in behaviour modification. A pilot project with parents of severely retarded children. Unpublished.

Cameron, R.J. (ed.) (1982) *Working Together: Portage in the UK*. Windsor: NFER-Nelson.

Cunningham, C. (1979) Parent counselling. In M, Craft (ed.) *Tredgold's Mental Retardation*, 12th edition. London: Ballière Tindall.

Cunningham, C. (1985) Training and education approaches for parents of children with special needs. *British Journal of Medical Psychology*, **58**, 285–305.

Cunningham, C.C., and Jeffree, D.J. (1971) Working with Parents: developing a workshop course for parents of young mentally handicapped children. Manchester: National Society for Mentally Handicapped Children (North West Region).

Dunst, C.J. (1985) Communicative competence and deficits: effects on early social interactions. In E. McDonald and D. Gallagher (eds) *Facilitating Social Emotional Development in Multiply Handicapped Children*. Philadelphia: Home of the Merciful Saviour for Crippled Children.

Felce, D., de Kock, U., Mansell, J., and Jenkins, J. (1984) Providing systematic individual teaching for severely disturbed and profoundly mentally handicapped adults in residential care. *Behaviour Research and Therapy*, **22**(3), 299–310.

Feldman, W.S., Manella, K.J., and Varni, J.W. (1983) A behavioural parent training programme for single mothers of physically handicapped children. *Child: Care, Health and Development*, **9**, 157–168.

Foxx, R.M., and Dufrense, D. (1984) 'Harry': the use of physical restraint as a reinforcer, timeout from restraint, and fading restraint in treating a self-injurious man. *Analysis and Intervention in Developmental Disablities*, **4**, 1–13.

Gardner, J.M. (1972) Teaching behaviour modification to nonprofessionals. *Journal of Applied Behaviour Analysis*, **5**, 517–521.

Georgiades, N.J., and Phillimore, L. (1975) The myth of the hero innovator and alternative strategies for organizational change. In C.C. Kiernan and E.P. Woodford (eds) *Behaviour Modification with the Severely Retarded*. Elsevier, N. Holland: Associated Scientific Publishers.

Heifetz, L.J. (1977) Behavioural training for parents of retarded children: alternative formats based on instructional materials. *American Journal of Mental Deficiency*, **82**, 194–203.

Hornby, G., and Singh, N.N. (1984) Behavioural group training with parents of mentally retarded children. *Journal of Mental Deficiency Research*, **28**, 43–52.

King, R.D., Raynes, N.V., and Tizard, J. (1971) *Patterns of Residential Care: Sociological studies in institutions for handicapped children*. London: Routledge and Kegan Paul.

Lovaas, O.I., Koegel, R., Simmons, J.Q., and Stevens, J. (1973) Some generalizations and follow up measures on autistic children in behaviour therapy. *Journal of Applied Behaviour Analysis*, **6**, 131–165.

Mansell, J., Felce, D., Jenkins, J., and Flight, C. (1983) *The Bereweeke Skill Teaching System*. Windsor: NFER-Nelson.

Martin, G.L. (1972) Teaching operant technology to psychiatric nurses, aides and attendants. In F. Clark, D.R. Evans and L.O. Hamerlynck (eds) *Implementing Behavioural Programs for Schools and Clinics*. Champaign, Ill.: Research Press.

Mira,, M. (1970) Results of a behaviour modification training program for parents and teachers. *Behaviour Research and Therapy*, **8**, 309–311.

Moos, R. (1974) *Evaluating Treatment Environments: A Social-Ecological Approach*. New York: Wiley.

Moos, R. (1976) *The Human Context: Environmental Determinants of Behaviour*. New York: Wiley.

Nihira, K., Meyers, E.C., and Mink, I.T. (1983) Reciprocal relationships between home environment and development of TMR adolescents. *American Journal of Mental Deficiency*, **88**, 139–149.

Nihira, K., Mink, I.T., and Meyers, C.E. (1984) Salient dimensions of home environments relevant to child development. In N.R. Ellis, and N.W. Bray (eds) *International Review of Research in Mental Retardation*, Vol. 12. Orlando: Academic Press.

O'Dell, S. (1974) Training parents in behaviour modification: a review. *Psychological Bulletin*, **81**, 418–433.

Raynes, N.V., Pratt, M.W., and Roses, S. (1979) *Organizational Structure and the Care of the Mentally Retarded*. London: Croom Helm.

Reppucci, N. (1977) Implementation issues for the behaviour modifier as institutional change agent. *Behaviour Therapy*, **8**, 594–605.

Reppucci, N.D., and Saunders, J.T. (1974) Social psychology of behaviour modification: problems of implementation in natural settings. *American Psychologist*, **29**, 649–660.

Revill, S., and Blunden, R.B. (1979) A home training service for pre-school developmentally handicapped children. *Behaviour Research and Therapy*, **17**, 207÷214.

Revill, S., and Blunden, R. (1980) *A Manual for Implementing a Portage Home Training Service for Developmentally Handicapped Preschool Children*. Windsor: NFER-Nelson.

Risley, T.R., and Favell, J. (1979) Constructing a living environment in an institution. In L.A. Hamerlynck (ed.) *Behavioural Systems for the Developmentally Disabled: II. Institutional, Clinic and Community Environments*. New York: Brunner/Mazel.

Sajwaj, T. (1973) Difficulties in the use of behavioral techniques by parents in changing child behavior: guides to success. *Journal of Nervous and Mental Disease*, **156**(1), 395–403.

Sandler, A., Goren, A., and Thurman, S.K. (1983) A training program for parents of handicapped pre-school children: effects upon mother, father and child. *Exceptional Children*, **49**, 355–358.

Schinke, S.P., and Wong, S.E. (1977) Evaluation of staff training in group homes for the retarded. *American Journal of Mental Deficiency*, **82**, 130–136.

Shearer, M.S., and Shearer, D.E. (1972) The Portage Project: a model for early childhood education. *Exceptional Children*, **39**, 210–217.

Sloper, P., Cunningham, C.C., and Arnljotsdottir, M. (1983) Parental reactions to early intervention with their Down's Syndrome infants. *Child: Care, Health and Development*, **9**, 357–376.

Stokes, T.F., and Baer, D.M. (1977) An implicit technology of generalization. *Journal of Applied Behaviour Analysis*, **10**, 349–367.

Tavormina, J.B. (1975) Relative effectiveness of behavioural and reflective group counselling with parents of mentally retarded children. *Journal of Consulting and Clinical Psychology*, **43**, 22–31.

Towell, D., and Harries, C. (eds) (1979) *Innovation in Patient Care*. London: Croom Helm.

Watts, F.N., and Bennett, D.H. (1983) Management of the staff team. In F.N. Watts and D.H. Bennett (eds) *Practice of Psychiatric Rehabilitation*. Chichester: Wiley.

Woods, P., and Cullen, C. (1983) Determinants of staff behaviour in long term care. *Behavioural Psychotherapy*, **11**, 4–17.

CONCLUSIONS TO PART 2

The use of basic behavioural principles has generated a wide range of tactics for helping the development and adjustment of people with severe learning disabilities. Such principles are universal in the sense that they reflect general laws of behaviour and are not specific to people with learning disabilities. Behavioural analysis is atheoretical and empiricist, proceeding from definitions of behaviour to be changed and discovering environmental influences that will effect such changes. It does not offer any theory as to the nature of severe learning disability in its many and varied forms. While it lays strong emphasis upon the individual as a focus study, there is little interest in individual differences except in so far as these reflect different learning histories.

This approach has yielded enormous dividends in the last twenty or so years. While recognizing these, Part 2 has also drawn attention to some of the limitations of this approach. These are of two kinds — empirical and analytic. Although the literature is large, the degree and type of validation for intervention techniques is variable. The behavioural literature does not provide a complete guide to effective and efficient teaching and management strategies. Some people make very slow progress, some gains made are of marginal significance, some gains made are later lost. Explanations for these facts can be offered at many different levels. However, it is a contention of this book that the growing knowledge of the nature and types of disability (as illustrated in Part 1) will need to be integrated with behavioural approaches to development and adjustment. There is need for a better conceptual framework within which to analyse individual differences. Such a framework will need to incorporate factors which inhere in the individual such as the presence of specific learning disorders, temperamental characteristics and aspects of biological functioning. In this way it will become possible to match more precisely intervention programmes to individual needs. It will also become possible to generate a wider range of intervention strategies.

Included in a broader conceptual framework will be a wider range of environmental variables. Attention was drawn at several points in this part to the limited analysis of environmental influence implicit in many applied behavioural endeavours. The need to recognize bidirectionality of influence and the role of general social setting and social system variables was stressed. Attention to these variables will lead to a better understanding of the problems for people with severe learning disabilities; and will help overcome the gap which already exists between knowledge and practice.

Thus, development can be seen as proceeding on two fronts. One is to develop better ways of helping people with severe learning disabilities. The other is to develop better ways of managing systems that provide services to these people so that they receive the best quality help. Much more attention has been given to the former than the latter endeavour. Yet it is the latter that in the end determines the quality of life experienced by the person with severe learning disabilities. Some of these issues will be touched upon in the third and final part which goes on to look in depth at two particular areas of help for people with severe learning disabilities.

Part Three

Remediating Severe Learning and Behavioural Disabilities: A Review of Two Specific Areas

INTRODUCTION TO PART 3

Research into understanding the nature of severe learning disabilities and into ways of helping people with these disabilities has proceeded relatively independently. It is a theme of this book that a much closer relationship between these two areas is necessary if further significant improvements in both understanding and help are to occur. This part will examine two areas of personal functioning which have attracted considerable interest from both experimental and applied researchers. It is hoped that this will support the contention that there *is* a great deal of common interest and much to be gained from closer collaboration. The main theme, however, is to illustrate in more detail than was possible in Chapter 6 the content and method of current techniques of practical help; and some of the limitations to our present knowledge base.

The two areas chosen are language and communication and self-control. These areas were chosen for several reasons. One is that they represent areas to which both experimental and applied workers have devoted considerable attention. The second reason is that these aspects of personal functioning relate closely to popular stereotypes about people with severe learning disabilities. Thus people so affected are often thought of as passive, dependent, lacking in initiative, unable to understand or communicate sensibly and effectively. If such myths are to be exposed then it is important to demonstrate that such characteristics are not inherent to severe learning disability; and that people with such disabilities can be active, independent, communicative and self-directed if helped in the right way — these skills are not beyond acquisition. This points up the third reason for choosing these areas — that they represent key skills in any curriculum aimed at social independence and helping people with disabilities find a satisfactory and accepted place in society. The fourth reason, perhaps obvious, is that these represent areas of special interest for the author.

Chapter 9

Language and Communication

INTRODUCTION

The next chapter will illustrate that close links exist between verbal language development and the development of self-control. In this sense language and individual thinking are very closely related. However, language arises in social contexts and acquiring a complex and creative system of verbal communication is one of the major achievements of human development. Although other organisms do have or can be taught systems of communication, none approaches the sophistication and flexibility of human language. It is almost one of the defining features of being 'human'. Language is essential for social adaptation, for relating to others, for expressing one's needs, for influencing the world around us.

Achievement in such an area of functioning is, therefore, essential for a person with learning disabilities. Yet of all the skills that must be acquired, language appears to present the greatest difficulty to those with such disabilities. It is failure in the verbal-academic aspects of the school curriculum that often identifies those who will be labelled as slow learners or mildly disabled. Among those identified as severely disabled language attainment often lags behind attainments in other areas of functioning (Lyle, 1961; Rosenberg, 1982). In this latter group up to one-third of those of school age are unable to produce recognizable words or to respond to simple instructions (Swann and Mittler, 1976). Understanding language development and language difficulties is a key area for efforts directed at helping improve the functioning and status of those with learning disabilties.

It is natural that in this endeavour as in others one should look to research on normal human development for ideas on both the content and method of help. This is an area of knowledge that has undergone rapid changes over the last twenty years. It is clear that the human language system can be viewed from a number of perspectives. The writings of Chomsky (e.g. 1965) drew attention to structural aspects of the language system, the rules which guide how sounds and words are combined — syntax. This was followed by a shift towards studying the meanings which are encoded in the language system — semantics (e.g. Miller and Yoder, 1974). Most recently attention has been drawn to the functions which language serves and the contextual determinants of what is said — pragmatics (e.g. Skinner, 1957; Bates, 1976; McLean and Snyder-McLean, 1984). Accompanying the shifts in perspective has been interest in the relationships between language and other areas of cognitive attainment such as concept formation and memory development, with considerable and continuing debate about the direction of any causal relationships (e.g. Cromer, 1974). Likewise Wing (1981) has drawn attention to the close relationship of language and social development. One final perspective is that derived from examination of the sound systems which underpin language — phonology. Thus there are many ways of looking at the development of normal human language and this can lead to the development of quite different 'curricula' for remediation.

The current emphasis upon pragmatic aspects of language is of particular interest for work with those who have severe learning disabilities. It accords well with the philosophy underlying many remedial efforts which focus upon the importance of social competence in 'normal' everyday environments. It emphasizes the embedding of language in social contexts. It also perhaps reflects the relative lack of success that language training efforts have achieved in the area of structural aspects of the language system (see Howlin, 1981). Most importantly, in drawing attention to the roots of communication in the earliest interactions of the child with its environment, long before the development of recognizable verbal language, the pragmatic perspective enables one to derive remedial strategies for those at the very earliest levels of development. The notion that the major functions of communication are expressed early, e.g. through gaze and hand gestures, and that later development serves to 'map' the more formal aspects of the language system on to these functions, is providing a major impetus in work with more severely disabled people (see Carr and Durand, 1984; Sternberg and Owens, 1985; Cirrin and Rowland, 1985).

Although it is clear that research on normal language development has an important contribution in suggesting suitable targets for remediation, its contribution to knowing how to achieve these targets is much more uncertain. Skinner's (1957) theoretical writing assigns a prime role to the environment in guiding language development via the processes of discrimination learning, stimulus control and reinforcement. Structuralists such as Chomsky rejected this notion and suggested instead that language development was controlled by an innate language acquisition device which was triggered by verbal input but otherwise was little controlled by environmental factors. This, of course, had the implication that little could be done in the event of damage to the device, damage such as one might expect to have occurred to people with severe learning difficulties. Others have adopted a midway position and looked for ways in which the environment might influence language development without determining it entirely. Bruner (1975) has drawn attention to important elements in the social context out of which communication skills develop — joint attention, shared activities, sensitive and responsive adults prepared to assign communicative significance to many aspects of the child's behaviour. From a quite different perspective the literature on institutionalization attests to the damaging effects that impoverished, unstimulating environments can inflict upon language development (e.g. Lyle, 1959, 1960). Other studies have sought to discover relationships at a more micro level between the type of language input to the child, the adult's way of responding to the child's initiations and specific aspects of the child's language development (e.g. the influence of adults' expansions of child utterances). However, at present far less is understood about *how* language is acquired under normal circumstances than about *what* is acquired (see Cromer, 1980).

LANGUAGE PROBLEMS AND SEVERE LEARNING DISABILITIES

The situation outlined in the introduction has meant that there are several views, sometimes contradictory, about how to conceptualize the language difficulties of those with general learning disabilities. At one level major debate has centred around whether the language development of people so affected is like that of others in terms of the stages of development and their ordering; or whether it is marked by deviant characteristics found rarely if at all in a non-impaired population. The point has been made frequently in this book that those labelled as having severe learning disabilities are an extremely diverse group of people so that a simple contrast of delay versus deviance applicable to the whole population is inappropriate. Much of the literature in this area has recently been reviewed by Rosenberg (1982). He points out that whatever evidence there is favours a developmental lag theory in the areas of syntax, semantics, phonology and pragmatics. However, it is also clear that language levels tend to remain lower than achievements in other areas of development, and that in some cases this discrepancy is very marked. A considerable number of this population fail altogether to develop useful language skills and there are others, often labelled as autistic, whose linguistic attainment may be marked by anomalies found only to a limited degree in the normal population (e.g. echolalia, prominal reversal, very restricted social usage of linguistic skills).

It would seem appropriate to move away from a simple delay versus deviance dichotomy. In a population with severe learning disabilities there will be some who are slow to develop but who pass through the normal stages, at least up to a certain point. However, there will be others suffering from specific linguistic-communicative impairments not explained in terms of overall rate of development. It might be helpful to look at the types of language disorders that can arise in the general population and map these on to the learning disabled population. Unfortunately there is as yet no agreed classification system for such language disorders. Martin (1980), in reviewing a large series of clinically referred cases of language difficulties, suggests a classificatory system based upon patterns of functioning in terms of chronological age, non-verbal level of development, verbal comprehension, verbal expression, hearing and speech. He indicates that most of his series could be subsumed under one of ten groupings (see Table 1). Fein *et al.* (1985) cluster analysed the cognitive test scores of 54 developmentally disabled children, many of whom were labelled autistic. They derived eight groups, not differentiated in terms of overall mental age, IQ or chronological age. Four of these are of particular interest from a language perspective. One group was marked by high non-verbal functioning and evenly low functioning in all areas of verbal development. A second group scored highest on non-verbal functioning and had comprehension skills exceeding their verbal expressive abilities. A third group were strongest in verbal areas but had relatively greater difficulty with expressive skills. A fourth group showed even development in all areas.

Cromer (1981) has offered a more theoretically based analysis of language problems and provided illustrations of how these can occur in practice. He points out firstly the need to understand the relationship between cognitive processes and language development. In particular he points to the link between concept formation and the semantic elements of a language system; and the role of memory which might be particularly influential upon the length and structural complexity of utterances. He also describes the different aspects of a language system which may be individually impaired — syntax, semantics, phonology and pragmatics. Of course, there remains the possibility of global impairments affecting all elements. By way of illustration he suggests that autistic children may experience particular difficulty with the pragmatic aspects of language whereas Down's syndrome children perhaps have difficulties with phonological aspects.

Although there are considerable differences in these approaches to classification there is also a considerable degree of overlap and it becomes possible to draw out a number of common threads which certainly coincide with experiences in clinical practice. It is worth stressing again that there is no simple correspondence between severe learning disability and a

Table 1
Ten Syndromes of Communication Disorders. (from Martin (1980) in Hersov,
Berger and Nicols (eds.) *Language and Language Disorders in Childhood*). Reproduced with
permission from the author and Pergamon Books Ltd.

Syndrome magnitude	VC	NVC	H	VX	S
1	2	0	2	2	1
2	0	0	0	0	1
	2	2	0	2	1
	0	0	0	2	1
	0	0	0	1	1
3	2	0	1	2	1
	0	0	1	0	0
	1	1	0	2	1
	2	1	0	2	1
	1	0	0	2	1

VC   verbal comprehension
NVC non-verbal comprehension
H   hearing
VX   verbal expression
S   speech

0   normal range of ability
1   moderate impairment
2   severe impairment

particular kind of language problem. For some there is a language delay. Others have language acquisition impaired by specific additional impairments which can accompany learning disabilities — hearing, visual and motor impairments being the most obvious. There are clearly also people who have a general learning disability and a specific language disorder; and as illustrated above such disorders may arise in several different forms.

In order to illustrate these different forms Table 2 sets out a number of groupings which are derived from the previously mentioned research and clinical experience. It must be stressed that these groupings are not meant to represent a comprehensive list of difficulties, nor are such groupings grounded in properly constructed research. However, it serves to illustrate the potential diversity of problems. This in its turn highlights the need to develop more adequate assessment methods in order to differentiate in objective fashion between such problems. This could be integrated with the findings from intervention research so that assessment and intervention can become linked in a more rational and individualized fashion (see later section).

Table 2 Problems in language and communication for the learning disabled

General Degree of Impairment	Verbal-Non-Verbal	Verbal-Comp. Exp.	Speech Sounds	Social	Imagina-tive Play	*Naturalistic*	*Sessional*
1. Moderate-severe	Even	VC=VX	/	/	/	Incidental teaching for semantic and pragmatic development	None
2. Profound	Even	VC=VX	/	/	X	Instruction following, vocal imitation, use of motor gestures and vocalizations	imitation – signing symbolic play Instruction
3. Moderate-severe	Even	VC<VX	/	/	/	Instruction following, concept formation	Verbal memory, verbal concepts
4. Moderate-severe	NV>V	VC=VX	/	X	X	Functional use of gestures and vocalization, joint activities to build sociability (adult and peer)	Vocal imitation, motor imitation – signing, symbolic play

#	General degree	Verbal–Non-Verbal	Verbal comp.–exp.	Speech sounds	Social	Imaginative play	Naturalistic	Sessional
5.	Moderate-severe	NV > V	VC >V	X	X	X	Functional use of gestures, joint activities to build sociability	Motor imitation – signing, symbolic play
6.	Moderate-severe	V NV	VC=V	/	/	/	Incidental teaching for semantic and pragmatic development	Concept formation
7.	Profound	NV >V	VC=V	X	X	X	Instruction following, functional use of gestures, joint activities to build sociability	Motor imitation – signing, symbolic play
8.	Profound	NV >V	VC >V	X	X	X	Functional use of gestures, joint activities to build sociability	Motor imitation – signing, symbolic play

LEGEND

General degree of impairment:	overall level of intellectual functioning
Verbal – Non-Verbal:	relative levels of development of verbal and non-verbal skills
Verbal comp. – exp.:	relative levels of development of verbal comprehension and expressive skills
Speech sounds:	whether speech sounds present (1) or not (X) in the individual's repertoire
Social:	whether individual is sociable (/) or impaired in social interactions (X)
Imaginative play:	whether individual shows evidence of symbolic, imaginative play (1) or not (X)
Naturalistic:	Interventions to be carried out in the individual's everyday environment(s)
Sessional:	Interventions to be carried out in specific training sessions

Up to this point language problems have been discussed primarily as a problem of individual functioning. The nature of the relationship between the environment and language development has already been mentioned as an area of considerable dispute. However, it is clear that people with learning disabilities have been exposed to environments that specifically impair language development, particularly large, unstimulating institutional settings (see earlier). It is equally clear that in these situations it is the least competent, i.e. those with the greatest language difficulty, who are exposed to the poorest quality linguistic input from their care staff (Grant and Moores, 1977; Raynes, Pratt and Roses, 1979). With the moves in many countries to run down such institutions and increase community provisions, it has been perhaps assumed that such problems no longer occur, i.e. community care is equated with high quality care. The general issues of environmental quality have been examined in Part 2 of this book but surprisingly little research has been conducted on the quality of the linguistic communicative environments to which people with learning disabilities are currently exposed. It has been shown at least with Down's syndrome children in the early years of life living at home, that their mothers are generally very sensitive to their developmental level and often provide language stimulation similar to that provided by the mothers of normal children at a simlar developmental level (Rondal, 1978; Buckholt, Rutherford and Goldberg, 1978; Mitchell, 1980). However, there is a tendency for the parental speech to be more directive with a large proportion of parent initiations; and for the child's communications to be less 'readable' for the parents so that some initiations by the child are not responded to (e.g. Dunst, 1985).

Research on teacher interaction with pupils who have severe learning disabilities suggests that the linguistic environment is marked by a high proportion of directive speech and low responsiveness to child initiations (Beveridge and Berry, 1977; Beveridge, Spencer and Mittler, 1978; Beveridge and Hurrell, 1980). How generalizable such findings are across age, diagnostic groups and living environments remains uncertain. It must also be stressed that it is not clear what impact such environmental factors are likely to have upon language development. However, developmental theorists (see Harris, 1984a) would certainly see such environments as inhibiting the development of a range of skills particularly in the areas of meaning and use. Such environments might also reduce overall level of child output and this must be of concern given the strong relationship between levels of output and development of linguistic complexity (Hart and Risley, 1980; Rogers-Warren and Warren, 1981).

These findings act as a reminder that in studying and understanding the communication difficulties of people with severe learning disabilities one must look at the nature of the environment to which people are exposed as well as the levels of functioning of the individuals. There are likely to be complex interactions between these two sets of factors which will also need to be understood if comprehensive approaches to remediation are to be adopted. As in other areas, development of remediational strategies has proceeded relatively independently of research on normal language acquisition and the nature and type of 'communication disorders'; and as in other areas there is a need for this gap to be bridged.

LANGUAGE REMEDIATION STRATEGIES

Language remediation with people who have severe learning disabilities was dominated initially by operant-behavioural approaches. However, there has been some influence from more developmentally oriented researchers who have sought to integrate knowledge from normal child development into strategies of help. There is, therefore, some diversity in strategies used and such diversity can be seen in several different areas:

1. *Curriculum:* Published work on language training suggests either explicitly or implicitly widely different curricula. The early behavioural programmes (e.g. Bricker, 1972; Guess, Sailor and Baer, 1976) laid strong emphasis upon a logical analysis of what skills were required of the learner and then teaching them in the sequence dictated by logic. Particularly strong emphasis was laid upon the role of imitation both of motor movements and of sounds although the role of imitation in normal language acquisition is not so central. Subsequent research has shown that motor and verbal imitation usually function as independent response classes (e.g. Garcia, Baer and Firestone, 1971). Nevertheless, imitation skills are an important early curriculum target of many logical-behaviour approaches and form a major method for teaching subsequent skills (see next section).

   Others have suggested curricula based upon the normal sequence of language development (see Yule and Berger, 1975). Within this group there has been variation in emphasis upon the different aspects of the language system — structure, meaning, function and the cognitive and social factors intimately related to language and communication (see Harris, 1984b, for a useful review of language training programmes). The recent growth in emphasis upon pragmatic aspects of language has seen the extension of the developmental curricula to include early pre-verbal forms of communication as legitimate targets for training (see McLean and Snyder-McLean, 1978; Sternberg and Owens, 1985; Cirrin and Rowland, 1985). There is as yet no research comparing the impact of different curriculum models and the instructional sequences that they imply (see Goetz, Schuler and Sailor, 1979).

2. *Teaching methods:* The early behavioural training studies relied heavily upon a discrimination learning paradigm, using the instructional tactics found effective in other skill areas. Thus there was emphasis upon restricting stimulus input, directly eliciting language or receptive responses through verbal instruction, questioning, demonstrating and physical prompting. Powerful reinforcers were used to immediately follow desired behaviour. Research on teaching methods within this framework has looked at the effects of teaching several responses at the same time as opposed to teaching one at a time, at whether each response should have a distinctive reinforcer of its own, and at whether reinforcers which are 'naturally' linked to the behaviour (e.g. saying 'ball' being reinforced by having a ball to play with) are more effective than those which are 'arbitrarily' linked (saying 'ball' followed by a spoon of ice cream). More recently interest has moved to looking at different stimulus control tactics which might enhance language development, e.g. use of pauses by teachers to allow initiation by the child, use of questioning following (rather than preceding) child initiations (Hart and Risley, 1975, 1980; Halle, Baer and Spradlin, 1981).

   More developmentally oriented researchers (e.g. Jones and Robson, 1979; Rutter, 1980; McLean and Snyder-McLean, 1984; Harris, 1984a) have suggested a number of other tactics which might enhance language development: simplifying input, repetition of the child's utterances, paraphrasing by the adult of the child's utterances, semantic expansion by the adult, responsiveness to communicative intent (rather than form) and establishment of joint social interactions. These remain as yet interesting possibilities untested for their impact upon people with severe learning disabilities.

3. *Teaching contexts:* The highly structured behavioural tactics outlined above have often been associated with individual sessional teaching in special teaching areas using a repeated trials procedure, i.e. the same response being elicited many times over within a session. Typically, also, the role of the student is relatively passive, being a respondent to the teacher's initiations. Several shortcomings of such an approach have been suggested. In the first place there often appears to be a lack of spontaneous generalization from the teaching contexts to more natural communicative contexts (see Garcia and De Haven, 1974; Goetz, Schuler and Sailor, 1979). This certainly does not invalidate such an approach as there are no other demonstrably effective strategies which do not suffer similar problems. However, it suggests the need to look at variables which improve generalization. The question of student passivity is

perhaps much more serious in that much of what is involved in communicative competence is the ability to initiate and comprehend utterances in dialogue contexts (Jones and Robson, 1979). These issues have stimulated interest in what has been called 'incidental' teaching, i.e. using the student's spontaneous initiations as the signal for the onset of training. This requires environments which are laid out to encourage opportunities for communication, e.g. favourite items visible but out of reach; adults who are clear about the student's current level of functioning and the next step in the learning sequence to be taught; and the use of 'naturalistic' stimulus control and reinforcement strategies (see above). As yet such approaches and their effects have only been well documented with pre-school disadvantaged children but their value at least with children whose level of disability is moderate is also suggested by Cheseldine and McConkey (1979) and Halle, Baer and Spradlin (1981).

THE EFFECTS OF LANGUAGE REMEDIATION

Attempts to influence directly the language skills of people with severe learning disabilities have been very diverse involving many combinations of curriculum, teaching method and teaching context. The students included in such work have ranged from young disadvantaged children to profoundly involved adults. In attempting to review the literature a number of methodological shortcomings are apparent. Many of these shortcomings have been raised in the context of other research areas discussed in this book. Thus subjects reported in research studies on communication skills are often poorly described in terms of level of functioning and types of disability. Independent variables are often described too imprecisely to permit others to replicate studies. The dependent variables measured are often extremely limited with little attempt to measure generalization across time, settings and people. Measurement procedures themselves are often subject to major potential error factors such as the lack of 'blind' assessment. Most studies have been carried out upon single cases or very small numbers of students, often using time-series designs. There are few group controlled studies. Likewise there are few studies lasting longer than a few months so that little is known about the long-term impact of any gains made — whether progress is maintained and what subsequent developments occur. Thus tentative conclusions will be offered although it is clear that very little can be said with any certainty (see Garcia and De Haven, 1974; Goetz, Schuler and Sailor, 1979; Howlin, 1981; Harris, 1984a,b; Mowrer, 1984, for useful reviews).

There are examples of operant sessional training effectively establishing within sessions a very wide range of receptive and expressive skills, including rule-governed grammatical forms such as plurals and verb tense endings. Such training often shows evidence of spontaneous generalization to other examples of the trained class within the training context. Hard evidence of spontaneous use of trained skills in natural contexts is not readily available although it is often stated that such generalization is the exception rather than the rule.

As regards specific teaching methods there is evidence that training in motor imitation does not facilitate verbal imitation; and that training receptive skills does not generalize to expressive skills, although the converse may not be true, i.e. teaching expressive skills may generalize to receptive skills (e.g. Watters, Wheeler and Watters, 1981). Teaching several responses concurrently and using multiple stimulus exemplars appear to be useful strategies and naturalistic and/or response-specific reinforcers appear more powerful than arbitrary reinforcers.

Incidental teaching strategies appear very powerful in raising the frequency of student initiations; and Hart and Risley (1980) found a strong correlation between the amount of talking and its degree of linguistic complexity. With the disadvantaged children that they studied Hart and Risley found that the impact of incidental teaching on these variables was far greater than the effect of individual sessional language training. Incidental teaching also seemed to lead to generalization of improvements beyond the exact responses that were targeted in the incidental teaching.

Although comparative studies are few, systematic and structured approaches to teaching do seem to achieve more in the short term than general attention or verbal enrichment (e.g. Nelson et al., 1976; Fenn, 1976). But it must also be said that many people with severe learning disabilities do acquire good grammatical speech without systematic teaching (see Howlin, 1981). Likewise there are some people who fail to make significant progress despite intensive individual training along operant lines (Lovaas, 1977; Ashdown, 1980; Howlin, 1981; Sailor, 1982).

In terms of curriculum goals there is more evidence to favour the impact of training upon the semantic content and functional use of speech than upon syntactic structure (see Hemsley et al., 1978).

Initial functional level is an important predictor of outcome. Children who have speech, even if echolalic, do better than those who are mute irrespective of whether they are exposed to systematic teaching (Howlin, 1981). Of those who lack any functional speech, people who have verbal imitative skills respond better to receptive language training (Carr, Prida and Dores, 1984). It is clear that the group for whom current training practices have been least effective are those who lack functional speech and who also make very few speech-related sounds. Such factors are not always associated with very low developmental levels (Carr *et al.*, 1984).

It is clear from this very brief review that there is as much diversity in outcome of training as there is diversity in the training itself. Earlier sections of this chapter sought to illustrate the wide range of communicative difficulties that are likely to be found in people with severe learning difficulties. Thus the question as to whether language training 'works' for such people has gradually become meaningless. It is rather a question of which aspects of communication in which clients respond to which interventions at which time in development.

In order to see what this might mean in practice Table 2 includes suggestions of how training approaches could be matched up to the specific types of disorder presented. It also illustrates the relevance of intervention in other areas of development (cognitive and social) so that communication is located within a broad context (see Introduction). Again it must be stressed that these suggestions are not in any way validated but are merely there to exemplify the diversity that is required once a framework is adopted which incorporates many individual differences. For example, in the table it is suggested that those who have language developing at a slow rate through the normal stages might benefit from naturalistic training strategies focused upon expanding semantic and pragmatic aspects of the language system. Such intervention would also probably raise the frequency of talking and hence facilitate grammatic complexity. Those at the early stages of verbal development may benefit from sessional imitation training and training in functional usage in order to get words into the repertoire that could be worked on through naturalistic teaching.

People with very few speech sounds in their repertoire may benefit from teaching focused upon following instructions and from naturalistic strategies that would reinforce pre-verbal forms of communication such as pointing, gazing or leading by the hand. Sometimes such strategies will have to be built around highly idiosyncratic wishes of the students such as the desire for string with which to twiddle. These are just a few examples and others are offered in the body of the table itself.

One important source of diversification in this area of work has been the development of approaches which are not based purely upon verbal language. This springs from a number of sources. As there has been a growing recognition of the individuality of people with severe learning disabilities there has been a heightened awareness of the needs of those who are deaf as well as having learning disabilities. Clearly, people who are deaf may have sign language as an alternative to the use of verbal language; and there is no *a priori* reason why this should be excluded for people who suffer from deafness and generalized learning disabilities. Research on the pragmatic aspects of language has drawn attention to the fact that in normal development communicative functions are expressed early through a range of gestures and non-verbal signals and this has also focused attention beyond the purely verbal system. A third factor has arisen from attempts to explore the possibility of animals, in particular primates, acquiring complex communicative skills. Such endeavours have necessitated the use of non-verbal systems such as signs or symbols as the vocal apparatus of these organisms is not suited to speech production (e.g. Gardner and Gardner, 1969; Premack and Premack, 1974). Finally, the failure of some people to benefit from systematic verbally based language training programmes has spurred interest in alternative approaches. Thus, for a number of reasons there has been a rapidly growing interest in the use of augmentative systems of communication, in particular sign and symbol systems, with those who have severe learning disabilities. Sometimes these are used as an alternative to verbal approaches, more commonly they are used as augmentative systems in conjunction with speech (see Kiernan, 1977, 1983; Carr, 1979; Bonvillian, Nelson and Rhyne, 1981; Musselwhite and St Louis, 1982; Remington and Light, 1983, for useful reviews in this area).

AUGMENTATIVE SYSTEMS OF COMMUNICATION

The reasons underlying interest in such systems have been outlined above and their use in practice has grown rapidly, in a relatively unplanned way, with little in the way of research-based knowledge to guide practice. As in the field of verbally based training reported programmes vary along a number of dimensions:

1. *Curriculum:* There has been a very wide range of sign and symbol systems used. Two natural sign languages for the deaf (American and British) have been used; and there have been a number of adaptations of these languages using the signs but imposing the word order and other syntactic constraints of spoken English, e.g. Signing Exact English, the Makaton vocabulary. The hand signals developed by American Indians who themselves spoke different languages have also been used. There are examples of specifically designed sign systems such as the Paget–Gorman system, based very much upon the form of spoken English. Among symbol systems, use has been made of pictures, Bliss symbols, and the arbitrary plastic symbols designed by Premack for his research on communication with primates. Of course, the written word is just such a symbol system; and the use also of a Rebus system, which

combines elements of picture symbols and written letters, has been suggested. In England and Wales such diversity in practice has decreased over the last few years as two clear 'market leaders' have emerged (Jones, Reid and Kiernan, 1982). These are the Makaton vocabulary and Bliss symbols, with schools designated for those with severe learning disabilities favouring signs, schools designated for the physically disabled favouring symbols. In the case of the former schools a large majority (about 75 per cent) report on some use of signing.

2. *Teaching method:* Published research often specifies poorly how augmentative systems are taught to students; but in general it seems that behavioural methods are used in much the same way as in verbal language training programmes with use of discrimination training, imitation, prompting and reinforcement techniques.

3. *Teaching contexts:* Many reported studies rely upon sessional training although some do report on the use of augmentative systems throughout the students' natural environment. Most seem to combine spoken language alongside the augmentative system. The survey of schools reported by Jones *et al.* (1982) indicates that as regards signing, only one-half of the schools reported that all staff members within a classroom used the system, only one-quarter indicated that all staff members within the school used the system, and only 10 per cent reported that there was use of the system by other children in the class.

It would seem clear therefore that much training takes place in relative isolation.

As with the verbal teaching studies people have been involved at all ages and at all levels and types of ability. Likewise, reported studies suffer from all the methodological defects outlined earlier. In particular there is an almost complete lack of controlled comparative studies, longitudinal studies, or studies on the natural spontaneous use of taught augmentative systems. Again these must be borne in mind when interpreting the general conclusions which can be drawn from presently available research.

Two major claims are made for augmentative systems. One is that they may be acquired as a useful form of communication. Secondly, it is sometimes claimed that the acquisition of such an augmentative system will also facilitate the development of speech. Clearly these are rather different aims and individual studies do not always distinguish between them. Certainly such systems have been used and success in their acquisition has been reported at all levels of ability. Bonvillian, Nelson and Rhyne (1981) suggest that in most sign studies students do master five or more signs. It is clear that outcome is better for children who are more able, particularly in terms of their verbal comprehension and verbal imitation. As with verbal language some also fail altogether to acquire signs or symbols (e.g. Carr and

Dores, 1981). This is particularly important in view of what has been shown with verbal language studies, i.e. that some will do well or badly irrespective of training input and that level of initial functioning is a very important predictor of long-term outcome. This highlights the need for controlled comparative research. Studies of generalization in the use of augmentative systems are almost entirely lacking although there are anecdotal reports on usage in spontaneous communication and generative usage of abstract concepts and syntax in sign systems (Carr, 1979). It does seem at least at the level of understanding signs, that students who lack functional speech and are poor at verbal imitation and who fail to master verbal understanding, may make progress in understanding signs (Carr, Prida and Dores, 1984). This would seem to be a particularly important finding and suggests that signing may have a distinctive contribution to a group which is unlikely to do well on purely verbal training methods. Whether signing also has a distinctive contribution to those who would do well on other approaches to training remains an open question.

However, it has been found that involvement in augmentative pro-grammes does not inhibit speech (Carr, 1979; Kiernan, 1983). It has also been shown in an experimental study by Reid (1983), using contrived signs and nonsense syllables, that the signs were learned faster as names for cartoon characters and that sign learning facilitated later learning of word labels. It will be interesting to see if such a finding could be replicated in applied programmes.

The research studies in this area offer little guidance as to which particular system is the most useful. There are no studies comparing augmentative or total communication training with purely verbal training: likewise there are no studies comparing different sign systems or sign-with-symbol systems. Nevertheless, there is a body of knowledge available, not directly related to the applied research, which offers some guidance about system selection. From a purely logical point of view symbol systems offer a number of advantages. They make a lower demand upon memory capacities, an important point given the difficulties that some people with learning disabilities may experience in this area (see Chapter 3). Symbol systems also make a lower demand upon imitation and motor skills, and enable very direct representation of syntactic rules such as word order. They require fewer social skills as immediate audience attention is not required, i.e. the communication is in the form of a permanent product available for inspection at any time. Symbol systems permit less ambiguity and can be linked very directly into well-recognized and understood communication systems such as pictures and words. It does seem rather surprising that symbol systems have attracted less attention than signs. Their main limitations are the restrictions imposed by having a limited set of communication elements available at any one time. Portability is also a problem in that a board and symbols must be present for communication to occur; but this would not seem to be an insurmountable problem outweighing all the many apparent advantages. This represents a good example of how research could help establish the validity (or otherwise) of the clear preference that is shown by teachers and language therapists for sign systems.

Sign systems themselves vary considerably and Kiernan (1983) reviews work, including that by himself and his colleagues, on features which determine ease of learning. For example, flat and fist hands are relatively easy postures to learn. Signs which involve one hand or both hands doing the same thing are easier than signs which involve each hand performing a different action. The degree to which a sign looks like the object that it represents (iconicity) or the likelihood that a naive observer will understand the sign (transparency) seem to have very little relationship to ease of acquisition. Kiernan (1983) stresses the value of adopting an information-processing approach in deciding the need for augmentative systems and to guide selection of a particular system. He suggests that there may be modality preferences which reflect stable individual differences in information processing. Thus, if an individual shows a preference for the visual modality, this might be taken to indicate the importance of using a sign or symbol system in communication. Alternatively, it might indicate the need to teach better attention to and processing of auditory information. In practice perhaps both strategies will be needed as the development of speech and verbal understanding must remain the main aim wherever possible if the integration of people with learning disabilities into wider society is to be assisted.

In addition to research on formal sign and symbol systems, research upon the pragmatic aspects of early communication in normal development has drawn attention to the general importance of non-verbal signals, (such as gaze and pointing). Recently the possible remedial significance of this has begun to be recognized. Clearly such a recognition has been aided by the fact that some people make as little progress with signing as they do with verbal training (a fact known more in practice than from reading the literature). Thus attention has been drawn to more 'natural' gestures and movements to see if these form an easier response class for training and strengthening in communicative contexts (see Cirrin and Rowland, 1985; Sternberg and Owens, 1985). The value of this approach is not yet established but marks an important extension of the 'communication curriculum' to take in those with the most profound degrees of disability.

Thus the area of augmentative communication is an exciting but rather confused one. It certainly offers another option in remediation but its precise and distinctive contribution has yet to be clearly established. However, if it is taken to include the use of more natural non-verbal signals, such systems may well have something to offer to those people who experience the greatest difficulties in verbal communication and do worst on verbally oriented training programmes.

CONCLUSIONS

Over the last twenty years the area of human language functioning and its remediation has seen an explosion of ideas and knowledge. In a comparatively short period of time the field of severe learning disability has passed through a phase of 'nothing can be done' to early tentative steps of limited remediation based upon operant laboratory tactics, and on to the enormous diversity in curriculum content, teaching methods and teaching contexts outlined in this chapter. It is clear that at all ages and all levels of ability people with severe learning disabilities can be helped to improve their language functioning; and that if the routes to verbal language are blocked for whatever reason there may be viable alternatives or supplements. At the same time it is clear that the language difficulties experienced are many and diverse. There is a lack of any adequate conceptual framework for interpreting this diversity. It is also clear that some people progress well without highly specific and intensive interventions; conversely, some people progress very slowly despite highly specific and intensive intervention. It thus becomes critical to engage in careful, controlled research to evaluate different programmes in relation to the various client groups — to find out who needs which programme at which point in development. The extraordinary and unsupported claims made for various programmes and approaches serve only to imperil this enterprise, with everyday practice being dictated by fashion rather than fact.

But as well as the need for better quality research on the impact of specific intervention strategies, there is a need to define the enterprise in a broader context. Language and communication development cannot be viewed in isolation from other aspects of cognitive development such as general symbolic capacities, memory and concept formation. Thus 'cognitive' interventions might be as important as 'language' interventions for some individuals. Most importantly the growing emphasis upon pragmatics stresses the interdependence of social and communication development. There can be no communication development where there is neither the wish nor the need to communicate. For those who suffer specific impairments in social development (often labelled as autistic) intervention will need to be targeted upon helping them to understand people, to interact with people and enjoy people if attempts to improve communication skills are to have any real chance of success.

Finally, the context in which communication skills are analysed must be broadened to include more general aspects of the living environment — What needs and opportunities are there to communicate? What are the attitudes and expectations of significant others? How responsive are others to initiations? What sorts of communication models are available?

Unless language and communication are viewed within this broader context, then it will be difficult to understand individual differences and to develop intervention strategies likely to achieve lasting and generalized progress. Language and communication together comprise perhaps the most central and complex area of need for people with severe learning disabilities. Many exciting developments have occurred, but these represent only a small beginning, a start in the process of developing a comprehensive strategy for help. Further progress will be dependent upon the closer integration of work from developmental, experimental, social and applied psychology — problems of communication and generalization are not confined to people with severe learning disabilities!

REFERENCES

Ashdown, R.W. (1980) The development of language skills of severely educationally subnormal children in a hospital setting. Unpublished Ph.D. Thesis, Faculty of Education, University College, Cardiff.

Bates, E. (1976) *Language and Context.* New York: Academic press.

Beveridge, M.C., and Berry, R. (1977) Observing interactions in severely mentally handicapped children. *Research in Education,* **17,** 13–22.

Beveridge, M., and Hurrell, P. (1980) Teacher's responses to severely mentally handicapped children's initiations in the classroom. *Journal of Child Psychology and Psychiatry,* **21,** 175–181.

Beveridge, M., Spencer, J., and Mittler, P. (1978) Language and social behaviour in severely educationally subnormal children. *British Journal of Social and Clinical Psychology,* **17,** 75–83.

Bonvillian, J.D., Nelson, K.E., and Rhyne, J.M. (1981) Sign language and autism. *Journal of Autism and Developmental Disorders,* **11,** 125–139.

Bricker, W.A. (1972) A systematic approach to language training. In R.L. Schiefelbusch (ed.) *Language of the Mentally Retarded.* Baltimore: University Park Press.

Bruner, J.S. (1975) The ontogenesis of speech acts. *Journal of Child Language,* **2,** 1–19.

Buckholt, J.A., Rutherford, R.B., and Goldberg, K.E. (1978) Verbal and non-verbal interaction of mothers with their Down's Syndrome and non-retarded infants. *American Journal of Mental Deficiency,* **82,** 337–343.

Carr, E.G. (1979) Teaching autistic children to use sign language: some research issues. *Journal of Autism and Developmental Disorders,* **9,** 345–359.

Carr, E.G., and Dores, P.A. (1981) Patterns of language acquisition following simultaneous communication with autistic children. *Analysis and Intervention in Developmental Disabilities,* **1,** 1–15.

Carr, E.G., and Durand, V.M. (1984) The social communicative basis of severe behavior problems in children. In S. Reiss and R. Bootzin (eds) *Theoretical Issues in Behavior Therapy*. New York: Academic Press.

Carr, E.G., Prida, L.C., and Dores, P.A. (1984) Speech versus sign comprehension in autistic children: analysis and prediction. *Journal of Experimental Child Psychology*, **37**, 587–597.

Charlop, M.H. (1983) The effects of echolalia on acquisition and generalization of receptive labelling in autistic children. *Journal of Applied Behaviour Analysis*, **16**, 111–126.

Cheseldine, S., and McConkey, R. (1979) Parental speech to young Down's Syndrome children: an intervention study. *American Journal of Mental Deficiency*, **83**, 612–620.

Chomsky, N. (1965) *Aspects of the Theory of Syntax*. Cambridge: MIT Press.

Cirrin, F.M., and Rowland, C.M. (1985) Communicative assessment of non-verbal youths with severe/profound mental retardation. *Mental Retardation*, **23**, 52–62.

Cromer, R.F. (1974) The development of language and cognition: the cognition hypothesis. In B. Foss (ed.) *New Perspectives in Child Development*. Harmondsworth: Penguin.

Cromer, R.F. (1980) Normal language development: recent progress. In L. Hersov, M. Berger and A.R. Nicol (eds) *Language and Language Disorders in Childhood*. Oxford: Pergamon.

Cromer, R.F. (1981) Developmental language disorders: cognitive processes, semantics, pragmatics, phonology and syntax. *Journal of Autism and Developmental Disorders*, **11**, 57–75.

Dunst, C.J. (1985) Communicative competence and deficits: effects on early social interactions. In E. McDonald and D. Gallagher (eds) *Facilitating Social Emotional Development in Multiply Handicapped Children*. Philadelphia: Home of the Merciful Saviour for Crippled Children.

Fein, D., Waterhouse, L., Lucci, D., and Snyder, D. (1985) Cognitive sub-types in developmentally disabled children: a pilot study. *Journal of Autism and Developmental Disorders*, **19**, 77–95.

Fenn, G. (1976) Against verbal enrichment. In P. Berry (ed.) *Language and Communication in the Mentally Handicapped*. London: Edward Arnold.

Garcia, E., Baer, D.M., and Firestone, I. (1971) The development of generalized imitation within topographcally determined boundaries. *Journal of Applied Behaviour Analysis*, **4**, 101–113.

Garcia, E.G., and De Haven, E.D. (1974) Use of operant techniques in the establishment and generalization of language: a review and analysis. *American Journal of Mental Deficiency*, **79**, 169–178.

Gardner, A., and Gardner, B. (1969) Teaching sign language to a chimpanzee. *Science*, **165**, 664–672.

Goetz, L., Schuler, A., and Sailor, W. (1979) Teaching functional speech to the severely handicapped: Current issues. *Journal of Autism and Developmental Disorders*, **9**, 325–342.

Grant, G.W.R., and Moores, B. (1977) Resident characteristics and staff behaviour in two hospitals for the mentally retarded. *American Journal of Mental Deficiency*, **82**, 259–265.

Guess, D., Sailor, W., and Baer, D.M. (1976). Functional Speech and Language Training for the Severely handicapped. Lawrence, Kansas: H & H Enterprises.

Halle, J.W., Baer, D.M., and Spradlin, J.E. (1981) Teacher's generalized use of delay as a stimulus control procedure to increase language use in handicapped children. *Journal of Applied Behaviour Analysis*, **14**, 389–409.

Harris, J. (1984a) Teaching children to develop language: the impossible dream? In D.J. Muller (ed.) *Remediating Children's Language: behavioural and naturalistic approaches.* London: Croom Helm.

Harris, J. (1984b) Early language intervention programmes: An update. *Association for Child Psychology and Psychiatry Newsletter,* **6**, 2–20.

Hart, B., and Risley, T.R. (1975) Incidental teaching of language in the pre-school. *Journal of Applied Behaviour Analysis,* **8**, 411–420.

Hart, B., and Risley, T.R. (1980) In vivo language intervention: unanticipated general effects. *Journal of Applied Behaviour Analysis,* **13**, 407–432.

Hemsley, R., Howlin, P., Berger, M., Hersov, L., Holbrook, D., Rutter, M., and Yule, W. (1978) Treating autistic children in a family context. In M. Rutter and E. Schopler (eds) *Autism: A Reappraisal of Concepts and Treatment.* New York: Plenum Press.

Howlin, P. (1981) The effectiveness of operant language training with autistic children. *Journal of Autism and Developmental Disorders,* **11**, 89–106.

Jones, L., Reid, B., and Kiernan, C. (1982) Signs and symbols: the 1980 survey. *Special Education: Forward Trends,* **9**, 34–37.

Jones, A., and Robson, C. (1979) Language training for the severely mentally handicapped. In N.R. Ellis (ed.) *Handbook of Mental Deficiency: Psychological Theory and Research.* New Jersey: Laurence Erlbaum Associates.

Kiernan, C. (1977) Alternatives to speech: a review of research on manual and other forms of communication with the mentally handicapped and other non-communicating populations. *British Journal of Mental Subnormality,* **23**, 8–24.

Kiernan, C. (1983) The exploration of sign and symbol effects. In J. Hogg and P. Mittler (eds) *Advances in Mental Handicap Research,* Vol. 2. Chichester: Wiley.

Kiernan, C. (1984) Language remediation programmes: a review. In D.J. Muller (ed.) *Remediating Children's Language: behavioural and naturalistic approaches.* London: Croom Helm.

Lovaas, O.I. (1977) *The Autistic Child: Language Development Through Behaviour Modification.* New York: Wiley.

Lyle, J.G. (1959) The effect of an institution environment upon the verbal development of imbecile children: I. Verbal intelligence. *Journal of Mental Deficiency Research,* **3**, 122–128.

Lyle, J.G. (1960) The effect of an institution environment upon the verbal development of imbecile children: II. Speech and language. *Journal of Mental Deficiency Research,* **4**, 1–13.

Lyle, J.G. (1961) Comparison of the language of normal and imbecile children. *Journal of Mental Deficiency Research,* **5**, 40–51.

McLean, I., and Snyder-McLean, L.K. (1984) Recent developments in pragmatics: remedial implications. In D.J. Muller (ed.) *Remediating Children's Language: behavioural and naturalistic approaches.* London: Croom Helm.

Martin, J.A.M. (1980) Syndrome delineation in communication disorders. In L.A. Hersov, M. Berger and A.R. Nicol (eds) *Language and Language Disorders in Childhood.* Oxford: Pergamon.

Miller, J., and Yoder, D. (1974) An ontogenetic language teaching strategy for retarded children. In R. Schiefelbusch and L. Lloyd (eds) *Language perspectives: Acquisition, Retardation and Intervention.* Baltimore: University Park Press.

Mitchell, D.R. (1980) Down's Syndrome children in structured dyadic communication situations with their parents. In J. Hogg and P. Mittler (eds) *Advances in Mental Handicap Research,* Vol. 1. Chichester: Wiley.

Mowrer, D.E. (1984) Behavioural approaches to treating language disorders. In D.J.

Muller (ed) *Remediating Children's Language: Behavioural and naturalistic approaches*. London: Croom Helm.

Musselwhite, C.R., and St Louis, K.W. (1982) *Communication Programming for the Severely Handicapped: Vocal and non-vocal strategies*. San Diego: College Hill Press.

Nelson, R.O., Peoples, A., Johnson, L.R., and Hay, W. (1976) The effectiveness of speech training techniques based on operant conditioning: a comparison of two methods. *Mental Retardation*, June, 34–38.

Premack, D., and Premack, A.J. (1974) Teaching visual language to apes and language deficient persons. In R.L. Schiefelbusch and L.L. Lloyd (eds) *Language Perspectives: Acquisition, retardation and intervention*. London: Macmillan.

Raynes, N.V., Pratt, M.W., and Roses, S. (1979) *Organisational Structure and the Care of the Mentally Retarded*. London: Croom Helm.

Reid, B.D. (1983) The acquisition and recall of spoken words and manual signs by mentally handicapped children. In J. Berg (ed) *Perspectives and Progress in Mental Retardation*: Proceedings of the Sixth Congress of the International Association for the Scientific Study of Mental Defiency. Baltimore: University Park Press.

Remington, R., and Light, P. (1983) Some problems in the evaluation of research on non-oral communication systems. In J. Hogg and P. Mittler (eds) *Advances in Mental Handicap Research*, Vol. 2. Chichester: Wiley.

Rogers-Warren, A., and Warren, S.E. (1981) Form and function in language learning and generalization. *Analysis and Intervention in Developmental Disabilities*, **1**, 389–404.

Rondal, J.A. (1978) Patterns of correlations for various language measures in mother–child interactions for normal and Down's Syndrome children. *Language and Speech*, **21**, 242–252.

Rosenberg, S. (1982) The langue of the mentally retarded: development, processes, and intervention. In S. Rosenberg (ed) *Handbook of Applied Psycholinguistics*. Hillsdale, NJ: Erlbaum.

Rutter, M. (1980) Language training with autistic children: how does it work and what does it achieve? In L.A. Hersov, M. Berger and A.R. Nicol (eds) *Language and Language Disorders in Childhood*. Oxford: Pergamon.

Sailor, W. (1982) Functional competence: issues in the teaching of a first vocabulary to severely handicapped students. Paper presented at the Sixth International Conference of the IASSMD, Toronto.

Seibert, J.M., and Oller, D.K. (1981) Linguistic pragmatics and language intervention strategies. *Journal of Autism and Developmental Disorders*, **11**, 75–88.

Skinner, B.F. (1957) *Verbal Behavior*. New York: Appleton-Century-Crofts.

Sternberg, L., and Owens, A. (1985) Establishing pre-language signalling behaviour with profoundly mentally handicapped students: a prelimary investigation. *Journal of Mental Deficiency Research*, **25**, 81–93.

Swann, W., and Mittler, P. (1976) Language abilities of ESN(S) children. *Special Education*, **5**, 24–27.

Watters, R.G., Wheeler, L.J., and Watters, W.E. (1981) The relative efficacy of two orders for training autistic children in the expressive and receptive use of manual signs. *Journal of Communication Disorders*, **14**, 273–285.

Wing, L. (1981) Language, social and cognitive impairments in autism and severe mental retardation. *Journal of Autism and Developmental Disorders*, **11**, 31–43.

Yule, W., and Berger, M. (1975) Communication, language and behaviour modification. In C.C. Kiernan and C.P. Woodford (eds) *Behaviour Modification with the Severely Retarded*. Elsevier, North Holland: Associated Scientific Publishers.

Chapter 10

Self-Control

INTRODUCTION

The term 'self-control' can have many different meanings. It will be used in this chapter to refer to that broad range of skills which enables the individual to monitor and direct his/her own behaviour. This will include the skills required to tackle and solve new problems as well as those required to deploy behaviours already in the individual's repertoire. The concept includes the skills themselves and the locus of control over their usage — that is, they are directed by the individual as opposed to some external source.

The development of self-control is of great importance for both philosophical and psychological reasons. Western capitalist societies strongly emphasize the value of the individual and personal achievement. A critical theme in the history of these societies is the struggle to establish the rights and freedoms of the individual against the coercive powers of the State and other minority interest forces. It is individual attainment, both economic and otherwise, which is highly valued; and the rise of the so-called meritocracy is marked by efforts to clear arbitrary obstacles from the path of the individual. Along with these values comes a concept of the individual as both capable of, and responsible for, directing his or her own destiny. Thus status is accorded not just in terms of attainment but how that attainment is reached. The self-made person has high status in many Western capitalist societies.

It is a central aspect of the philosophy of normalization that people with impairments and disabilities should acquire the skills and behaviours regarded as valuable by the society in which they live. If the status of disabled people is to be raised in societies such as those described above, then acquiring the capacity for self-direction will be important.

There are, in addition, more mundane psychological reasons behind the growing interest in the development of self-management skills. At several points in the chapters on teaching new skills and managing problem behaviours, reference was made to difficulties in generalizing progress It may be difficult to get a behaviour change to maintain over time. It may be difficult to get changes made in one situation to generalize to other situations — other places, other people, other times. It may be difficult to get a specific change in behaviour to generalize and be incorporated into other skills where the behaviour is relevant. For example, teaching someone to thread beads does not necessarily help that person learn to do up buttons, even though there are a number of common skill components. If this problem of generalization cannot be overcome then it begins to look as though development for people with severe learning disabilities will require a never-ending amount of specific skill teaching and a very detailed structuring of every aspect of their lives for all time. If, however, one could teach the learner to absorb more general principles of problem- solving, to analyse situations, to know when and how to initiate required skills and behaviours, and to gain insight into and monitor his or her own behaviour, then there may be some prospect of more generalized behaviour change.

The failure to resolve satisfactorily these difficulties in generalization raises the third and most fundamental reason for underlying interest in self-control. If effecting useful generalization requires the life-long commitment to teaching and environmental structuring outlined above, then economic issues become pertinent. It seems quite unlikely that society will make available the manpower and other material resources required for such an endeavour. The basic economic limitations create pressure for an alternative approach to learning and development, and the general area of self-control offers one such possibility.

Although there are many reasons for taking an interest in self-control, work at present remains rather unfocused. There is enormous variation in the theoretical background to published work. There is enormous variation in the specific skills targeted for teaching and in the skills and behaviours which are the object of such self-control procedures. The next section will provide an overview of some aspects of this variation and the chapter will then go on to look at the empirical studies which have been carried out within the various experimental traditions.

CONCEPTS OF SELF-CONTROL: AN OVERVIEW

The development of self-control has been studied in a variety of ways. One area of variation has been the type of skills referred to as 'self-control'.

Defining the Skills of 'Self-control'

Four traditions can be distinguished in the literature: cognitive–experimental; operant–behavioural; cognitive–behavioural; and self-advocacy.

Cognitive-Experimental Chapter 3 reviewed the development that had taken place in experimental studies of information handling by people with learning disabilities. One major shift has been from the study of structural limitations towards greater concern with functional aspects of information processing. Particular interest has been attached to the use of both specific and general strategies by people with learning disabilities in problem-solving situations. It appears that people with such disabilities often lack strategies or, if they have them available, they fail to use them. This has generated interest in the teachability of specific task-relevant strategies, as when Brown and Barclay (1976) taught their students to self-test on list-learning tasks (see later). Limited achievements from teaching specific strategies prompted interest in trying to teach more general problem solving. Thus Borkowski and Varnhagen (1984) combined specific strategy teaching with the teaching of more general self-instructions to solve problems (see later). Such studies represent attention to improving performance outcomes and the process by which such outcomes are achieved. They are an attempt to teach generalizable self-directed problem-solving strategies and this is one important aspect of self-control.

Indeed the strategies taught by Borkowski and Varnhagen (1984) are almost identical to strategies explicitly labelled as self-control but derived from a quite different experimental tradition. This tradition reflects the work of Russian psychologists, in particular Luria (1961) and Vygotsky (1962). Russian formulations see self-control as intimately related to the development of verbal language and the directive role that it comes to assume over other behaviour. This role of language as a tool in thinking is seen as arising in the period of normal development between four and ten years of age. Such a use of language is thought to grow out of the child's social interactions — the child uses the skills that it has witnessed used towards itself and that it has developed for communication with others, both to reflect upon and guide its own behaviour. A child moves from talking out loud when solving problems towards internalizing this type of speech. As well as speech becoming internalized, the child is seen as becoming increasingly sophisticated at being able to use speech to choose between actions and plan their execution as opposed to speech just being used to accompany and describe actions and objects. Such ideas have been expressed in the teaching of self-instructional skills, particularly in relation to academic tasks. Thus, individuals can be taught a series of verbal instructions which help them to analyse tasks, initiate action and monitor performance, both errors and successes. This approach was first described by Meichenbaum and Goodman (1969, 1971) and has become extensively used with a range of childhood difficulties (see Kendall, 1984).

Both the above traditions assign a key role to verbal language in the development of self-control. Indeed, self-control is identified with verbal control of behaviour. However, in a useful review of developmental aspects of self-control, Kopp (1982) points out that this may be only one factor influencing the control that an individual will exert over his or her own behaviour. She argues that the roots of self-control antedate the acquisition of language skills. She highlights the importance of general cognitive development, the role of external controls and of the social relationships within which the development of self-control is embedded. Self-control is seen as emerging through a series of phases over a period of years by the interaction of child and environment. She draws attention to its roots in the very first year of life with the adjustment of biological functions such as sleep or feeding to temporal aspects of the environment. Similar processes can be seen in the way infants learn strategies for coping selectively with incoming sensory information. She sees self-control as related to the development of a sense of identity, to an awareness and recall of externally imposed rules, to linguistic development and the ability to think representationally and monitor one's own behaviour. In other words self-control is seen as intimately related to many areas of social and cognitive development. Kopp draws particular attention to self-control as part of social development and awareness of socially approved behaviours. But it can also be seen as part of general intellectual development related to problem solving in both social and non-social areas. In either case self-control is seen as having its roots in external control and direction with a gradual shift over time towards internal regulation. Thus, the development of self-control becomes intimately related to the nature of care giver interactions and the delicate balance between external and internal control. These ideas have yet to find expression in planned interventions to develop self-control in people with serious learning difficulties. The chapter on social cognition (Chapter 4) did describe a number of interventions which might help people analyse social situations and direct their behaviour in these situations. This is a specific example of self-control although still relying heavily upon verbal elements. Kopp is suggesting a much more broad-based approach to our understanding of the developmental aspects of these abilities. This would seem very appropriate for people who have serious generalized learning difficulties and opens up the possibility of working on self-control at the earliest developmental levels.

Operant-Behavioural Within this approach self-control is interpreted as the acquisition by the learner of the principles and methods of operant behaviour analysis and their application to the individual's own behaviour. Thus the skills taught include self-observation, self-recording, self-cueing and self-reinforcement. There is some overlap with the self-instruction techniques previously described, in the approach known as 'correspondence training'. This uses basic operant methods (prompting and fading, reinforcement) to teach the individual to get actions to correspond to words. The individual is taught to express verbally an intention to do, or not to do, certain things and is then reinforced if subsequent behaviour 'corresponds' to this intention. Further integration of the cognitive–experimental and operant–behavioural approaches is exemplified in the third distinguishable approach to self-control.

Cognitive-behavioural This approach blends the two traditions described above but is usually applied in psychiatric contexts. The people who describe and research cognitive–behavioural techniques are people charged with resolving clinical problems — that is, serious difficulties in day-to-day personal functioning rather than the more academic experimental perspective. This tends to involve the use of intervention 'packages' as a way of maximizing the likelihood of a positive, socially meaningful outcome. Such packages may incorporate techniques drawn from a number of areas which individually are regarded as of proven value with such clinical problems. Self-instruction training is, in practice, often a form of cognitive-behaviour therapy because it combines well-known and researched behavioural techniques (such as reinforcement) with the more cognitive developmental approach of self-instruction. However, there are more broad-spectrum packages of which one relevant example is that of anger management, as described by Novaco (1976a,b, 1977). This incorporates teaching analysis of social situations, self-awareness, empathy, self-instructions, self-monitoring, relaxation and appropriate assertive skills. It is, therefore, drawing on a much wider range of techniques than self-instructional training; it has been primarily developed in relation to adults rather than children; and will be given separate consideration in this chapter.

Self-advocacy This is a broad term referring to a number of specific activities such as making one's own decision, demanding one's entitlements and asserting rights. It may be an individual act or a group enterprise involving people with a common cause. It is a fast growing area of development for people with serious learning difficulties (Williams and Schoultz, 1982; Crawley, 1983). Its origins lie in the concern for the human rights of people with disabilities and handicaps, but it has many psychological implications. The practice of self-advocacy requires the ability to analyse problems, make decisions and act effectively to implement those decisions either on one's own or as a group. It is a means whereby the individual or group will effect change towards a desired goal by their own efforts. It is, therefore, an area of self-control, particularly in relation to problem solving in real-life practical situations.

Methods of acquiring self-control

The developmental literature as exemplified in the Russian work and Kopp's (1982) review indicates that the skills required for self-control develop normally over a period of many years. The experimental literature has produced evidence that generalized use of taught self-control strategies is only likely when development has reached around the eight-year level (e.g. Higa, Tharp and Calkins, 1978; Schleser et al., 1984).

It is something of a surprise that the applied literature on self-control skills seems to devote very little time to teaching these skills — several hours at most. Training is usually carried out on an individual basis using a variety of techniques such as modelling, rehearsal, direct instruction, reinforcement and discovery learning. There has been little comparative study of how to teach target self-control skills effectively and efficiently. At this stage little can be said except that something more than direct verbal instructions may be needed, i.e. there seems to be an active rehearsal component required (see, for example, Schleser et al., 1984). It also seems likely that the training time necessary to teach generalized skills to disabled learners with serious problems in day-to-day functioning is likely to be far greater than anything so far reported in the literature (Kendall, 1984).

The aims of self-control

Many different behaviours have been targeted for self-control in the reported literature. These include completion of assigned work in classroom or laboratory settings, learning self-care skills, managing job changes in vocational settings and meal cookery in residential settings, appropriate assertiveness of one's rights, and organizing and running a self-advocacy committee. Problem behaviours targeted have included inattentiveness, leaving one's seat in class, inappropriate verbalizations, temper outbursts, excessive dribbling, nose picking and head shaking. It is clear that the literature is mainly concerned with finding specific self-control techniques for a relatively narrow range of behaviours. There is little concern with the more general issues of how to develop broad-based self-control skills relevant to many areas of individual functioning. These are more the issues with which developmental theorists are concerned, and certainly, if the so-called problem of generalization is ever to be tackled then a more broad-based notion of the skills to be taught and the behaviours to be targeted, will need to be considered.

Thus, the present applied literature illustrates considerable variation in the self-control skills taught, the amount and method of teaching and the behaviours targeted for control. In addition, the clients involved in these studies have ranged from normal pre-schoolers to adults with profound impairments. Most research is of the single case or small groups univariate type. It will, therefore, be very difficult to draw any firm conclusions from this literature, but an overview of some of the work emanating from each theoretical background may help give an idea of what can and might be achieved.

EMPIRICAL STUDIES OF SELF-CONTROL

Cognitive–Experimental The developmental and experimental literature has so far generated one major strategy for applied work — that of self-instruction training. Much of the work using self-instructional training follows closely in content the original study by Meichenbaum and Goodman (1971). That is, those involved are taught in specific training sessions to use a series of self-statements. These are usually taught in relation to table-top visual–perceptual problems. Clients are taught to define the problem (what must I do?), to focus attention (where do I start?), to cope with mistakes (I've made a mistake but I can sort it out by . . .) and to acknowledge successes (that's good). Sometimes the instructions taught are specific to the task material; sometimes more general questions and statements applicable to any task are taught. Clients learn first to say these out loud to themselves and then are taught to reduce gradually the volume of their speech until they are saying them silently to themselves. The main methods of teaching are verbal instruction, modelling and prompting. The rationale for such training is that it may help people who have problems with the verbal mediation of their behaviour. The most common target group has been impulsive children showing problems of concentration and activity level. Initial studies suggested that such skills could be acquired by these children even at the pre-school level, and that the effects of training generalized from the training sessions into the classroom setting and maintained over time (Meichenbaum and Goodman, 1971; Bornstein and Quevillon, 1976). The main effect sought has been upon task performance in the classroom situation. However, it has also been thought that such training might aid in the control of problem behaviours, particularly in view of Camp's (1977) finding that compared to normal boys, aggressive six- to eight-year-old boys show clear evidence of a deficit in their ability to use speech to direct their behaviour and to know when such a strategy is relevant. Although studies on the value of self-instruction have used children within the normal range of intelligence, their ages have been as low as four years old which, in developmental terms, would make the procedures potentially relevant to older children with serious learning difficulties. This client group has not yet, however, been researched.

Within the normal group studies, conflicting findings have emerged (see Kendall, 1977, 1984; Bornstein, 1985, for reviews and comments). Some studies have shown that a combination of self-instruction training with external contingency management produces greater and more lasting effects than the use of contingency management on its own. But there are other findings which do not support this, and often the only effects that can be shown are upon academic tasks similar to those used in training and in situations very similar to the training situation itself. That is, the same problems of generalization are found as with more straightforward behavioural techniques. An attempt to replicate one of the original and most influential studies (Bornstein and Quevillon, 1976) was able to show no effect of self-instruction training on the classroom behaviour of three disruptive four to five year olds (Billings and Wasik, 1985). Bryant and Budd (1982) had, however, been able to show some small generalized effects upon a similar group, and also highlighted clear individual differences in response to training.

Such conflicting findings and the evidence for the role of individual differences have led reviewers to pin-point a number of important issues. One is the selection of clients. Many of the subjects included in experiments are not children presenting with clinical problems. It may be that the more serious the problems of the children the more difficult it is to achieve significant results. This must be particularly important in view of the very limited time devoted to self-instructional training — usually several hours at most (cf. earlier). Another key factor highlighted by reviewers is the cognitive level of the subjects (cf. earlier). Higa, Tharp and Calkins (1978) point out that a number of studies suggest that reliable verbal direction of behaviour is not normally shown before five to six years of age. They then went on to show that having to verbalize in a discrimination training task impaired the performance of five year olds, but not that of six to seven year olds. In a similar vein, Schleser et al. (1984) were able to offer some evidence with seven to eight year olds that although both pre-operational and concrete-operational children could benefit from self-instruction training in terms of task performance; only the concrete operational children seemed able to generalize what they had learned to an untrained task.

The influence of cognitive level and amount of training is clearly of critical significance when it comes to using these procedures with those who have known developmental difficulties. The limited amount of research with people who have intellectual impairments is somewhat surprising. Such clients are often characterized as 'impulsive'. Indeed, Russian theorists have suggested that it is one of the central features of intellectual impairment that verbal skills fail to gain directive control over behaviour. One might use this view to argue that such training should be a central focus in the education of people with serious learning difficulties. It is certainly proposed as such by Feuerstein (1979), using rather different terminologies and techniques but stressing the need to develop mediated learning (see Chapter 3). A study by Davison (1984) also indicates the potential of this approach. She worked with adults whose verbal understanding was between the $5\frac{1}{2}$- and 11-year level. She taught a table-top game, encouraging one group to ask specific task-related questions about their own and others' performances, and instructing a comparison group in a more traditional didactic way. While both groups mastered the task equally well, the group given a questioning strategy maintained better performance on follow-up and did better on a generalization task. No direct relationship could be found between the use of the strategy and level of performance. These findings are very similar to some of those emanating from studies of human performance in laboratory settings.

In Chapter 3, it was pointed out that such laboratory work has moved away from studying capacity deficits in specific information-processing components towards the study of strategy usage. There is evidence that people with serious learning difficulties may lack information-processing strategies or, if they have them, may not know when and how to deploy them. It has proved possible to teach a range of specific strategies to such learners, particularly in relation to memory tasks, and the strategies show some evidence of maintaining over time. However, there has been less evidence that clients are able to transfer strategies from one task to another. Brown and Barclay (1976) trained their subjects to use a self-testing routine to help their performance on a list-learning task. They showed that subjects at both the six- and eight-year developmental levels could learn and benefit from this strategy, but that only the developmentally older made spontaneous use of it. They were then able to show, in a follow-up study, that this latter group were also able to make use of the strategy taught in a quite different task (Brown, Campione and Barclay, 1979). They argued that it would be fruitful to teach people with learning difficulties more generalized strategies which were not tied to specific tasks, and would be relevant in real-life situations. In this spirit, Borkowski and Varnhagen (1984) looked at the effects of teaching eleven year olds, who were functioning at about the eight-year level, both specific task strategies and a more general self-instructional strategy similar to that described above. With a fairly minimum training time they were able to find some evidence for generalization of strategies taught, but this could not be clearly attributed to the self-instructional training. They did, however, feel that for some of their subjects self-instruction did help them generalize specific strategies to new tasks.

There is, therefore, some empirical reason to take seriously the potential value of cognitive training. Such training might be of value both in relation to skill acquisition and to behavioural control. Perhaps it is in the former area that the most exciting prospects reside. If a person with learning difficulties can be taught problem-solving strategies with broad applicability, then independent and discovery learning become real possibilities. The effect that this might have upon number of skills learned, and the general psychological adjustment of the learner (e.g. confidence and self-image) are incalculable. It is clear that with current teaching technologies a large amount of teaching time would need to be invested in such an endeavour. It is clear also that such an approach is likely to have greatest impact upon those whose developmental level is at least in the five- to eight-year range. But this is a substantial number of people, and the potential of this area requires very serious consideration.

Operant Behavioural One set of self-control skills that has received considerable attention in this literature is the development of self-observation and self-recording skills. Shapiro (1982) reviews a series of studies by Litrownik and colleagues who worked in a laboratory setting with children and adolescents who had a moderate degree of learning disability. They were able to show that it was possible to teach their subjects to observe and record their own behaviour on table-top tasks such as bead stringing. They were also able to show that their subjects could set their own standards and learn to reinforce themselves appropriately. These skills were acquired with very limited training input, showed some generalization across tasks and were retained in the short term. However, the acquisition of such skills appeared to do little to improve actual task performance. Some evidence was found for reactivity, that is, the fact that simply recording behaviour may act to change it. Reactivity is a common phenomenon in people without learning difficulties and appears to hold for people with such difficulties. In more applied studies, teaching people to observe and record their own behaviour has been shown to increase appropriate verbalizations in a discussion group for nine adults with mild degrees of intellectual impairment (Nelson, Lipinski and Boykin, 1978). It acted to decrease the nose picking and head shaking of two adults in the study by Zeigob, Klukas and Junginger (1978), even though the accuracy of the recording in this study was quite low.

An alternative approach to self-management in the operant- behavioural literature has been to provide the individual with meaningful cues for appropriate behaviour but cues which the client retains under his or her own control. This method has been called 'antecedent cue regulation'. For example, Martin et al. (1982) taught three people with mild to moderate degrees of learning difficulty to use picture card sequences to take them through the cooking of complex meals. The authors were able to demonstrate a very marked increase in the number of steps the clients were able to carry out independently when they had the cards compared to when they were provided with instructions, prompting and feedback from a trainer. Likewise, Sowers et al. (1985) taught four young adults with a similar degree of difficulty to use picture sequences to manage their change from one job to another on an independent basis. In some respects, picture sequences are a form of external control but there are elements which suggest they are a legitimate aspect of self-control. In the first place, the use of such cues remains under the control of the individual him/herself. In the second place, these cues clearly reduce dependence on a very important source of external control — other people. They are also a form of self-management commonly used by most people, although their form is adapted to the needs of those with learning disabilities. Thus, many ordinary people rely on recipe books and shopping lists to aid their memories. The great attraction of the antecedent cue regulation studies is that they open up self-management possibilities to people with very limited language skills. Many other techniques are heavily dependent upon a considerable degree of verbal comprehension and expression.

A number of operant–behavioural studies have used a package of self-control techniques in combination with externally controlled reinforcement programmes. Robertson et al. (1979) report on a study with twelve disruptive children who had mild to moderate degrees of learning difficulty. In a classroom setting the authors provided feedback to the children on their behaviour and tokens for appropriate behaviour. They also taught these pupils to rate accurately their own behaviour and award themselves reinforcement on the basis of these ratings. The level of all behaviour problems in the class decreased throughout the study, the improvements generalized to periods outside of the training sessions, and the improvements maintained once all interventions had been faded out, in the last few days of the study. Because of the design of the study it is impossible to pin-point the factors responsible for such changes. Nevertheless, the results are impressive and have, to some extent, been replicated by Shapiro and Klein (1980) and Shapiro, McGonigle and Ollendick (1981). In a single case study of an adult with a moderate degree of disability Gardner, Clees and Cole (1983) reported similar success in decreasing high-rate disruptive vocalizations. The client was taught to discriminate appropriate from inappropriate vocalizations, to monitor his own vocalizations, and to reinforce himself for appropriate behaviour. Again, this intervention was combined with an externally controlled schedule of differential reinforcement for other behaviour and a response–cost procedure. Nevertheless, substantial improvements were achieved and maintained at six months and one year follow-up after all interventions had been withdrawn. A similar package for teaching self-care skills to adults with degrees of disability, varying from moderate to profound, was reported by Matson, Marchetti and Adkins (1980). They examined the teaching of shower use and a range of skills relevant to the maintenance of a personal living area. They compared a group of people given standard operant training involving prompting and reinforcement by a trainer, to a group given both this training and additional help to rate their own performance over the previous week, and judge if it merited special recognition (a publicly posted star). There was also a no-treatment group. Over the six-week training period, only the group with the self-evaluation component showed any significant gains. While the design permits one to infer a specific contribution of the self-management component of training, the numerical gains were not large and it remains something of a puzzle as to why the standard operant training had no effect at all.

These studies do not permit any firm conclusions about the value of operant–behavioural self-control techniques. However, they do clearly demonstrate that even people with quite severe learning difficulties are able to master the skills of monitoring, cueing, evaluating and reinforcing their own behaviours. They certainly suggest the potential of these techniques, and the value of more controlled experimentation to look at their effect upon generalization and maintenance, both in regard to skill training and problem behaviour management.

The role of verbalization in the above studies is not clearly specified. However, other studies within the operant–behavioural tradition have specifically made use of verbal behaviours as a means of controlling other forms of behaviour. Thorbecke and Jackson (1982) report a case study with a young person with a moderate degree of learning disability who dribbled excessively. They taught the individual to monitor and evaluate this behaviour, to self-correct the dribbling and to self-reinforce dryness. They also taught her to verbalize her intentions. The client was reported as acquiring the skills and the programme proved effective; but again the self-control aspect of the intervention followed a period of successful external control, which had used a combination of correction for dribbling and differential reinforcement of any non-dribbling behaviour. Whitman *et al.* (1982) report a series of classroom studies involving children with mild degrees of intellectual impairment. They used the correspondence training paradigm which required the individual to state in advance, or otherwise show, an intention to carry out certain behaviours. After a period of time the person is asked to review his or her behaviour to see if it has corresponded to the initial statement. If it has, then reinforcement is given. Whitman *et al.* were able to achieve improvements in out-of-seat behaviour and posture and attention in class. There was some evidence for generalization beyond training sessions both to other sessions and over time. Although, again, it is possible that the reinforcement alone was responsible for the changes, it was interesting in these studies that maintenance was achieved even when reinforcement was provided only for the initial statement of intention.

Cognitive-Behavioural The work of Novaco (1976a,b, 1977) with psychiatric and non-psychiatric adult clients may well have relevance for helping people with learning difficulties overcome behavioural problems. He has worked on the self-management of anger and its inappropriate behavioural expression, particularly through aggression. His 'package' trains people in three areas of self-control. The first is teaching people to interpret the social situations which lead to the arousal of anger. This involves learning how to monitor level of anger arousal, identify the triggers for anger, identify any irrational beliefs and look at alternative ways of interpreting the situation. The second training element teaches the client how to control level of emotional arousal through self-induced relaxation or humour. The third element teaches alternative ways of behaving in anger-arousing situations — how to use self-instructions to plan the desired outcome for the situation and monitor progress towards this outcome.

This is a complex series of interventions and Novaco (1976a, b) has produced some evidence that the package works better than the separate components individually. Relaxation techniques have been used in a number of studies for people with serious learning problems and behaviour difficulties but the evidence for their value has been equivocal (e.g. Luiselli, 1980). Benson, Miranti and Johnson (1984) reported on a controlled group study using Novaco's techniques with adults who had a mild to moderate degree of intellectual impairment. Unfortunately these were not people for whom anger control was presenting serious difficulties. The research design compared a group who received a Novaco package with groups who received an individual component of the package (relaxation training, self-instruction training and training in social problem solving). There was no group which received no treatment or equivalent attention only. Outcome was measured in terms of self-report, performance in role-play situations and vocational supervisor ratings. All groups showed improvement, with no clear advantage to any one particular group. There was some indication that relaxation only and the self-instruction group only groups did marginally better, and that the clients found social problem-solving training difficult to understand. This last point serves as another reminder about the need to consider more extensive training as only twelve to fifteen hours of group training were provided overall in this study.

This kind of approach, which incorporates ideas from research on social cognition, general cognition and cognitive and behaviour therapy, is certainly of interest. There is, however, the need for much more research about the applications of such a package. It certainly seems that many of the individual elements can be taught to people with learning difficulties. Whether they can be taught to combine and use these techniques in day-to-day situations has yet to be demonstrated. Whether their use would improve behavioural functioning for people with serious learning difficulties has also yet to be demonstrated. In future research, it will be essential to clarify the required level of functioning needed to derive benefit from these techniques and also the amount of training that is going to be required. It will also be important to detail the type of problem behaviours susceptible to such an approach. It is already clear that a far greater investment of time is going to be needed if such complex skills are going to be taught to people with serious learning difficulties compared to the amount of time allocated to people whose functioning is within the normal intellectual range.

Self-advocacy   Although there is a considerable literature on self-advocacy which describes some of the skills required and training programmes used to teach these skills, there is little in the way of scientific research about the efficacy of such training. Crawley (1983) surveyed self-advocacy practices, as expressed through committees of trainees attending adult centres. She described factors which are likely to influence the success of such trainee committees, factors such as their structure, size and involvement of staff and parents. She also describes a training programme, using both didactic and enactive methods, which serves to prepare trainees for operating such a system. The programme described includes training in verbal and non-verbal communication skills, how to assert oneself appropriately and how to perform the various role functions in a formal committee (e.g. chairing meetings, taking minutes).

There is common ground between the programme described by Crawley and general social skills training. There is also common ground with other problem-solving techniques as those involved have to learn how to define a problem and select an action to resolve it. It would certainly be fruitful to define these skills more clearly and relate their development to other areas of self-control. This would help elucidate the psychological foundations for self-advocacy and see it as one area to which self-control skills could be deployed.

CONCLUSIONS

Applied research on self-control for people with severe learning disabilities is more notable for its potential than for its demonstrable achievements. At least it has been established that this particular client group can acquire, given adequate help, a range of skills relevant to self-control. This, in its turn, suggests a modification in expectations towards people with these difficulties, and towards viewing them as people with a potential for self-efficacy, rather than as being forever passive and dependent, requiring a high degree of external control. However, the development of this potential will require active educational intervention from the environment as these skills may not be spontaneously acquired through simple maturation or exposure. Indeed, the tendency of 'normal' people to anticipate the needs of people with learning difficulties, and to expect little in the way of self-direction, may act positively to discourage the development of better self-control.

At this stage it is not clear what exactly can be achieved for which people. The best validated area of applied work lies in the acquisition by people with serious degrees of disability of basic operant–behavioural self-control skills. These skills (self-observation, self-recording, self-evaluation, antecedent cue regulation and self-reinforcement) appear useful in helping clients make independent use of skills already acquired to some extent and in assisting self-management of behaviour difficulties. They are usually used in conjunction with more externally controlled interventions and it is not as yet clear to what extent self-control does facilitate generalization and maintenance.

More controversial are the cognitive approaches to self-control particularly the general area of self-instruction. The promise is that there may be general problem-solving strategies which are teachable and which might enhance the acquisition of a wide range of skills. Such strategies would constitute learning to learn, and would provide an invaluable adjuvant to teaching — perhaps enabling learners to direct their own learning more and benefit from less structured environmental input. Whether such a promise can be fulfilled will depend on a much clearer articulation of what these general problem-solving strategies might be. It will also require far greater investment in training time well beyond the few hours reported in the experimental literature. This is particularly true if such skills are to be taught to those with more severe degrees of learning difficulty. For any real progress to be made it looks as though such skills would need to become a legitimate part of an educational curriculum and be the subject of long-term teaching endeavours. There is perhaps enough evidence to encourage such an investment, at least on a research basis.

This, in its turn, leads on to the need for considering self-control in a more general context. Both developmental and experimental research demonstrates that self-control in those without intellectual impairment takes many years and grows through the interaction of general level of understanding, verbal development and external environment factors. If true progress towards self-control is to be achieved, all these aspects will need consideration. It will be necessary to define more clearly the sort of problem areas in which self-control is relevant. It will be necessary to establish the actual skills that are required for the exercising of self-control. It will be necessary to determine the factors which influence whether those skills are acquired *and* applied in relevant contexts. Such factors will involve consideration of the role of developmental level, general external environmental conditions (setting conditions such as parent–child interaction style) and specific methods of teaching. The development of self-control thus represents an exciting interface between developmental, experimental, ecological and behavioural psychology. There now exists the foundation, in terms of an understanding of general developmental processes, intellectual impairment and intervention technologies to develop a more rational and comprehensive approach to this most exciting and potentially fruitful area.

REFERENCES

Benson, B.A., Miranti, S.V., and Johnson, C. (1984) Self control techniques for anger management with mentally retarded adults. Paper presented in the AABT Convention, Philadelphia.

Billings, D.C., and Wasik, B.H. (1985) Self-instructional training with pre-schoolers: an attempt to replicate. *Journal of Applied Behaviour Analysis*, **18**, 61–67.

Borkowski, J.G., and Varnhagen, C.K. (1984) Transfer of learning strategies: contrast of self-instruction and traditional training formats with EMR children. *American Journal of Mental Deficiency*, **88**, 369–379.

Bornstein, P.H. (1985) Self-instructional training: a commentary and state of the art. *Journal of Applied Behaviour Analysis*, **18**, 69–72.

Bornstein, P.H., and Quevillon, R.P. (1976) The effects of a self-instructional package on overactive pre-school boys. *Journal of Applied Behaviour Analysis*, **9**, 179–188.

Brown, A. L., and Barclay, L.R. (1976) The effects of training specific mnemonics on the metamnemonic efficiency of retarded children. *Child Development*, **47**, 70–80.

Brown, A.L., Campione, J.C., and Barclay, L.R. (1979) Training self-checking routines for estimating test readiness: generalization from list learning to prose recall. Child Development, **50**, 501–512.

Bryant, L.E., and Budd, K.S. (1982) Self-instructional training to increase independent work performance in preschoolers. *Journal of Applied Behaviour Analysis*, **15**, 359–271.

Camp, B.W. (1977) Verbal mediation in young aggressive boys. *Journal of Abnormal Psychology*, **86**, 145–157.

Crawley, B. (1983) Self Advocacy Manual. An overview of the development of self-advocacy by mentally handicapped people and recommendations for the development of trainee committees. Paper No. 49, Habilitation Technology Project. Manchester: Hester Adrain Research Centre.

Davison, H.A. (1984) The effects of verbalization as a tool in problem solving and task acquisition in mentally handicapped adults. Unpublished M.Phil. Thesis, University of London.

Feuerstein, R. (1979) *Instrumental Enrichment: Redevelopment of cognitive functions of retarded performers*. Baltimore: University Park Press.

Gardner, W.I., Clees, T.J., and Cole, C.I. (1983) Self-management of disruptive verbal ruminations by a mentally retarded adult. *Applied Research in Mental Retardation*, **4**, 41–58.

Higa, W.R., Tharp, R.G., and Calkins, R.P. (1978) Developmental verbal control of behaviour: implications for self-instructional training. *Journal of Experimental Child Psychology*, **26**, 480–497.

Jackson, H.J., and Boag, P.G. (1981) The efficacy of self-control procedures in motivational strategies with mentally retarded persons: A review of the literature and guidelines for future research. *Australian Journal of Developmental Disabilities*, **7**, 65–79.

Kendall, P.C. (1977) On the efficacious use of verbal self-instructional procedures with children. *Cognitive Therapy and Research*, **1**, 331–341.

Kendall, P.C. (1984) Cognitive–behavioural self-control therapy for children. *Journal of Child Psychology and Psychiatry*, **25**, 173–179.

Kopp, C.B. (1982) Antecedents of self-regulation: a developmental perspective. *Developmental Psychology*, **18**, 199–214.

Luiselli, J.K. (1980) Relaxation training with the developmentally disabled. *Behaviour Research of Severe Developmental Disabilities*, **1**, 191–213.

Luria, A.R. (1961) *The Role of Speech in the Regulation of Normal and Abnormal Behaviour*. Oxford: Pergamon.

Martin, J.E., Rusch, F.R., James, V.L., Decker, P.J., and Trtol, K.A. (1982). The use of picture cues to establish self-control in the preparation of complex meals by mentally retarded adults. *Applied Research in Mental Retardation*, **3**, 105–119.

Matson, J.L., Marchetti, A., and Adkins, J.A. (1980) Comparison of operant and independence–training procedures for mentally retarded adults. *American Journal of Mental Deficiency*, **84**, 487–494.

Meichenbaum, D., and Goodman, J. (1969) The development of control of operant motor responding by verbal operants. *Journal of Experimental Child Psychology*, **7**, 553–565.

Meichenbaum, D., and Goodman, J. (1971) Training impulsive children to talk to themselves: a means of developing self-control. *Journal of Abnormal Psychology*, **77**, 115–126.

Nelson, R.D., Lipinski, D.P., and Boykin, R.A. (1978). The effects of self-recorders' training and the obtrusiveness of the self-recording device on the accuracy and reactivity of self-monitoring. *Behaviour Therapy*, **9**, 200–201.

Novaco, R.W. (1976a) The functions and regulation of the arousal of anger. *American Journal of Psychiatry*, **133**, 1124–1128.

Novaco, R.W. (1976b) Treatment of chronic anger through cognitive and relaxation controls. *Journal of Consulting and Clinical Psychology*, **44**, 681.

Novaco, R.W. (1977) Stress inoculation: a cognitive therapy for anger and its application to a case of depression. *Journal of Consulting and Clinical Psychology*, **45**, 600–608.

Robertson, S.J., Simon, S.J., Pachman, J.S., and Drabman, R.S. (1979) Self control and generalization procedures in a classroom of disruptive retarded children. *Child*

Behaviour Therapy, **1**, 347–362.

Schleser, R., Cohen, R., Meyers, A.W., and Rodick, J.D. (1984) The effects of cognitive level and training procedures on the generalization of self-instructions. *Cognitive Therapy and Research*, **8**, 187–200.

Shapiro, E.S. (1982) Self-control procedures with the mentally retarded. In M. Hersen, R.M. Eisler and P.M. Miller (eds) *Progress in Behavior Modification*, Vol. 12. New York: Academic Press.

Shapiro, E.S., and Klein, R.D. (1980) Self-management of classroom behaviour with retarded disturbed children. *Behaviour Modification*, **4**, 83–97.

Shapiro, E.S., Mcgonigle, J.J., and Ollendick, T.H. (1981) An analysis of self-assessment and self-reinforcement in a self-managed token economy with mentally retarded children. *Applied Research in Mental Retardation*, **1**, 227–240.

Sowers, J.A., Verdi, A., Bourbeau, P., and Sheehan, P. (1985) Teaching job independence and flexibility to mentally retarded students through the use of a self-control package. *Journal of Applied Behaviour Analysis*, **18**, 81–85.

Thorbecke, P.J., and Jackson, H.J. (1982) Reducing chronic drooling in a retarded female using a multi-treatment package. *Journal of Behaviour Therapy and Experimental Psychiatry*, **13**, 89–93.

Whitman, T.L., Scibak, J.W., Butler, K.M., Richter, R., and Johnson, M.R. (1982) Improving classroom behaviour in mentally retarded children through correspondence training. *Journal of Applied Behaviour Analysis*, **15**, 545–564.

Williams, P., and Schoultz, B. (1982) *We Can Speak for Ourselves*. London: Souvenir Press.

Vygotsky, L.S. (1962) *Thought and Language*. Cambridge, Mass: MIT Press.

Zeigob, L., Klukas, N., and Junginger, J. (1978) Reactivity of self monitoring procedures with retarded adolescents. *American Journal of Mental Deficiency*, **83**, 156–167.

CONCLUSIONS TO PART 3

The chapters in this section provide a brief overview of some of the work relevant to the development of communication and thinking skills in those with severe learning disabilities. These two areas of development are central, almost by definition, to working with people affected by these disabilities. It is hoped that some impression has been given of what sorts of skills have been taught and what methods have been used to teach them. It seems clear that much can be done to help people with severe learning disabilities acquire skills in these two areas; and that techniques of help have a specific contribution to make. In general, giving structured, focused help seems more likely to lead to development than unstructured 'wait and see' approaches. However, it is equally clear that success is not always achieved and a number of limitations in our present knowledge base have been apparent with present intervention techniques. Some skills (for example, syntactic aspects of language) may yield in only a limited way; some advances (for example, in problem-solving strategies) may fail to generalize;

some clients (for example, those whose degree of impairment is profound) may be very difficult to help effectively with present techniques.

Further advancement of our intervention strategies will probably depend upon at least three kinds of development. There is a great need for more research — there are simply too few studies available to support wide-ranging applied endeavours. This was particularly evident in the section on self-instruction training in Chapter 10, and indeed the literature on the whole area of self-control is pitifully small. Even where a considerable literature exists, as for communication skills, the quality of the research is poor. There are too few properly controlled studies, too few longitudinal studies and too few multi-variate studies. There are a range of other methodological shortcomings, and overall the research base does not yet provide a secure foundation for applied work.

The third area in which development is needed is at the conceptual level. A better framwork is needed for interpreting individual differences. While the literature is full of specific ways to teach specific skills, there has been little comprehensive analysis of what is involved in the development of 'communication' and 'self-control'. Such major areas encompass many different skills acquired through many processes over a long period of time. It has been the argument of this section, and indeed of the book in general, that a fuller understanding will require the integration of knowledge from many areas of psychology, and much closer contact between experimental and applied endeavours. Only if this can be effected is it likely that there will be significant advances in our ability to analyse and understand individual differences and a significant expansion and refinement of present intervention techniques. Behavioural approaches have contributed enormously to 'breaking the mould', to shattering the expectations of those without learning disabilities about those who have them. They have clearly established that much can be done in all areas of development, with all types and levels of disability. But if this impetus is to be sustained then there needs to be more reliable feed-through from the rapidly expanding knowledge base of other areas of psychology into applied work. If this can be effected then the exciting advances of the last twenty years will be at the very least matched in the next twenty years, and more probably exceeded.

Chapter 11

Conclusions

This book has attempted to summarize in a limited way the present state of knowledge regarding the nature of intellectual impairment and severe learning disabilities, and some of the ways of helping people so affected. It has focused upon the psychological aspects of these difficulties and has drawn primarily upon the 'scientific' literature. Philosophy and ideology are recognized as important determinants of any scientific endeavour. They are crucial in determining what the important questions are, but they must not be allowed to determine what the answers might be. A totally objective science is an illusion, but that does not mean that the struggle for the maximum objectivity possible should be abandoned. The belief underlying this book is that scientific methods are critical to furthering our understanding of people with severe learning disabilities. Without such a belief, people with disabilities become prey to the fashions and fantasies of those without disabilities. The exaggerated claims of nineteenth-century practitioners contributed to a backlash against 'progressive' attempts to help people with disabilities. It is only recently that services have begun to emerge from the 'Dark Age' philosophies and practices that began in the second half of the nineteenth century. It would be a disaster if new developments were to flounder because of the excessive claims for particular techniques of help or types of service provision.

A balanced but dynamic relationship is essential between new philosophies, new ideas and scientific research. Science obviously proceeds on a number of fronts, and a division is sometimes made between basic and applied research. Thus research aimed at understanding the nature of intellectual functioning has been constructed and developed quite independently from the practical work of helping people suffering from impairments in intellectual functioning. There have been dutiful expressions about basic research providing useful practical knowledge 'in the long term'; but applied research has by and large had to develop quite independently, using a different conceptual framework (behavioural rather than cognitive) and different scientific methods (time series single case analysis rather than group comparison analysis). In reviewing the status of present efforts to help people with learning disabilities it became clear that important advances had been made in the last twenty years but that there remain severe limitations in knowledge and technology. It has been argued in the text that these limitations are more likely to be overcome if better communication and collaboration can be effected between basic and applied researchers. In reviewing work in each area concrete examples were offered of shared interests, useful ideas and (hopefully) exciting possibilities for advance through a more collaborative approach.

It has also been argued that there needs to be a shift in the way that severe learning disabilities are conceptualized. This might be summarized as the need to shift from a univariate linear approach to a multivariate interactive approach. Thus cognitive researchers have tended to view learning disabilities in terms of a single dimension (IQ) and what determines the individual's place along this dimension. In seeking an explanation for this 'place' a single source of difficulty (e.g. memory) has been sought. Behavioural researchers have likewise tended to view 'disability' in terms of some aggregate dimension of the number of skills an individual has — improvement means giving an individual more skills and all skills are much the same, to be taught in the same way. Explanations for problem behaviours and techniques for teaching have been conceptualized along a single temporal dimension — the antecedents and consequences of behaviour.

Useful though these models have been, they do not reflect the current state of knowledge. In order to understand the nature of an individual's functioning it is necessary to look at multiple aspects of the information–processing system which may be relevant — number of areas processed, preferences, speed of processing, storage and retrieval capacities, and organizing strategies. Biological features of the individual may be critically involved in these processes. There are factors such as personality, chronological age and personal history which have received scant attention in this book; but all contribute to the understanding of individual functioning. This multidimensional approach, which is clearly relevant to understanding any human behaviour, requires explicit acknowledgement when understanding people with severe learning disabilities, so often characterized as 'simple'.

Likewise when viewing the environment and its influence it is clear that no simple model will hold. There are both quantitative and qualitative aspects of the environment which will critically determine how an individual functions. A number of these were illustrated in the text — factors such as level of stimulation, level of demand, social cohesion and harmony, the attitudes and expectations of significant others, responsivity and physical characteristics of the environment as well as the detailed moment-to-moment behavioural interactions so clearly exemplified in applied behavioural work. The environment too needs to be conceptualized multidimensionally.

Once such a multidimensional framework is adopted it becomes possible to analyse more easily interactive effects — how specific individual characteristics interact with specific environmental characteristics. An environment high in direct demands might prove more difficult for some people (for example, those with 'autistic-type' learning difficulties) than others. Detailed behavioural teaching techniques might be more relevant to some individuals at some points in their development than others. Level of stimulation may be a more critical determinant of functioning at some stages in development than others. Problem behaviours may seriously affect the general functioning of an environment as well as vice versa. Level of disability affects environmental functioning as well as vice versa. It is often stated that people categorized as 'severely intellectually impaired' show enormous variance in their performance. As a more multidimensional approach to both the individual and the environment is adopted, it will become easier to understand the reasons for such variance, rather than it being regarded as some sort of 'error' term. Unpredictability is not a characteristic of the person with learning disabilities. It reflects a limited understanding of that disability and the environment within which the individual operates.

Adopting an interactive approach between the individual and the environment implies a crucial role shift for the person with severe learning disabilities. People so affected are often cast in the passive, dependent role. Models of understanding and techniques of change have tended to collude with this role. Little attention has been given to individual differences; general prescriptions of change suited to everyone are offered; the control of the individual's behaviour is seen as entirely residing in the external environment. The interactive model points up this imbalance and suggests the individual as a source of change as well as an object of change. The individual with learning disabilities becomes an active part of the social dynamic, influencing and being influenced, a subject as well as an object.

Such a role shift has implications beyond that of improving our ability to understand and help people with learning disabilities. It enables us to see people with these difficulties as contributors to, as well as consumers of, scientific progress. Thus, in understanding learning disability light will be shed upon many aspects of the human information-processing system and the nature of developmental processes. Understanding the very specific biological anomalies which affect individual functioning will illustrate more general aspects of bio-behavioural relationships. Society's response to people with disabilities does much to exemplify the formation and function of social attitudes. Study of the individual's response to the disabled person acts as a source of insight into personal attitudes, emotions and coping strategies. From these many points of view the person with severe learning disabilities has as much to teach as to learn and as much to give as to take. As this is understood it becomes possible to move from an attitude of pity or cold scientific objectivity towards an attitude of respect.

Author Index

Adkins, J.W. 92, 166
Agras, s. 103
Allen, L.M. 86
Alpert, M. 66
Anderson, L. 66
Anderson, N.B. 30
Andrews, R.J. 72
Arbitman-Smith, R. 36
Armstrong, P.M. 90, 91
Arnljotsdottir, M. 118
Arnold, R. 63, 64
Ashdown, R. 144
Ashman, A.F. 10
August, G.J. 66, 67
Azrin, N.H. 90, 91, 99, 105

Baer, D.M. 89, 92, 116, 141, 142, 143
Bailey, S.L. 30
Baker, B.L. 90, 118
Balazs, R. 68
Balla, D. 37, 38
Barclay, L.R. 34, 35, 157, 163
Baron-Cohen, S. 50, 56
Barrera, F. 104
Barrett, R.P. 103
Bartak, L. 87
Barton, E.S. 104
Bates, E. 134
Bates, M.V. 69
Baumeister, A.A. 24, 25, 103, 105, 107
Baumrind, D. 99
Begab, J. 90
Belmont, J.M. 34
Bendall, S.A. 121
Bennett, D.H. 123
Benson, B. 44, 47, 52, 167
Berger, M. 137, 141

Berkowitz, B.P. 117
Berkson, G. 93, 100
Berry, P. 72
Berry, R. 55, 140
Beveridge, M. 55, 140
Bialer, I. 71
Billings, D.C. 162
Bilovsky, D. 71
Binkoff, J.A. 102, 107
Blacher, J. 49
Blair, J.A. 68
Blewitt, E. 100
Bluma, S.M. 121
Blunden, R. 90, 92, 100, 121
Boe, R.B. 107
Bonvillian, J.D. 146, 147
Borkowski, J.C. 31, 33, 34, 35, 157, 163
Bornstein, P.H. 161, 162
Boykin, R.A. 164
Bransford, J.D. 36
Bricker, W.A. 141
Brightman, R.P. 118
Broadbent, D.E. 19
Brooks, P.H. 24, 36
Brooksbank, B.W.L. 68
Brown, A.L. 34, 35, 157, 163
Brown, W.J. 67
Bruner, J.S. 135
Bryant, L.E. 162
Bucher, B. 30, 103
Buckholt, J.A. 140
Budd, K.S. 162
Buium, N. 70
Bull, M. 65
Burchard, J.D. 104
Butterfield, E.C. 34, 35
Byck, M. 37

Calkins, R.P. 160, 162
Callias, M. 91, 117, 118
Cameron, R.J. 121
Camp, B.W. 162
Campione, J.C. 34, 35, 163
Cardoso-Martins, C. 70
Carpenter, N.J. 67
Carr, E.G. 99, 101, 103, 107, 134, 144, 145, 146, 147, 148
Carr, J. 69, 71, 90, 91
Cavanaugh, J.C. 34
Centerwall, C.A. 86
Centerwall, W.R. 86
Chadwick, O. 100
Chandler, M.J. 43, 48, 51
Cheseldine, S. 143
Chomsky, N. 133, 134
Christie, R. 68
Ciccetti, D. 70
Cirrin, F.M. 134, 141, 149
Claridge, G.S. 37, 38
Clarke, A.D.B. 86
Clarke, A.M. 86
Clees, T.J. 165
Cleland, C.C. 100
Clements, P.R. 69
Cohen, R.D. 63
Cole, C.I. 165
Corbett, J. 98, 103
Cowie, V. 69
Cox, G.R. 98
Crapper, D.R. 70
Crawley, B. 70, 159, 168
Cromer, R.F. 134, 135, 136
Cullen, C. 119
Cunningham, C. 69, 72, 86, 90, 94, 98, 117, 118

Dalton, A.J. 70
Damberg, P.R. 31
Dancis, J. 66
Davison, H. 163
Dawson, M.J. 103
De Haven, E.D. 142, 143
De La Cruz, F. 66, 67
Deitz, S.M. 106
Denham, S. 47
Detterman, D.K. 33
Dodd, B. 71
Doleys, D.M. 104
Doran, J. 30

Dores, P.A. 144, 148
Dorsey, M.F. 103
Drabman, R.S. 109
Dufrense, D. 108, 116
Dunst, C.J. 22, 24, 43, 53, 54, 69, 70, 118, 140
Durand, V.M. 99, 101, 102, 134
Dye, H.B. 86

Easterbrook, J.A. 30
Edelson, S.M. 102
Edmondson, B. 47, 51
Ellis, N.R. 33
Epstein, L.H. 105
Ersner-Hershfield, B. 103
Esser, A.H. 100
Etzel, B.C. 29, 20
Evans, D. 71
Evans, P.L.C. 37

Fantz, R.L. 72
Favell, J.E. 97, 100, 109, 120, 121
Fein, D. 136
Felce, D. 121
Feldman, W.S. 118
Fellner, M. 100
Fenn, G. 144
Ferretti, R.P. 35
Feuerstein, R. 36, 37, 163
Finger, I. 70
Firestone, I. 141
Fisher, M.A. 25
Forehand, R. 104
Foxx, R.M. 90, 98, 101, 105, 106, 108, 116
Frith, C.D. 71
Frith, U. 50, 71

Garber, H.L. 90
Garcia, E.G. 141, 142, 143
Gardner, A. 146
Gardner, B. 146
Gardner, J.M. 117
Gardner, W.I. 165
Genung, T. 44, 97
Georgiades, N.J. 122
Gersten, R. 30
Gesell, A. 45
Gillberg, C. 67
Glidden, L.M. 34
Glossop, C. 86

Glover, A. 70
Goetz, L. 142, 143
Goldberg, K.E. 140
Goldiamond, I.E. 99, 106
Goodman, J. 158, 161
Goren, A. 118
Goren, E.R. 103
Gould, J. 44, 101
Grant, G.W.R. 140
Graziano, A.M. 117
Green, R. 33
Greene, R. 103
Gresham, F. 47, 52
Griffiths, R. 45
Gross, A.M. 109
Guess, D. 141
Gunn, P. 72
Gustavson, K.H. 67

Hafer, M. 69
Halle, J.W. 142, 143
Harper, R.S. 44, 97
Harries, C. 123
Harris, J. 140, 141, 142, 143
Harris, S.L. 103
Hart, B. 140, 142, 144
Haywood, H.C. 36, 90
Heaton-Ward, A. 98
Heifetz, L.J. 117, 118
Hemsley, R. 91, 144
Henderson, S.E. 71
Hereford, S.M. 100
Hermelin, B.M. 34, 71
Herriot, P. 33, 34
Hersov, L. 137
Higa, W.R. 160, 162
Hoats, D. 103
Hobbs, S.A. 104
Hobson, R.P. 49, 50, 51
Hogg, J. 37
Holland, A. 69
Holland, J.G. 30
Holz, W.C. 99
Hornby, G. 118
Horner, R.D. 100
House, E.J. 24, 25, 26, 27
Howard-Peebles, P. 67
Howlin, P. 134, 143, 155
Hurrell, P. 55, 140

Itard, J. 82
Iwata, B.A. 102

Jackson, H.J. 166
Jeffree, D. 31, 32, 118
Jett, A.D. 49
Jenkins, J.A. 118
Johnson, C. 52, 167
Johnson, W.L. 106, 107
Jones, A. 142, 143
Jones, L. 147
Jones, M. 38
Jones, O.H.M. 72
Junginger, J. 164

Katz, M. 98
Kendall, L.C. 34, 158, 160, 162
Kent, L.R. 90
Kephart, N. 82
Kiernan, C. 38, 146, 147, 148, 149
King, R.D. 86, 87, 119
Klein, R.D. 165
Klinnert, M.P. 48
Klukas, N. 164
Koegel, R.L. 30, 32
Koller, H. 98
Kopp, R. 158, 160
Krenn, M.J. 91
Kurt, R.C. 34
Kurtz, P.D. 36
Kushlick, A. 86, 98, 121

Lally, M. 25
Langdell, T. 50
Laura, R.S. 10
Lavecchio, F. 65
Le Blanc, J.M. 29
Le Jeune, J. 67
Leeming, R.J. 68
Leslie, A.M. 50
Levin, H. 51
Lewis, C.C. 99
Libet, J. 103
Light, P. 146
Lincoln, A.J. 70, 71
Lipinski, D.P. 164
Litrownik, E. 164
Livesay, J. 98
Lockhart, L.H. 66, 67
Lovaas, O.I. 30, 101, 102, 103, 107, 116, 144
Lucero, W.J. 104
Ludlow, J.R. 86
Luiselli, J.K. 106, 167
Luria, A.R. 37, 157

Lutzker, J.R. 103
Lyle, J.G. 86, 133, 135

McCartney, J.R. 90
McCauley, C. 24, 36
Maccoby, E.E. 51
McConkey, R. 33, 143
MacDonough, J.S. 104
McDowell, J.J. 102
McGimsey, J.F. 100
McGonigle, J.J. 165
McLean, I. 134, 141, 142
McMillan, D.L. 24, 25
Mahoney, G. 70
Mahoney, K. 36
Mahoney, M.J. 36
Maisto, A.A. 25
Manella, K.J. 118
Manning, P.J. 103
Mansell, J. 121
Marcell, M.M. 49
Marchetti, A. 92, 166
Markely, J. 91
Martin, E.D. 105
Martin, G.L. 117, 118
Martin, J.A.M. 136, 137
Martin, J.E. 165
Martin, N.D.T. 63
Martin, P. 103
Martin, P.L. 101
Mason, W.A. 100
Matson, J.L. 90, 91, 92, 105, 166
Meichenbaum, D. 158, 161
Meisel, C.J. 30
Mervis, C.R. 70
Meyers, C.E. 24, 25, 87, 100, 119
Miller, J. 134
Mims, M.G. 67
Miniszek, N.A. 69
Mink, I.T. 87, 100, 119
Mira, M. 117
Miranda, S.B. 72
Miranti, S.V. 52, 167
Mitchell, D.R. 140
Mittler, P. 55, 133, 140
Monson, L.B. 49
Montessori, M. 82
Moores, B. 140
Moos, R. 119
Morris, J. 71
Mosk, M.D. 30
Mowrer, D.E. 143

Mulick, J.A. 107
Murphy, G.M. 118
Murphy, L.M. 103, 105
Musselwhite, C.R. 146

Neisworth, J.T. 36
Nelson, K.E. 146, 147
Nelson, R.D. 164
Nelson, R.O. 144
Nettlebeck, T. 25
Newson, R.D. 32, 102, 107
Ney, P.G. 91
Nicol, A.R. 137
Nihira, K. 87, 100, 119
Nirje, B. 8
Novaco, R.W. 52, 159, 167
Nuffield, E.J. 87

O'Connor, N. 34, 37, 38
O'Dell, S. 117
Oliver, C. 69
Ollendick, T.H. 103, 105, 165
Owens, A. 134, 141, 149

Paluck, R.J. 100
Palvesky, A.E. 91
Peck, V.A. 31
Pendergrass, V.E. 104
Penrose, L.S. 68
Peterson, C.R. 100
Peterson, G.A. 70
Phillimore, L. 122
Porterfield, J. 100
Pratt, M.W. 87, 97, 119, 140
Premack, A.J. 146
Premack, D. 146
Prida, L.C. 144, 148

Quevillon, R.P. 161, 162

Raynes, N.V. 86, 87, 97, 119, 120, 140
Reid, B. 147, 148
Reid, M.K. 34
Reiman, S. 86
Remington, R. 146
Repp, A.C. 106
Reppucci, N. 122
Revill, S. 90, 92, 121
Rhyne, J.M. 146, 147
Richardson, A.M. 53
Richardson, S.A. 98
Richmond, G. 103

Ricks, D.M. 54
Rilling, M. 28
Rincover, A. 28, 29, 30, 100
Risley, T.R. 107, 120, 121, 140, 142, 144
Robertson, I. 53
Robertson, S.J. 165
Robson, C. 142, 143
Rogers-Warren, A. 108, 140
Rojahn, W. 107, 108, 109
Rollings, J.P. 105, 109
Romanczyk, A.G. 103
Romer, D. 93
Rondal, J.A. 140
Rosefsky, Q.B. 83
Rosen, M. 52
Rosenberg, S. 133, 135
Roses, S.S. 87, 97, 119, 140
Rowland, C.M. 134, 141, 149
Rutherford, R.B. 140
Rutter, M. 46, 64, 87, 99, 142
Rynders, J. 70

Sailor, W. 141, 142, 143, 144
St. Louis, K.W. 146
Sajwaj, T. 103, 107, 122
Sandler, A. 118
Sandow, S.A. 90
Saunders, J.T. 122
Schaeffer, R.M. 90
Schalock, R.L. 44, 97
Schantz, C.V. 43, 47, 48, 51
Schell, R.M. 100
Schilmoeller, G.L. 28, 30
Schinke, S.P. 117
Schlesser, R. 160, 162
Schlotterer, G.R. 70
Schoultz, B. 159
Schover, L.R. 32
Schreibman, L. 30, 32 107
Schroeder, S.E. 107, 108, 109
Schuler, A. 142, 143
Sears, R.R. 51
Seguin, E. 82
Senatore, V. 91
Serafica, F.C. 70
Shapiro, E.C. 36, 103, 164, 165
Shapiro, S.T. 106
Share, J. 71
Shearer, D.E. 121
Shearer, M.S. 121
Sherrod, K.G. 70
Simeonsson, R.J. 49

Simmons, J.Q. 101, 103
Singh, N.N. 103, 118
Skeels, H.M. 86
Skeffington, M. 31, 32
Skinner, B.F. 77, 134
Sloper, P. 118, 121
Smith, J. 86, 121
Smith, R.S. 91
Snodgrass, G.J.A.I. 63
Snyder-McLean, L.K. 134, 141, 142
Solnick, J.V. 100, 109
Sowers, J.A. 165
Spencer, J. 55, 140
Spradlin, J.E. 142, 143
Sroufe, L.A. 70
Steiner, R. 82
Sternberg, L. 134, 141, 149
Sternlicht, M. 82
Stoddard, G.R. 67
Stokes, T.F. 89, 92, 116
Stolz, S.B. 103
Strain, P.S. 44
Sutherland, D.G.R. 66
Swann, W. 133
Szymanski, L.S. 83

Tarpley, H.D. 107
Taubman, M.T. 102
Tavormina, J.B. 118
Terrace, H.S. 28
Tharp, R.G. 160, 162
Thorbecke, R.J. 166
Thurman, S.K. 118
Tizard, J. 86, 87, 100, 118
Towell, D. 123
Turnure, J. 70
Twardosz, S. 107

Udwin, O. 63, 64

Varnhagen, C.K. 35, 157, 163
Varni, J.W. 118
Venables, P. 30, 171
Vygotsky, L.S. 33, 157

Wahlstrom, J. 67
Walls, R.T. 28
Warren, S. 108, 140
Wasik, B.H. 162
Watters, R.G. 144
Watters, W.E. 144
Watts, F.N. 123

Watts, R.W.E. 65
Whiteley, H.H. 91
Weeks, S.J. 49
Wesch, D. 103
Wesolowski, M.D. 91
Wheeler, L.J. 144
Whitman, T.L. 166, 167
Williams, J.L. 100, 104, 109
Williams, P. 159
Wilson, B. 103
Wing, L. 44, 46, 98, 101, 134
Wolfensberger, W. 2, 8, 11
Wong, S.E. 117

Woods, P. 119
World Health Organization 1

Yoder, D. 134
Youngston, S.C. 53
Yule, W. 63, 90, 141

Zawlocki, R.J. 28
Zeaman, D. 25, 26, 27, 30
Zeigob, L. 164
Zigler, E. 37, 38
Zisfein, L. 52
Zisk, P.K. 71

Subject Index

Advocacy 12

Aggression 65, 97, 100, 102, 103, 104, 105, 107, 109, 162, 167

Alzheimer's disease 69

Amniocentesis 9

Antecedent cue regulation 165, 169

Anxiety 55, 56, 64, 65, 66, 109

Assessment 1, 4, 5, 6, 38, 45, 72, 73, 137

Attention 19, 20, 21, 25, 26, 30, 31, 36, 38, 50

Attitudes, 2, 3, 4, 5, 7, 10, 87, 123, 124, 151, 175, 177

Augmentative communication systems 72, 138, 139, 145, 146–150

Autism 28, 30, 32, 43, 44, 46, 49, 50, 54, 56, 67, 91, 97, 135, 136, 150, 176

Behaviour problems 44, 62, 64, 66, 67, 77, 82, 83, 85, 87, 91, 94, ch. 7 passim, 116, 118, 119, 120, 127, 160, 162, 164, 165, 166, 167, 168, 175, 176

Behavioural contrast 109

Brain damage 60

Classification 136

Cognitive behaviour therapy 52, 167–168

Cognitive functioning Ch. 3 passim, Ch. 4 passim, 150, 157, 158, 159, 161, 162, 163, 167, 168, 169, 170
see also Information processing

Cognitive training 47

Communication 12, 36, 63, 65, 67, 70, 71, 72, 86, 90, 91, 93, 99, 101, 102, 132, Ch. 9 passim, 157, 172, 173

Community care 3, 8, 12, 61, 140

Consent 9, 10

Contingency management 77, 84, 87, 99, 101, 106, 108, 162

Correspondence training 159, 166

Counselling 64, 66, 68, 73, 82

Delay-deviance models 4, 11, 135, 136

Depression 44, 47, 97, 109

Development 22, 43, 44, 45, 46, 48, 49, 51, 53, 56, 61, 67, 69, 70, 86, 90, 99, 118, 119, 120, 127, 133, 134, 136, 141, 142, 146, 149, 150, 157, 158, 160, 162, 163, 169, 170, 172, 173, 176

Differential reinforcement 106, 107, 166

Discrimination learning 19, 25, 27, 28, 29, 30, 31, 32, 134, 142, 147

Down's syndrome 9, 54, 55, 63, 66, 68–72, 86, 94, 136, 140

Dressing 90

Drugs 67, 83

Early intervention 90, 93, 121, 143

Education 3, 73, 83, 87, 106

Environment 12, 48, 53, 54, 55, 56, 76, 77, 83, 84, 86, 92, 93, 94, 97, 98, 99, 102, 108, 109, 110, 111, 120, 134, 135, 140, 151, 170, 175

Epidemiology 66, 98, 134, 147

Errorless learning 28, 88

Ethics 3, 8, 9, 10, 11, 13, 14, 103, 104, 105, 106, 110

Expectations 61, 87, 92, 151, 175

Facial screening 103

Fading 28
Families 64, 66, 68, 73, 86 87, 100, 119,
    120, 121, 122, 123, 124, 125
Feeding 90, 91
Fragile-X 62, 63, 66–68
Functional analysis 77, 101, 102

Generalization 30, 34, 35, 46, 53, 89,
    92, 116, 142, 144, 148, 151, 156, 161
    162, 163, 164, 165, 166, 167, 169,
    172
Genetics 60, 62, 65, 66, 67, 68, 72

Imitation 71, 120, 138, 139, 141, 144,
    145, 147, 148
Incidental teaching 138, 139, 143, 144
Individual differences 12, 57, 77, 93,
    102, 127, 149, 151, 162, 173, 176
Infantile hypercalcaemia 63–64
Information processing Ch. 3 *passim*,
    Ch. 4 *passim*, 70, 72, 76, 149, 157,
    163, 175, 176
Institutionalization 8, 61, 62, 86, 90,
    97, 100, 120, 135, 140
Integration 3, 8 61

Lesch-Nyhan disease 63, 65–66

Memory 11, 19, 20, 21, 22, 33, 34, 37,
    70, 134, 136, 138, 148, 150, 163, 175
Methodology 6, 7, 23–25, 45–48,
    89–92, 108–110, 118, 143, 174–175
Modelling 53, 88, 160, 161
Motivation 23, 30, 37, 38, 44, 45, 47,
    48, 55, 56
Mucopolysaccharidoses 62

Normalization 8, 61, 155

Organizational factors 87, 120, 121,
    122–123, 124
Overcorrection 104, 105
Overselectivity 30

Parent-child interaction 48, 51, 54, 55,
    70, 99, 100, 117, 118–119, 140, 158
Personality 37, 38, 175
Phenylketonuria 62
Philosophy 2, 8, 124, 155, 174
Physical cognition Ch. 3 *passim*, 168
    see also Cognitive Functioning,
    Information Processing

Physical handicap 65
Physical restraint 103, 104, 105, 108
Precision teaching 88, 89, 91, 92, 93,
    117
Prevention 9, 62
Problem solving 19, 20, 22, 24, 35, 36,
    38, 52, 76, 155, 156, 157, 160, 167,
    168, 169, 172
Prompting 28, 30, 88, 142, 147, 161,
    165, 166
Psychotherapy 82, 91
Punishment 9, 66, 83, 89, 99, 101, 102,
    103, 104, 105, 108, 109, 119

Reaction time 31, 71
Reinforcement 38, 83, 89, 98, 101, 102,
    105, 106, 107, 109, 119, 134, 142,
    143, 144, 147, 159, 160, 165, 166,
    167
Relaxation 52, 159, 167
Response cost 166
Restraint 65
Rights 3, 4, 8, 13, 61, 103, 159, 160
Role factors 87, 123, 124, 176

Segregation 97
Self-advocacy 159, 160, 168
Self-control 12, 36, 37, 99, 132, 133,
    Ch. 10 *passim*, 173
Self-injurious behaviour 9, 44, 65, 97,
    101, 102, 103, 104, 105, 106, 107,
    108, 110
Self-instruction 35, 36, 52, 157, 159,
    161, 162, 164, 167, 169, 173
Self-monitoring 36, 92, 159, 164, 165,
    166, 167, 169
Self-reinforcement 159, 164, 165, 166,
    169
Setting conditions 83, 85, 87, 93, 99,
    100, 101, 116, 120, 122, 123, 128,
    170
Shaping 28, 30, 53, 89
Social cognition 22, 23, 39, Ch. 4
    passim, 158, 167, 168
Social competence 19
Social impairment 44, 45, 46, 97, 150
Social interaction 93, 100, 102, 109,
    142, 157
Social policy 2, 4, 5, 8, 10, 55, 61, 62,
    176
Social relationships 54, 56, 63, 64, 90,
    97, 101, 158

Social skills 44, 47, 48, 50, 51, 52, 53, 54, 55, 56, 91, 93, 148, 159, 160, 168
Stereotyped behaviours 87, 93, 97, 100, 103, 105, 106
Stigmatization 11, 103
Stimulus control 28, 77, 83, 84, 87, 98, 99, 101, 107, 108, 116, 134, 142, 143, 165
Strategies 20, 21, 30, 33, 34, 35, 36, 37, 38, 43, 50, 157, 163, 164, 172, 177

Stress 52, 123
Systems approach 119, 120, 121, 122, 123, 124, 125, 128

Task analysis 88
Terminology 1
Time-out 66, 100, 101, 104, 105, 109
Toileting 90, 91, 100
Training staff or parents 116, 117–120, 124